Handbook on Developing Curriculum Materials for Teachers

Lessons From Museum Education Partnerships

Handbook on Developing Curriculum Materials for Teachers

Lessons From Museum Education Partnerships

edited by

Gerald Bailey
Tara Baillargeron
Cari D. Barragree
Kansas State University

Ann L. Elliott
Auburn Washburn Unified School District

Raymond Doswell
Negro Leagues Baseball Museum

Information Age Publishing, Inc.
Charlotte, North Carolina • www.infoagepub.com

Library of Congress Cataloging-in-Publication Data

Handbook on developing online curriculum materials for teachers : lessons from museum education partnerships / edited by Gerald Bailey ... [et al.].
    p. cm.
    Includes bibliographical references.
    ISBN 978-1-60752-323-9 (paperback) — ISBN 978-1-60752-324-6 (hardcover) — ISBN 978-1-60752-325-3 (e-book) 1. Web-based instruction. 2. Education, Higher—Computer-assisted instruction. 3. Museums—Educational aspects. I. Bailey, Gerald.
    LB1044.87.H347 2010
    371.33'44678—dc22

                                                                    2009042502

Printed in the United States of America

CONTENTS

FOREWORD

Museums across the United States and around the world view education as the core of their missions. The museum and heritage preservation industry has made the promotion of "life-long learning" the key tenant of their existence. Institutions large and small have reached out in their communities in dynamics ways, formal and informal, to enhance learning and citizenship in their respective communities. For institutions whose primary aim is to preserve and showcase history and social studies, these efforts are becoming increasingly essential to their sustainability. The current education climate values the application of technical and scientific skills as more applicable to a productive global economy than the analytical, leadership building skills from lessons in the social sciences. Yet, museums serve as unparalleled resources for communities eager to build the capacity of its citizens to connect to each other and issues in deep, meaningful ways.

A common way for museums to help build the intellectual capacity of the community is through development of materials for schools. Students routinely represent the lion's share of museum goers. Museums have been aggressive in providing resources that empower teachers to affect student achievement. The Negro Leagues Baseball Museum, Inc. (NLBM) is no exception. The NLBM exists to preserve research and disseminate the history of African American baseball from the late 1800s-1960s. The story of the Negro Leagues bridges the gap in African American history from the Civil War to the Civil Rights movement; a story that

Handbook on Developing Curriculum Materials for Teachers:
Lessons From Museum Education Partnerships, pp. vii–viii
Copyright © 2010 by Information Age Publishing

empowers learners in lessons of diversity, entrepreneurship, leadership, sportsmanship, and perseverance. Through published teachers' guides and voluminous information Web sites, the NLBM has made every effort to reach this vital audience with these lessons.

The efforts of the NLBM would not have been possible without the support of its primary partner, the College of Education at Kansas State University. Through the leadership of Dr. Gerald Bailey, and generously supported by the leadership of the college, the university has marshaled its resources of intellect and human energy to bring the rich history of African American baseball to thousands of students and teachers. This book is the successful continuation of that effort. The detailed efforts of Dr. Cari Barragree, Dr. Ann Elliot, and Dr. Tara Baillargeon have produced a resource that will be useful to the NLBM, school leaders, and museum educators for years to come.

With extreme gratitude, the NLBM is pleased to support this volume of informative resources, immediately applicable to the needs of museum and education leaders everywhere.

—Raymond Doswell,
Deputy Director and Chief Curator
Negro Leagues Baseball Museum
Kansas City, Missouri

PREFACE

This book is a product of 5 years of collaborative work by a group of researchers. We came together at Kansas State University through a partnership forged with the College of Education and the Negro League Baseball Museum, located in Kansas City, Missouri. Through this collaboration, the museum discovered that there was a great interest among educators seeking resources to motivate students through subjects like baseball, and to enhance multicultural content for their classroom lessons. Because museums articulate their mission to include education, our group, identified as the Negro League Baseball Scholars program, produced a number of initiatives and products for the Negro League Baseball Museum. These products were designed to assist students and teachers to better understand the social studies themes found in Negro Leagues history.

Negro Leagues Baseball (NLB) Scholars developed curriculum materials and an eMuseum featuring Negro Leagues history as a platform for teaching American history. Secondary educators, with emphasis on the needs of high school teachers, were the target audience. The lessons are interactive and multimedia based. The lessons effectively incorporate National Council for the Social Studies (NCSS) standards, specific state social studies standards, and the International Society for Technology in Education (ISTE) standards. The curricular focus of the lessons demonstrates how themes and issues reflected in studying African American baseball are rooted in U.S. history and social studies. These themes

Handbook on Developing Curriculum Materials for Teachers:
Lessons From Museum Education Partnerships, pp. ix–xii
Copyright © 2010 by Information Age Publishing
ix

include, but are not limited to, economic, social and political studies, family history and genealogy, education, military history, and civil rights.

Each set of lesson plans was subjected to a series of field tests by high school educators. Feedback derived from these tests was used to revise and improve lesson plan components such as learning objectives, resources, activities, assessments and accommodations. This material synthesizes the most reliable primary and secondary source materials on the subject in a useful format for educators; a goal of the Negro League Baseball Museum whose mission was to authenticate and preserve the history of this important story.

In order to expand the reach of the product, materials were made accessible through Web-based technologies and included resources for diverse learners. This process allowed NLB Scholars to identify potent methods educators from schools and museums could use to modify any curriculum material they choose. Techniques for adding multi-sensory dimensions, learning scaffolds and opportunities to match individual learning styles were outlined.

Once the set of lesson plans was validated via the field testing process, NLB Scholars designed the Negro Leagues eMuseum. This digital repository contains archival content from the Negro Leagues Museum including player interviews and photos in a searchable format. Lesson plans are displayed by topic and timeframe and are accompanied by all the supplemental learning materials a teacher may need to reach a wide variety of learners. The eMuseum circumvents the limitations of geography and time to capture the important story of Negro Leagues history for researchers and teachers.

Upon completion of these projects NLB Scholars have had the opportunity to share their work with other education professionals from both schools and museums. We received many questions from others seeking to work collaboratively in order to maximize the potential learning experiences museums offer. In response to this interest, handbooks were developed to outline the three stages of our process, (1) creating eMuseums, (2) developing museum/school partnerships in order to produce curriculum, and (3) modifying and expanding that curriculum to reach diverse learners. This book represents the compilation of the three handbooks into one comprehensive guide for museum and school professionals to make almost any subject more relevant to students' lives, increase students' interests, and make learning more effective. The book contains three sections.

Section I: Planning Developing, and Evaluating eMuseums guides the reader through the stages of planning, creating, an evaluation a user-centered eMusuem. This section provides an overview of the process, giving small- and medium-sized museums the framework and guidance needed to create an eMuseum.

Section II: Museum and Public School Partnerships: A Step-by-Step Guide for Creating Standards-Based Curriculum Materials in High School Social Studies includes how to (1) form a partnership, (2) create standards-based curriculum materials, and (3) evaluate curriculum material.

Section III: Developing Accessible Museum Curriculum: A Handbook for Museum Professionals and Educators outlines specific strategies that can be applied to curriculum to expand its application to broader audiences. These tools will assist professionals to deliver content to patrons with increasingly diverse interests, skills and learning needs. The section includes (1) content presentation, (2) content process, and (3) content product.

Throughout the book, materials created from the Negro Leagues Baseball Museum and the Kansas State University partnership are included as product examples.

The Negro Leagues Baseball Scholars extend special thanks to the following individuals for their support and guidance throughout the development of the eMuseum project:

Dr. Michael Holen, Dean, College of Education, Kansas State University

Dr. David Thompson, Chair, Educational Administration and Leadership, College of Education, Kansas State University

Don B. Motely, Executive Director, Negro Leagues Baseball Museum

Mary Hammel, Associate Director for Creative Services, The Catalyst, College of Education, Kansas State University

SECTION I

Planning, Creating, and Evaluating eMuseums

A Step-by-Step Handbook for Museum Professionals

by

Tara Baillargeon
Kansas State University

Cari D. Barragree
Kansas State University

Ann Elliott
Auburn Washburn Unified School District

Gerald D. Bailey
Kansas State University

CONTENTS

INTRODUCTION

The purpose of this handbook is to guide the reader through the stages of planning, creating, and evaluating a user-centered eMuseum. Several guides to building Web sites and digital libraries exist, but none of these guides explain the process, from beginning to end, of planning, creating and evaluating an eMuseum. This handbook does not focus on technical details, but instead provides an overview of the eMuseum creation process. Those interested in technical details such as developing metadata and digitizing materials have other resources to turn to, many of which are referenced in this handbook. The purpose of this handbook is to provide an overview of the process of planning, creating, and evaluating an eMuseum, giving medium- and small-sized museums the framework and guidance needed to create an eMuseum.

The eMuseum Development Model (see Figure 1) illustrates the steps involved in creating an eMuseum. Each chapter of this book details a step in the development process. Chapter 1 begins with defining an eMuseum. By understanding what an eMuseum is, it can be determine if an eMuseum will benefit the organization. Once a decision has been made that an eMuseum will be beneficial to the organization and its users, the audience is identified and partnerships are developed. Chapter 2 explains the value of external partnerships and some of the ways that museums can collaborate with outside organizations.

Chapter 3 discusses how to identify audiences and target the eMuseum to specific audiences. As indicated by the eMuseum Development Model, audience identification and partnership development can occur sequentially, or simultaneously. There are times when the audience will determine who should be involved in the partnership, and there are other times museum's partnerships will determine who the target audience

Handbook on Developing Curriculum Materials for Teachers:
Lessons From Museum Education Partnerships, pp. 1–4
Copyright © 2010 by Information Age Publishing

should be. For example, when Kansas State University's College of Education partnered with the Negro Leagues Baseball Museum in Kansas City, together they identified the primary audience for their eMuseum as middle school teachers. If the Negro Leagues Baseball Museum had been partnering with local high school teachers to create the eMuseum, the target audience would have been high school teachers instead of middle school teachers.

Once the audience has been identified, a vision can be developed for the eMuseum. The vision will guide the direction that development of the eMuseum will take during the next stage of development—design of the eMuseum. Chapter 4 describes the process of developing a vision and how that vision guides the growth of the eMuseum. Chapters 5 and 6 detail what is involved in designing an eMuseum and offers guidance on technology decisions made about the eMuseum. During the design of the eMuseum, evaluation of the format and content of the Web site will occur. Once development of the eMuseum is complete, a summative evaluation of the entire site is conducted. Revisions to the eMuseum site are based on the summative evaluation results. Chapter 7 explains how to evaluate the eMuseum through formative assessment and summative evaluation. Throughout the process of the developing the eMuseum, funding will need to be secured. External and internal funding sources are needed to support not only the initial implementation of the eMuseum, but to support the long-term maintenance of the Web site. Developing and implementing an eMuseum is not a one-time project, but instead a long-term commitment that needs to be maintained. Chapter 8 addresses issues related to maintaining the eMuseum once developed and ideas for finding funding to start up and sustain the eMuseum.

Many of the examples used in this handbook are a result of partnership between Kansas State University (K-State) in Manhattan, Kansas and the Negro Leagues Baseball Museum (NLBM) in Kansas City, Missouri. In 2005, graduate students and faculty from K-State's College of Education collaborated with the NLBM to create the Negro Leagues Baseball eMuseum (NLB eMuseum). This collaborative experience is the basis for much of the content in this handbook.

WHO SHOULD USE THIS HANDBOOK

This book is intended for leaders in medium- and small-sized museums interested in collaborating with community stakeholders to create an eMuseum. This includes museum curators, directors, and educators. The handbook will also be of interest to those thinking about developing partnerships with outside organizations. Throughout the handbook coverage

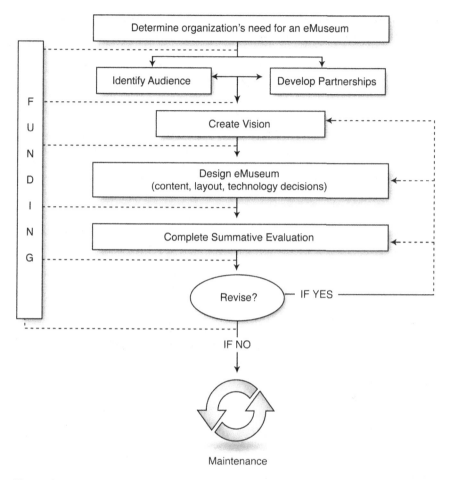

Figure 1.   eMuseum Development Model.

is given to the development of collaborative relationships and the steps involved in creating an eMuseum.

HOW TO USE THIS HANDBOOK

The guide is written so that readers can read the book from beginning to end, or skip ahead to the chapter that best meets their needs. Many Web-based resources are recommended throughout the book, making the text a useful reference guide for those wanting to create eMuseums or focus more narrowly on something such as implementing Web 2.0 technologies into a currently existing Web site.

ICONS USED IN THIS HANDBOOK

The pencil icon identifies a reference indicating that more information is available on the topic. The reference will be for a Web site, book, or article.

Whenever you see the exclamation mark, look for a tidbit that might save you time and trouble.

The wrench icon indicates the recommendation of tools to assist the reader in the process of creating an eMuseum.

CHAPTER 1

DETERMINE ORGANIZATION'S NEED FOR AN eMUSEUM

DEFINING THE EMUSEUM

In 1934, Paul Rea described the mission of museums as "the acquisition and preservation of objects, the advancement of knowledge by the study of objects, and the diffusion of knowledge for the enrichment of the life of the people" (United States President's Research Committee on Social Trends, 1934, p. 995). Today's museum still abides by Rea's mission description, but the methods have changed by which museums share knowledge with the public. Museums are no longer limited to physical spaces as use of the Internet as an interactive communication tool contributes to the development of new ways for museums to share knowledge with the public.

An eMuseums is an online space that provides multiple levels, perspectives, and dimensions of information about a museum and its collections. An eMuseum is much more than a museum Web site with a simple searchable database and a few small online exhibits. eMuseum content targets specific audiences who are identified as educators, children, researchers, lifelong learners, vacation planners, or others. Information in the eMuseum is tailored to meet the needs of these different audiences.

Take a moment and think about what an eMuseum might look like if it reached out to its audiences through an interactive online space. Web 2.0

Handbook on Developing Curriculum Materials for Teachers:
Lessons From Museum Education Partnerships, pp. 5–10
Copyright © 2010 by Information Age Publishing

technologies mean that eMuseums and their audiences can actively engage with each other. This envisioned eMuseum would have an area designed for educators consisting of detailed lesson plans, student assessment tools, and a forum for teachers wishing to share lesson ideas. There would be an area in the eMuseum for children containing an interactive game and stories that could be read online in a text format or downloaded for listening on an MP3 player, allowing children to choose the format that matches their preferred learning style. The eMuseum would also feature digital collections and online exhibits that researchers could access from their own computers. Online exhibits allow museums to make their collections accessible online and connect with audiences that would have previously been impossible to reach because of geographic distance. These are just a few of the ways that eMuseums can use the Internet to reach their audiences.

NEED FOR EMUSEUMS

Consider the following:

- Most visitors to museums in North America have access to the Internet.
- Many visitors come from outside the museum's state or country.
- The Internet has become the main vehicle for accessing information for all types of research.

Museums can do more to expand opportunities for people to engage with their collections. The large size of many museum collections compared to the size of their physical display space means that most items museums own can never be displayed. Museums are poised to use new technologies to make it easier to offer access to their collections. As technology becomes less expensive and more accessible, museums can offer visitors a variety of pathways to their collections. In particular, eMuseums can reach unprecedented numbers of audiences, including students and their teachers.

Online Museum Exhibits Transcend the Barriers of Time, Distance, and Space

Online exhibits overcome barriers of time by being available to audiences 24/7 instead of only during the gallery's hours that are open to the public. By being accessible online, museum exhibits can transcend distance by being visited by anyone with an Internet connection, regardless of their geographic location. Some online exhibits incorporate additional features that physical exhibits cannot offer. With online exhibits, museums are not limited by the physical space available in their galleries.

The Web provides museums with new ways of interacting with the public. With something as simple as hypertext linking, eMuseums can provide online patrons the opportunity to further explore information available about an item in a collection. With Web 2.0 capabilities, further explained in chapter 6, museum educators can engage audiences by using interactive and collaborative technologies such as blogs and wikis.

Researchers Increasingly Expect to Find Resources Available Online

Many museum collections are underused by not being displayed, published, or used for research (Museums Association, 2005). In-house displays are no longer the only and most relevant way of presenting a museum's collections, nor have physical displays been adequate to encompass the volume of materials that museums hold. Putting collections online give people more opportunities to engage with collections by releasing more information and generating knowledge.

Impact of eMuseums on Front Door Attendance

Getting visitors through the doors of the museum is an important goal for museums and its ability to meet the bottom line. Museum professionals wonder if creating an eMuseum means that less people will visit their institutions because potential visitors can find what the information they want online. eMuseums do not replace the experience of visiting a museum in person, but instead, should motivate online visitors to visit the museum in person. As museum informatics researcher Paul Marty (2008) points out:

> Visitors to physical museums should feel similarly inspired to visit the museum's Web site, using the Web site as a bridge to connect their pre-visit and post-visit activities by learning more about the museum and its collections. If all goes well, the resulting feedback loop should lead to increased visitation and overall visitor satisfaction. (p. 337)

Marty also reports that a number of surveys provide compelling evidence that online museums actually drive physical museum attendance instead of discouraging physical visits (Marty, 2008). An eMuseum does not replace a visit to the physical museum, but instead enhances visitors' experiences by making information and resources available both before and after a visit.

THE CHALLENGES OF CREATING AN EMUSEUM

Increases in visitors to museum Web sites have pressured museums to provide more useful information online than ever before. Major museums such as the Smithsonian's National Museum of American History hire professional firms like Second Story to create their Web site, giving their online exhibits a professional feel (see http://americanhistory.si.edu/militaryhistory/exhibition/flash.html). Smaller museums' Web sites sometimes have more of a homemade look when compared to museums using professional Web development companies. Without the funding available to large museums like the Smithsonian, small museums are left to their own devices for developing an online presence.

There are many costs involved in planning, creating, and maintaining an eMuseum for the long term. Consequently, it is a challenge for small museums to find the skills and resources needed to make their collections available online. The total cost of making a museum collection accessible online is not always obvious (see Table 1.1) for examples of items to consider when budgeting for the eMuseum). When planning the creation of an eMuseum, focus tends to be on the literal costs of moving documents into digital form, such as paying someone to type a handwritten document or employing a student to operate a scanner. There are other crucial and expensive parts of the process, especially preparing and selecting the materials to be digitized and assembling metadata about the materials. Roughly, only one third of the costs in digitization projects stem from actual digital conversion; an equal third goes toward cataloging and descriptive metadata and the final third is spent on administrative costs, overhead, and quality control (Cohen & Rosenzweig, 2006; Collaborative Digitization Program, 2006; Lesk, 2004; Puglia, 1999). Without the staff, expertise, and resources available to large museums, small museums are left alone to face the challenges and costs involved in developing a digital collection. Therefore, developing partnerships is an effective way for museums to undertake some of these challenges.

REFERENCES

Cohen, D. J., & Rosenzweig, R. (2005). *Digital history: A guide to gathering, preserving, and presenting the past on the Web*. Philadelphia: University of Pennsylvania Press.

Table 1.1.   Cost Considerations When Budgeting for the eMuseum

Human resources	Hiring new staff when turnover occurs, staff development and training, planning, and estimating workflow. Also consider the costs of setting up meetings, especially if partnering institutions are not located in the same city. Short-term project costs can be estimated by examining the hourly salary of each eMuseum team member.
Materials and equipment	Costs include equipment, hardware and software, such as scanning equipment and image manipulation software.
Space and facilities	Adequate space and facilities are needed for equipment and any necessary new staff
Web site design and database development	If a staff member with database development and Web-design skills is not available, then someone will need to be hired to design and create the eMuseum Web site.
Assessment of audience needs and eMuseum Web site	Assessment of audience needs and eMuseum Web site requires conducting focus groups, usability studies, and other methods of user input.
Selection and preparation of material	Materials need to be selected and prepared for digitization. Content for the eMuseum needs to be planned and written.
Conservation and preservation	Items selected for online exhibits and digital collections may need conserving and digital preservation. Materials, such as audio cassettes or video in beta or VHS, will be converted into a digital format.
Transportation and handling	If materials are digitized by an outside source, costs for transportation and handling should be included. Items being transported should be insured.
Metadata management	Digital items in the eMuseum need to be assigned metadata, such as titles, subject headings, and other descriptions.
Copyright and licensing issues	Someone on the eMuseum team should be knowledgeable about and responsible for copyright and licensing issues. If the eMuseum team decides to use materials for which the museum does not own the copyright, permission must be obtained from the copyright owner, usually for a price.
Documentation and quality control	Once procedures have been developed and implemented, they should be documented and assessed for improvement.
Long-term storage	The eMuseum requires a server on which digital objects will be stored on a long-term basis.
Ongoing maintenance	Once the eMuseum is initially developed, the site will need to be maintained and updated.

Collaborative Digitization Project. (2006). *Toolbox*. Retrieved March 20, 2009, from http://www.bcr.org/cdp/digitaltb/index.html

Lesk, M. (2005). *Understanding digital libraries*. New York: Morgan Kaufmann.

Marty, P. (2007). Museum websites and museum visitors: Before and after the museum visit. *Museum Management and Curatorship*, 22(4), 337-360.

Museums Association. (2005). *Collections for the future: Report of a Museums Association inquiry*. Retrieved March 20, 2009, from http://www.museumassociation.org/asset_arena/text/ns/policy_collections.pdf

Puglia, S. (1999). The costs of digital imaging projects. *RLG DigiNews, 3*(5).

Smithsonian National Museum of American History. (2006). The price of freedom: Exhibition. Retrieved March 20, 2009, from http://americanhistory.si.edu/militaryhistory/exhibition/flash.html

United States President's Research Committee on Social Trends. (1934). *Recent social trends in the United States: Report of the President's Research Committee on Social Trends*. New York: McGraw Hill.

CHAPTER 2

MUSEUM PARTNERSHIPS

Museums wanting to create an eMuseum encounter many difficult questions including:

- Who needs to be involved in creating the eMuseum?
- Which technologies should be incorporated?
- How should the process be managed?

Meeting the demands of users who want to access the collection is not as simple as just digitizing a collection and creating links from the museum's homepage. Ensuring that users' information seeking behaviors lead them to find what they are looking for is a complex task and museums have yet to achieve what libraries and archives have been doing for decades to facilitate access to their holdings (Bevan, 2005; Coburn & Baca, 2004; Marty & Twidale, 2004). Museums and libraries that partner can learn from each other's expertise. Libraries can learn from museums that provide learning opportunities for different types of learners by making information available in multiple formats (e.g., audio, visual, and tactile formats) (McNichol & Spry, 2003).

Handbook on Developing Curriculum Materials for Teachers:
Lessons From Museum Education Partnerships, pp. 11–18
Copyright © 2010 by Information Age Publishing

NEED FOR PARTNERSHIPS

When developing an eMuseum, it is often more economical to form partnerships with a consortia of museums, libraries or other entities who have the technological infrastructures to store digitized materials for the long term. These partnerships can offer infrastructure at a fraction of the cost of "going it alone." Links between museums and higher education are far less developed than they could be (Museums Association, 2005). Enhancing the research culture in museums requires hybrid solutions. Museums need to promote their collections to potential researchers, a role that has been less well developed in museums than in libraries and archives (Museums Association, 2005). Museums can do more to establish links with higher education and be recognized as places where different users can carry out research at different levels.

Higher education has resources available that are worth the pursuit of museums, especially since higher education has a history of being a source of funding for museum projects (Cohen & Rosenzweig, 2006). According to the 2005 *Collections for the Future* report from the Museums Association, museums should pool their resources by working across institutional boundaries, to begin addressing the shortfall of expertise, and find ways of making better use of underused collections. Groups of museums who have worked together have been able to use external expertise from higher education, industry, and enthusiasts' groups.

Libraries and educators also have reasons for wanting to partner with museums. In a 2002 study, Bennett, Sandore, and Pianfetti found that teachers were attracted to collaborating with museums and libraries because it provided them an opportunity to match mandated state learning standards with classroom activities. Curators and librarians indicated they were motivated to collaborate because the partnership provided them with the impetus to do a number of things they considered institutional priorities but had been unable to fund including, focusing on a community outreach program, forming new partnerships with previously unserved or underserved groups, and identifying and assessing collections for digitization.

EVOLUTION OF THE KANSAS STATE UNIVERSITY–
NEGRO LEAGUES BASEBALL MUSEUM PARTNERSHIP

The Negro Leagues Baseball eMuseum (NLB eMuseum) is a result of the collaborative relationship between Kansas State University's (K-State) College of Education and the Negro Leagues Baseball Museum (NLBM). The NLBM is located at 18th and Vine in the heart of Kansas City,

Missouri. The NLBM was founded in 1990 and is a privately funded, non-profit organization dedicated to preserving the rich history of African American baseball. Visitors can tour multimedia displays, a grandstand theater, a baseball diamond with life-size statues of NLB players, the museum store, and artifacts dating from the late 1800s through the 1960s. The NLBM opened a permanent 10,000 square foot facility in 1997 and shares the new 18th & Vine museum complex with the American Jazz Museum. K-State's College of Education began a partnership with the NLBM in 1998. Until recently, their collaboration consisted mainly of developing teacher materials for the museum, such as a teacher's field-trip guide.

In spring of 2005, K-State's Dr. Gerald D. Bailey recruited four graduate students from the Educational Leadership Department to become members of the inaugural Negro Leagues Scholars Academy. The doctoral research of the Negro Leagues Scholars focused on working with the NLBM to create curriculum materials and an eMuseum to house these teacher-focused materials. The NLB eMuseum was created as an online resource where teachers, students, and researchers can access NLB Museum materials, including lesson plans, a teacher's toolkit, digital resources, and other curriculum related materials. Since 2005, several graduate students have become involved in the NLBM projects. Dissertations and internships by K-State graduate students have become unexpected benefits to students who would not normally be afforded these opportunities.

The partnership between K-State's College of Education and the NLBM has resulted in several positive outcomes for the museum, including:

- The ability to reach wide numbers of educators to tell the story of the Negro Leagues. Locally and nationally, teachers and students are visiting the NLBM in greater numbers.
- The resources to undertake projects that would not normally be covered by a limited budget, such as the creation of standards-based curriculum materials and the eMuseum Web site.
- The ability of the NLBM to promote the *untold* story of the Negro Leagues—the social, political, economic, and leadership impact on American and world history. In the past, baseball historians and teachers have focused on the Negro Leagues Baseball game, statistics, and the players' accomplishments.
- The other partners have brought "new eyes" to the role and mission of the museum. As a consequence, multiple educational

perspectives are considered when developing the long-term agenda of the NLBM (Doswell, Bailey & Lumley, 2006).

SELECTING THE EMUSEUM TEAM

Putting together a team to develop the eMuseum involves gathering members from a range of disciplines. When deciding on roles for the eMuseum team, some staff may cover more than one role. The roles involved in the eMuseum team might include:

- museum curator or director;
- project director;
- education consultants;
- Web designer;
- technical staff;
- editor;
- information manager; and
- copyright expert.

Museum Curator or Director: The museum curator or director guides the development of the vision for the eMuseum. The curator is responsible for the intellectual content of the eMuseum. Overall responsibility for final decisions about the eMuseum is the responsibility of the museum's director or curator.

Project Director: The project director is the person who directs the project by scheduling meetings and determining timelines and project plans. The project director also develops documentation for the project. This role may be assigned to the museum curator or director, or other team member.

Education Consultant(s): The role of the education consultant is to make certain that the eMuseum's educational materials meet the needs of a wide range of learners. Education consultants can contribute to the development of lesson plans and related curriculum materials for a targeted age group or subject area. In the case of the NLB eMuseum, education consultants consisted of a curriculum director, two social studies teachers, and a special education teacher. Together, the education consultants developed the curriculum materials for the eMuseum. The curriculum director coordinated the lesson planning, ensuring that state and national curriculum standards were met, and the special education teacher made modifications to the curriculum materials to meet the needs of diverse learners. All of the educators involved in the creation of lesson plans were enrolled as graduate students in the College of Education at K-State. These educators/graduate students received course credit for contributing lesson plans to the NLB eMuseum.

Web Designer: The web designer's expertise is needed to translate ideas into the creation of a usable Web space. Ideally, the Web designer has the technical skills and graphic arts talent necessary to create the eMuseum. The Web designer is able to take the team through the Web site's stages of development, implementing changes suggested by the team.

Technical Staff: Technical staff are needed to digitize items and contribute to database development, script writing, and programming. During the development of the NLB eMuseum, student workers were hired to scan photographs and digitize oral history videos for the Web site.

Editor: Having an editor to proofread the text in an eMuseum is essential for correcting typos and other mistakes.

Information Manager: The information manager is responsible for organizing the eMuseum's content in a way that makes information accessible and intuitive to users. A librarian is well-suited for the role of information manager. The information manager's duties include defining and implementing standards and processes for the eMuseum's content management, including schema development, metadata management, and item classification.

Copyright Expert: For those who have begun thinking about developing an eMuseum, copyright is an issue. Museums are forced to make decisions between making materials accessible and following copyright law, often without the help of those with copyright expertise. Ensuring that use of materials in the eMuseum does not infringe on copyright law or licensing agreements is an important task. If objects from other institutions or individuals are being used, the museum needs to get permission to use those objects. The role of the team's copyright expert could be an additional task assigned to the site's editor or information manager.

The NLB eMuseum team was led by four doctoral students in education who were members of K-State's Negro Leagues Scholars program. These students were part-time doctoral students who, together, had professional experience in curriculum development, information science, special education, and museum curatorship. Their doctoral program centered on the development of the NLB eMuseum and each student was assigned a lead role in the project based on their area of expertise. For instance, the student with a background in information science filled the roles of project director, information manager, and copyright expert. Also, master's level students in education, undergraduate interns, teachers, and a graphic designer contributed content throughout the project. The time between when the eMuseum was first conceptualized and its completion was approximately 3 years. The main reason development of the eMuseum took 3 years was because the team members were only able to contribute limited, regular hours to working on the eMuseum project.

CULTIVATING THE eMUSEUM TEAM

The eMuseum team members need sufficient time to explore each others' areas of expertise in order to develop a sense of being a part of a multi-disciplinary team. One of the techniques for team building used by the NLB eMuseum team was to begin each meeting with a "whip activity" and end each meeting with "fish bowling." Whip activities are an engaging way to begin a meeting because it allows team members to bond by sharing information with the team while building trust among team members (see examples of whip activities below). Fish bowling occurs at the end of a teaming session and is an effective way of debriefing the meeting in order to reflect and determine progress. An example of fish bowling includes going around the table and asking each team member what they learned from today's meeting.

Whip and Fishbowl Activities

Try beginning a meeting with one of these whip activities:

- Ask each team member to describe the top three outcomes they want to achieve through today's meeting.
- Have each team member write down on a piece of paper three things they learned from the last meeting. Pass the piece of paper to their neighbor on the left and have each person share one item from their neighbor's list.

Fish bowling activities include:

- Ask each team member to finish the following two sentences:
  o "I feel good about ..."
  o "I am still concerned about ..."

 For more teaming ideas go to *101 Tips, Traps, and To-Dos for Creating Teams: A Guidebook for School Leaders* (1998) by Gerald D. Bailey, Tweed Ross, Gwen L. Bailey, and Dan Lumley, National Educational Service.

REFERENCES

Bailey, G. D., Bailey, G. L., & Lumley, D. (1998). *101 tips, traps, and to-dos for creating teams: A guidebook for school leaders.* Bloomington, IN: National Educational Service.

Bennett, N. A., Sandore, B., & Pianfetti, E. S. (2002) Illinois digital cultural heritage community-collaborative interactions among libraries, museums and elementary schools. *D-Lib Magazine, 8*(1). Retrieved March 20, 2009, from http://www.dlib.org/dlib/january02/bennett/01bennett.html

Bevan, B. (2005). Starting with what we know: A CILS framework for moving from physical to virtual science learning environments. In L. Tan & R. Subramaniam (Eds.), *E-learning and virtual science centers* (pp. 68-92). Hershey, PA: Information Science.

Coburn, E., & Baca, M. (2004). Beyond the gallery walls: Tools and methods for leading end-users to collections information. *Bulletin of the American Society for Information Science and Technology, 30*(5), 14-19.

Cohen, D. J., & Rosenzweig, R. (2005). *Digital history: A guide to gathering, preserving, and presenting the past on the web.* Philadelphia: University of Pennsylvania Press.

Doswell, R., Bailey, G. D., & Lumley, D. (2006). Educational partnerships: Times, traditions, and technology-teaching the Negro Leagues. In E. J. Rielly (Ed.), *Baseball in the classroom: Essays on teaching the national pastime* (pp. 33-39). Jefferson, NC: McFarland.

McNichol, S., & Spry, J. (2003). *Learning in museums and libraries.* Retrieved March 20, 2009, from http://www.ebase.uce.ac.uk/docs/Learning_in_museums.doc

Marty, P. F. & Twidale, M.B. (2004). Lost in gallery space: A conceptual framework for analyzing the usability flaws of museum *Web sites. First Monday, 9*(9). Retrieved March 20, 2009, from http://firstmonday.org/htbin/cgiwrap/bin/ojs/index.php/fm/article/view/1171/1091

Museums Association. (2005). *Collections for the future: Report of a Museums Association inquiry.* Retrieved March 20, 2009, from http://www.museumassociation.org/asset_arena/text/ns/policy_collections.pdf

CHAPTER 3

TARGETING THE eMUSEUM'S AUDIENCE

Early in the undertaking of an eMuseum project an important task is identifying the eMuseum's intended audience. The audience should be narrowly defined to help determine the parameters of the project. What are the needs of the eMuseum's identified audience and how can they best be served? The answers to these questions will determine the content and interfaces of the eMuseum.

Audiences can be divided into primary, secondary, and tertiary user groups. In the case of the Negro Leagues Baseball (NLB) eMuseum, the primary audience is K-12 teachers interested in incorporating Negro Leagues history into their social studies curriculum. The secondary audience consists of people interested in learning about Negro Leagues history. This secondary audience includes students working on school projects, Negro Leagues scholars, and hobbyists interested in Negro Leagues history. Tertiary users consist of Internet users at large who may not have been looking for the Negro Leagues Baseball information, but find themselves on the Web site after following links or doing a search in a search engine. Tertiary users are not necessarily looking for information from the NLB eMuseum, but their search for information leads them to the Web site. For example, someone searching the Web for information about the Kansas City Royals might end up on the NLB eMuseum site if they did a search for "Kansas City and baseball." A search engine might

Handbook on Developing Curriculum Materials for Teachers:
Lessons From Museum Education Partnerships, pp. 19–23
Copyright © 2009 by Information Age Publishing

direct such a user to the NLB eMuseum because the Web site contains information about the Kansas City Monarchs, a Negro Leagues team from Kansas City.

Get to Know the Primary Audience

When working on the Negro Leagues Baseball eMuseum, teachers interviewed indicated that the majority of the schools in their district use Macs instead of PCs. This prompted our decision to make material on the Web site both Mac and PC compatible.

METHODS FOR ASSESSING AUDIENCE NEEDS

Once the target audience is determined, assessing their needs helps the eMuseum team decide what content to include in the eMuseum. There are several ways, depending on your resources and budget, that audience needs can be assessed. An audience needs assessment can be accomplished by soliciting user feedback through focus groups and surveys.

Focus Groups (Patron Profiling)

Patron profiling can be accomplished before the Web site is developed by using focus groups to get user feedback. Focus groups are an increasingly popular way to learn about opinions and attitudes. Focus groups can be used before and after the eMuseum's interface is developed.

The museum can recruit participants by placing ads on the museum Web site, in the museum building, and in local newspapers. Best practice is to recruit focus group participants from the eMuseum's primary and secondary audiences. It is essential to offer incentives for participants, such as free passes to visit the museum, a T-shirt, or even a small amount of money. When developing questions for focus groups, use open-ended questions and avoid close-ended questions ("yes" or "no"), and best practices indicate that "why" questions should be avoided. A focus group should consist of six to 12 people. The focus group is an opportunity to ask questions such as:

- What would you like to see in our eMuseum?
- What would make you want to visit our eMuseum?
- What do you think teachers would like best about this Web site?

> *For more information on conducting focus groups see:*
> "Focus Group Interviews in Qualitative Research," by Melinda Lewis (http://www.scu.edu.au/schools/gcm/ar/arr/arow/rlewis.html)

Surveys

Surveys are a quick and effective way to solicit feedback about the museum and what audiences would like to see in an eMuseum. Access to a survey can be provided both onsite at the museum and on the museum's Web page. If the museum has a mailing list, consider sending list members the survey. Conducting a Web-based survey is an inexpensive way to get feedback about the eMuseum.

> *Examples of tools for creating online surveys:*
>
> - AdvancedSurvey
>   http://www.advancedsurvey.com
> - EZquestionnaire
>   http://www.ezquestionnaire.com
> - SurveyKey
>   http://www.surveykey.com
> - Survey Monkey
>   http://www.surveymonkey.com

> *For more information about creating surveys see:*
>
> - *What Is a Survey? The National Opinion Research Center* (http://www.whatisasurvey.info/)
> - *Conducting Research Surveys via E-mail and the Web,* by Matthias Schonlau, Ronald D. Fricker, Jr., Marc N. Elliott (http://www.rand.org/pubs/monograph_reports/MR1480/index.html)

BUILDING THE AUDIENCE

An eMuseum will not promote itself. Fortunately, there are many things that can be done to ensure that the eMuseum is publicized. Museum staff should use every opportunity to encourage patrons to visit the eMuseum site. The Web site URL should be included on the museum's Web site, admission tickets, brochures, newsletters, business cards, and all other communication materials. Continual marketing and promotion is necessary for a Web site to be successful. Begin building an e-mail list by including an information sheet at the museum's information desk, by asking people to subscribe through a form on the museum's Web site, by including an "opt-in" question any time an e-mail address is provided by a patron. E-mail the list regularly about updates to the eMuseum.

Share the eMuseum URL with professional associations by presenting at workshops, events, conferences, and professional meetings. Museum colleagues are interested in hearing about and learning from other museums' experiences in creating an eMuseum. Post the eMuseum's URL to listservs and connect with other communities by linking the eMuseum to community-based Web sites. Ask other Web sites (e.g., educational Web sites, library Web sites) to add a link to the eMuseum's Web site. Register the eMuseum Web site in search engines such as Google and Yahoo!. Optimize the eMuseum's pages through the use of meta keywords and descriptions so that the site ranks higher in search engine results.

- *Promoting Your New (or Redesigned) Web Site: Ten Cost-Effective and Easy Ways to Generate a Buzz,* by Leanne Bergey (http://www.techsoup.org/learningcenter/webbuilding/page5958.cfm)
- *Search Engine Watch* helps Web site owners trying to improve their ability to be found in search engines (http://searchenginewatch.com

REFERENCES

Advanced Survey. (2009). Retrieved March 20, 2009, from http://www.advancedsurvey.com

Bergy, L. (2006). Promoting your new (or redesigned) Web site: Ten cost-effective and easy ways to generate a buzz. *TechSoup.* Retrieved March 20, 2009, from http://www.techsoup.org/learningcenter/webbuilding/page5958.cfm

EZquestionnaire. (2008). Retrieved March 20, 2009, from http://www.ezquestionnaire.com

Lewis, M. (1995). Focus group interviews in qualitative research. *Action Research Electronic Reader.* Retrieved March 20, 2009, from http://www.scu.edu.au/schools/gcm/ar/arr/arow/rlewis.html

National Opinion Research Center. (n.d.). *What is a survey?* Retrieved March 20, 2009, from http://www.whatisasurvey.info

Schonlau, M., Fricker, R. D., and Elliott, M. N. (2003). *Conducting research surveys via e-mail and the web*. Retrieved March 20, 2009, from http://www.rand.org/pubs/monograph_reports/MR1480/index.html

Search Engine Watch. (2009). Retrieved March 20, 2009, from http://searchengine-watch.com

Survey Monkey. (2008). Retrieved March 20, 2009, from http://www.surveymon-key.com

SurveyKey. (2008). Retrieved March 20, 2009, from http://www.surveykey.com

CHAPTER 4

CREATING THE VISION

Museums, schools, and libraries should not let technology dictate how they will use technology to reach their vision. For example, just because a museum has the capability of using technology (e.g., audio tours) to lead patron tours does not mean that the use of docents should be discontinued. Instead, think about the eMuseum's vision and how technology can help the eMuseum meet its goals. Consider first what the eMuseum's needs are and then determine how new technological tools might meet those needs.

MISSION AND VISION OF THE MUSEUM

The mission of the eMuseum describes the purpose or reason for its existence. The vision is a description of how the eMuseum expects to see itself in the foreseeable future. The vision is broad and future oriented, whereas the mission is specific and goal oriented.

The eMuseum's vision conveys the desired image for the future of the Web site. The vision represents an ideal of what the eMuseum will become. A good way to begin developing the vision for the eMuseum is to look at the mission of the institution. The mission of the eMuseum should reflect the mission of the physical museum. Once the vision for the eMuseum is determined, the vision will guide you through developing the Web site and influence every decision made about the eMuseum.

Handbook on Developing Curriculum Materials for Teachers:
Lessons From Museum Education Partnerships, pp. 25–28
Copyright © 2010 by Information Age Publishing
All rights of reproduction in any form reserved.

The mission of the Negro Leagues Baseball Museum is to preserve the rich history of African American baseball. The Negro Leagues Baseball eMuseum helps the museum meet this mission by being an online space where the history of African American baseball is preserved through the digitization of oral histories, photographs, and biographical information. Another mission of the Negro Leagues eMuseum is to develop and provide access to curriculum materials that use Negro Leagues history as a platform for teaching social sciences. Teachers, specifically middle school and high school teachers, are the target audience for lesson plans aligned with regional and national teaching standards and include resources for diverse learners. The story of Negro Leagues Baseball goes beyond one subject matter or one discipline. The story cuts across all subject areas including history (social studies), math, science, reading, art, English, and special education.

DEVELOPING THE VISION

Visions have several components, including the following:

- A vision features a compelling picture or image of what the eMuseum can become in the future.
- A vision is feasible and attainable.
- A vision is connected to and articulates deeper values and hopes for the future.
- A vision needs to be translated into actions and plans that can be and are implemented.
- A vision will die if it is not regularly communicated. Putting a vision statement into a drawer will achieve nothing and might be counter-productive (adapted from the North Central Regional Educational Laboratory Web site: http://www.ncrel.org/sdrs/areas/issues/educatrs/leadrshp/le1comps.htm).

A white paper is an article that states the organization's position or philosophy about a subject. To begin developing a vision, write a white paper describing the features, goals, and audience of the eMuseum. Think about how the eMuseum will appear in 5 years. When writing the paper, consider audience needs and the museum's mission. Read the vision and mission statements of comparable organizations when developing the vision paper. Be sure to collaborate with or get input from stakeholders. Developing the vision in isolation can mean that that those who were left out of the process will not buy into it. Ask coworkers and colleagues in other organizations to read the vision paper and give honest feedback. This document can help guide the team through the development process. Since the vision paper is written before the development of the eMuseum begins, do not be surprised if not everything described in the vision is realized. Through the course of development, it may be discovered that certain elements in the white paper turn out to be larger than the scope of the project allows. For example, the vision paper for the Negro Leagues eMuseum describes the eMuseum as having three separate, but exhaustive portals catering to the needs of teachers, scholars, and students. Having a limited amount of time for graduate students to work on the site led to downscaling the project to focus only on completing a portal for teachers. In the future, the museum hopes to expand the eMuseum site for scholars by collaborating with Kansas State University Libraries to create a digital archive accessible to the public.

Developing the Vision Tips

- Write a white paper describing the eMuseum 5 years down the road.
    o Ask colleagues to read the paper and give honest feedback.
- Consider audience needs and the museum's mission.
- Get input from stakeholders.
- Read mission and vision statements of comparable organizations.

REFERENCES

North Central Regional Educational Laboratory. (2004). *Components of a vision.* Retrieved March 20, 2009, from http://www.ncrel.org/sdrs/areas/issues/educatrs/leadrshp/le1comps.htm

CHAPTER 5

DESIGNING THE ᴇMUSEUM

Try not to limit the eMuseum's design to traditional print collection lay-
outs. It is not uncommon to have someone suggest that an online collection reflect the looks of a paper-based collection. This is apparent when
sites make use of "virtual book shelves" or "virtual picture albums." Since
the possibilities inherent to online formatting are numerable, do not be
afraid to try new things. Resources will be used differently in an online
environment than in person. For example, a user cannot use a keyword to
"search" a collection of paper books, but online that is a completely reasonable and expected function. Hyperlinking is another function that is
inherent to online environments. A hyperlink is an element in an electronic document or Web page that links to another place in the same document or to an entirely different document. Online capabilities should be
kept foremost in mind when deciding how to present content.

SEVEN STEPS TO DESIGNING THE ᴇMUSEUM

Good design is crucial for any Web site. A poorly designed and presented
Web site can create a negative reaction to the organization and can hurt
its public image. When the time came to design the NLB eMuseum, the
eMuseum team depended on the work of a graphic artist who had Web
design skills. The eMuseum's information professional led the implementation of the design process by getting input from team members and act-

Handbook on Developing Curriculum Materials for Teachers:
Lessons From Museum Education Partnerships, pp. 29–38
Copyright © 2010 by Information Age Publishing

ing as the team liaison to the graphic Web artist. Design of the eMuseum includes the following steps:

- **Step One:** Preparation of the creative brief
- **Step Two:** Evaluation and feedback from team members
- **Step Three:** Selection of objects (images, videos, lesson plans)
- **Step Four:** Drafting of text to accompany objects and webpages
- **Step Five:** Preparation of objects (digitization, graphic design)
- **Step Six:** Graphic design and webpage creation
- **Step Seven:** Final editing

Step One: Creative Brief

The creative brief is a one-page document that outlines the strategic direction for creative development of the eMuseum. The creative brief guides the eMuseum development process and provides the background necessary for the Web designer to conceptualize the project. For an example of a creative brief used for the NLB eMuseum, see Figure 5.1. The creative brief includes the following components:

1. Description of the project's concept;
2. Project objectives/goals;
3. User value/benefits;
4. User interface considerations;
5. Audience;
6. Assumptions and research;
7. Competitive landscapes; and
8. Structure flowchart.

Begin the creative brief with a description of the project's concept which consists of a two- to three-sentence description of the purpose of the eMuseum. Once a description of the eMuseum has been developed, list the top three to five goals for the eMuseum. The third component of the creative brief consists of user value and benefits. In this section, describe what the value of the eMuseum project is and how users will benefit from its existence.

The fourth component of the brief is used to list user interface considerations for the eMuseum. The user interface consists of the elements of the computer screen that users interact with. Decisions about user interface elements will influence how the Web site will look. Be sure that the

NLB eMuseum Creative Brief
This document provides a brief description of the NLB eMuseum. It outlines the objectives, audience, and assumptions for the project and details the creative concept the team intends to use moving forward.

Project Concept
The NLB eMuseum will be an electronic space that complements the physical spaces of the Negro Leagues Baseball Museum and the Buck O'Neil Research and Education Center. This project's portion of the eMuseum will be a web-based resource for teachers to find curriculum materials and primary sources related to Negro Leagues history to use in the classroom.

Project Objectives / Goals
1. Expand access to the collections of the NLBM and the Buck O'Neil Research and Education Center.
2. Establish and share innovative models for distributing image, audio, and video artifacts via the eMuseum.
3. Integrate a variety of museum/archival artifacts and resources in a variety of formats.
4. Share technology-infused social studies curriculum materials with K-12 teachers.

User Value / Benefits
1. A repository for materials related to NLB
2. A positive social environment that meets the curriculum and research needs of teachers interested in NLB.
3. Teacher ready curriculum materials – easy to integrate into the classroom.
4. Facilitates a better understanding of Negro Leagues and African American history and how it connects to Social Studies.
5. Information is user-centered, interactive, and available in a variety of formats (audio, video, text), including formats suitable for diverse learners.

User Interface Considerations
Static content: copyright notice, logo, bread crumbs, global navigation links (e.g. home, teachers, students, virtual exhibits, players, etc)
Dynamic requirements: User sign up page for newsletter, log on page for users, searching, downloading

Audience
1. Primary audience: Middle and high school teachers
2. Secondary audience: Middle and high school students
3. Museum education professionals
4. Negro League scholars
5. Baseball enthusiasts

Assumptions and Research
1. Content available in text, video, audio.
2. Content suitable for all types of learners.
3. Use of metadata to describe objects (e.g. video clips, lesson plans, audio clips, etc.)
4. User-created areas (e.g. discussion boards, posting student projects, sharing NLB stories, connecting NL people with students and teachers)
5. Curator blog
6. Usability studies

Competitive Landscape

Exploratorium	Baseball Hall of Fame
http://www.exploratorium.com/	http://www.baseballhalloffame.org/
BrainPOP	Louisville Slugger Museum
http://www.brainpop.com/	http://www.sluggermuseum.org/

Figure 5.1.   Creative brief prepared for the NLB eMuseum.

eMuseum team includes representatives from the primary audience (e.g. social science teachers). They will have insight about what should be considered when developing the Web site's interface. There is also great benefit to getting feedback from nonteam members who represent the eMuseum's targeted audience (see chapter 3 for more information on assessing the audience's needs).

Component five of the creative brief consists of a description of the eMuseum's audience (for audience definitions, see chapter 3). Describe the primary and secondary audiences for the eMuseum and include available information about those audiences (e.g., demographics, etc.). Section six of the brief is used to present information about assumptions and research related to the project. Use this section to state the elements or characteristics of the eMuseum that must be included in the project (assumptions), as well as any data, usability analysis, and research that could inform the project's design (research).

The sixth component of the creative brief is an overview of the museum's competitive landscape. Surveying the landscape is an effective way to get ideas about how the eMuseum should look when completed. To survey the landscape, look at the Web sites of comparable museums and make a list of what you like and do not like about each one. Think about which features on these Web sites are essential. Try starting the museum Web site search with a museum directory Web site.

These sites list links to various museum Web sites

- The Museum of Online Museums (MoOM)
  http://www.coudal.com/moom.php
- Virtual Library Museum Page
  http://vlmp.icom.museum/

The last component of the creative brief is the structure flowchart. The structure flowchart is a method for visualizing the components and structure of the eMuseum and how each page in the site relates to one another. During the development of the NLB eMuseum, a structure flowchart described which team members were responsible for each section of the eMuseum.

Step Two: Evaluation and Feedback From Team Members

Once a draft of the creative brief is completed, the document should be evaluated by team members and feedback gathered to make necessary adjustments to the creative brief. Once the creative brief is complete, share it with the graphic Web designer who will use it to guide the creation of the eMuseum.

5.1.3 Step Three: Selection of Objects

At this point in the process, final selection of objects to be included in the eMuseum is determined. Objects to be included in the eMuseum consist of items such as images, video, audio, curriculum materials, and historical content. Objects should be selected for inclusion in the eMuseum based on their ability to meet the needs of identified audiences. There is no need to digitize materials that are widely available elsewhere on the Internet. Objects should be unique and reflect the strengths of the museum's collection. Criteria to consider when selecting objects for the eMuseum include:

- Museum has copyright clearance of object.
- Objects are suitable for digitization because of their format, condition, or other characteristics.
- Collection depicts broad or deep coverage of a specific subject or theme.
- Objects are new acquisitions or used in exhibitions.
- Collection has the potential to attraction donors or be used in promotional publications.
- Objects have a special public or educational appeal and are not widely represented elsewhere on the Internet.

When the time came for the NLB eMuseum team to select objects for the Web site, curriculum materials for the Web site were already developed. Curriculum materials, including lesson plans, resources for diverse learners, and a teacher's toolkit were completed before work began on creating the eMuseum. That left the team with the task of selecting items for digitization (videos and photographs) for inclusion on the Web site.

For more information on selecting objects for digitization see:

- *Capture Your Collection: A Guide for Managers,* by the Canadian Heritage Information Network (http://www.chin.gc.ca/English/Digital_Content/ Managers_Guide/index.html)
- *Digitisation Guidelines: A Selected List,* a collection of resources compiled by Minerva (a European Union organization concerned with the digitization of cultural heritage collections) (http:// www.minervaeurope.org/guidelines.htm).

Step Four: Drafting Text to Accompany Objects and Web Pages

Audiences browsing the eMuseum will want to know what they are viewing on the Web site. Scripts need to be developed for each page on the eMuseum. Drafting of the text may be the responsibility of one team member, such as the museum's curator, or can be divided among team members. Once someone has written an original draft, fellow team members review and edit the text. Once corrections and changes are made to the text, the final draft is ready to be added to the eMuseum.

Limit Jargon!
When museum professionals are involved in the design and development of museum Web sites, designers risk creating Web sites that use organizational schemes and vocabularies unfamiliar to nonmuseum professionals.

Step Five: Preparation of Objects (Digitization, Graphic Design)

Once selected for inclusion in the eMuseum, the format of many objects will need conversion to a digital format. This includes digitizing images and converting audio and video to a format compatible with the eMuseum. Metadata should be constructed for objects (see chapter 6).

For in-depth information on best practices in digital imaging see:

- *The Collaborative Digitization Program Digital Toolbox* (http://www.bcr.org/cdp/digitaltb/index.html)

Step Six: Graphic Design and Web Page Creation

Now that the content for the eMuseum has been prepared, the graphic Web designer can begin designing and putting the Web site together. If the organization does not have enough money to hire an experienced graphic designer, consider offering an internship to a graphic design student. Both the organization and the student will learn from the experience.

Share layout decisions with the graphic Web designer. The layout for the site's content can be organized systematically, thematically, by material type, and/or by using multiple schemes. Content organized systematically might appear chronologically or alphabetically. Thematically organized materials are grouped by themes that tell a story. Sometimes content is organized by original material type, such as photographs. When organizing by a multiple schemes, hyperlinking allows users to follow their own learning paths by clicking on the hyperlinks that interest them most.

> ***Information on the art and science of creating good Web sites:***
>
> • Web site Architecture—University of Greenwich (http://www.Web sitearchitecture.co.uk)

Step Seven: Final Editing

Once the graphic Web designer creates preliminary drafts of the Web site, the eMuseum team assesses the Web site and gives feedback to the designer. It is common for graphic designers to provide two designs and have the team discuss what they like and dislike about each. Final additions, changes, and corrections are made to the eMuseum.

COMPONENTS TO INCLUDE ON THE eMUSEUM HOMEPAGE

• *Identification and Branding:* This includes the museum's name and logo. This information helps users determine if they are visiting an authoritative and reliable Web site. The opening page of the NLB eMuseum identifies the site as collaborative project between K-State and the NLBM.

Include links to pages containing:

• *Copyright and Usage Policy:* A statement of copyright and usage policies are commonly included in an online exhibit or library. The "Research Library" section of the NLB eMuseum includes many photographs and video interviews, therefore, copyright information and a usage policy was included:

Negro Leagues eMuseum Library Materials Usage Policy

Written materials, art work and photography on this site are copyrighted by the Negro Leagues Baseball Museum, other writers, photog-
raphers, and organizations. Materials on these pages may be distributed
and duplicated if unchanged in format and content. They may also be
e-mailed from person to person unaltered. Educators may alter the
materials for personal classroom use to meet their and their students'
needs. All other uses, transmissions and duplications or alterations are
prohibited unless permission is granted expressly.

- *FAQs:* Frequently Asked Questions (FAQ) is a list of the Web site's
  most commonly asked questions and their responses. The FAQ list

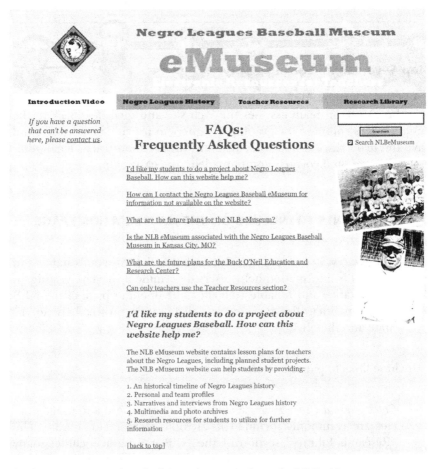

Figure 5.2.   Frequently Asked Questions page from the NLB eMuseum

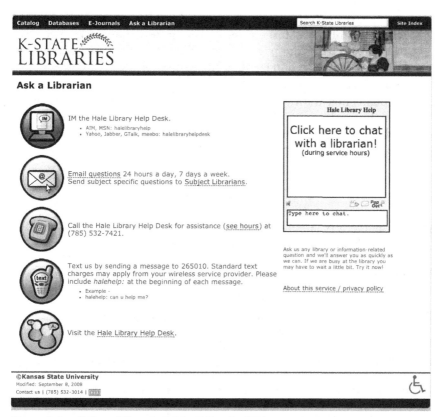

Figure 5.3. K-State Libraries' *Ask a Librarian* Web page.

is a quick way for eMuseum visitors to get answer to some of their questions before contacting someone from the museum. Below is the FAQ page from the NLB eMuseum (see Figure 5.2). As more questions from visitors arise, they will be added to the list.

- *Contact Us:* A "contact us" link should be prominently displayed on the eMuseum's homepage in case a visitor has a question or comment to share with eMuseum staff. The "contact us" link can be used to connect to a staff member's e-mail address or to open a page with a form that the visitor can fill out and send to a staff member. Some Web sites give users the option to chat with a staff member online. K-State Libraries "Ask a Librarian" page allows visitors several choices for contacting a staff member, including the option to chat with a librarian (see Figure 5.3).

- *About This Site:* Every Web site should have an "About Us" or "About This Site" page. The purpose of the About This Site page is to explain the eMuseum's purpose, enabling visitors to assess whether the goals of the eMuseum meet their information seeking needs. The About This Site page is also a place where information about the people involved in creating the eMuseum can be listed.

- *Privacy Policy:* A privacy policy is a disclaimer on the Web site that explains how information gathered from users will be used such as whether or how their information is shared with parent companies, subsidiaries, or third parties. Often the privacy policy also explains how or if the Web site uses cookies.

REFERENCES

BCR Collaborative Digitization Program. (2004). *Digital toolbox*. Retrieved March 20, 2009, from http://www.bcr.org/cdp/digitaltb/index.html

Bowen, J. (2006). *Virtual Library Museums Page*. Retrieved March 20, 2009, from http://vlmp.icom.museum

Kalfatovic, M. R. (2002). *Creating a winning online exhibition: A guide for libraries, archives, and museums*. Chicago: American Library Association.

Canadian Heritage Information Network. (2002). *Capture your collection: A guide for managers*. Retrieved March 20, 2009, from http://www.chin.gc.ca/English/Digital_Content/Managers_Guide/index.html

Coudal Partners. (2009). *The Museum of Online Museums (MoOM)*. Retrieved March 20, 2009, from http://www.coudal.com/moom.php

Minerva. (2004). *Digitisation guidelines: A selected list*. Retrieved March 20, 2009, from http://www.minervaeurope.org/guidelines.htm

University of Greenwich, School of Architecture and Construction. (2008). *Website architecture*. Retrieved March 20, 2009, from http://www.websitearchitecture.co.uk

CHAPTER 6

TECHNOLOGY DECISIONS AND WEB 2.0

When developing the eMuseum, technology decisions will be made throughout the process. There are many pros and cons to consider with each technology decision. Using the latest, most innovative technology might make the eMuseum cutting edge, but using the newest technologies can alienate users whose computers and Internet connections are not fast enough to use the eMuseum's technological features or are not familiar with how to use the newest technologies.

MEETING THE NEEDS OF THE PRIMARY AUDIENCE

The information seeking needs of the primary audience should be considerd when determining how the eMuseum's interface will best serve users. Consider the ways in which audiences are used to accessing information on a Web site. Google and Amazon are examples of heavily used Web sites that have come to define user expectations. The eMuseum team will also need to decide if information in the eMuseum can be browsed or if a Web site search feature is needed.

Handbook on Developing Curriculum Materials for Teachers:
Lessons From Museum Education Partnerships, pp. 39–58
Copyright © 2010 by Information Age Publishing

Figure 6.1.   NLB eMuseum homepage.

Make Information Seeking User-Friendly

Channels of access are the ways in which users seek information on a Web site. Each channel should meet the specific needs of a particular type of user. For the NLB eMuseum we identified the primary audience as teachers and secondary audiences as students and other people interested in learning about Negro Leagues history. Therefore, for the eMuseum entry page we developed three main channels of access by creating three entry points: Negro Leagues History, Teacher Resources, and Research Library. Audiences interested in general information about Negro Leagues history can explore the Negro Leagues History section of the eMuseum. The Teacher Resources section of the eMuseum is for the primary user group—teachers interested in working Negro Leagues history into their curriculum. The Research Library section is for audiences interested in looking at primary and secondary materials related to Negro Leagues history (see Figure 6.1).

KEYWORD SEARCHING VERSUS BROWSING

One of the primary goals of any digital resource is to make information as accessible as possible to users. One of the decisions that needs to be made is whether or not your digital collection is searchable, browsable, or both. Browsing a digital collection involves scanning lists of items available in the eMuseum whereas keyword searching directs the computer to look for a word or a combination of words from the author, title, subject, or other fields in a record. There are several factors to consider when deciding if a digital collection should be searchable. Not all information can be found by searching. The ability to find items through a search function will depend on the keywords used in the search and how the items being searched are indexed. A user's success in using a Web site's search engine relies on whether the keywords searched by the user match the words indexed by the creators of the Web site. Browsing is a good option when a user is uncertain about what they are looking for or if they want to get an idea of what is available on the Web site.

Key Factors in Deciding to Create a Searchable Digital Collection

- Is the size of the collection browsable or is a search function necessary to optimize usage? Browsing works well for small collections where a listing of items can fit on one page. If the eMuseum has too many items to browse through effectively, then a search function is useful.
- Are the items in the collection (files, images, text, etc.) already indexed with subject headings? Adding subject headings can be time consuming, expensive or difficult if they are not a priority. For a search to be effective, items will need to be indexed with subject headings.
- What resources are available for the project? It can be costly to make a collection searchable (e.g., hiring people to classify, catalog, and index digital materials).
- What do you want to be searchable? A site search allows users to search the entire eMuseum including items stored in separate databases (e.g. images, text, audio, curriculum materials).

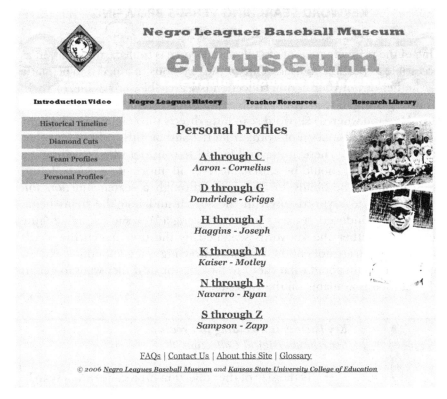

Figure 6.2.   Player profiles browseable by last name.

Browsing the eMuseum

If the amount of material available in the eMuseum is limited, there may not be a need to implement a search engine. Some resources can be accessed easily by browsing, especially if items are browsable by subject or date. Some of the items browsable in the NLB eMuseum include player biographical information, team profiles, lesson plans, and video oral histories. Player profiles can be browsed alphabetically by a player's last name (see Figure 6.2) and teams can be browsed by state.

To determine how teachers would want to browse lesson plans in the eMuseum, the NLB eMuseum Team met with teachers. By meeting with teachers, the team discovered that teachers in the classroom feel pressure to meet state and national standards such as those from the National

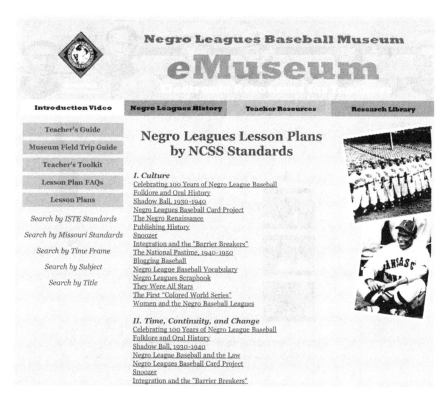

Figure 6.3.   Lesson plans browsable by NCSS Standards.

Council of Social Studies (NCSS Standards) and the International Society for Technology in Education (National Educational Technology Standards). Keeping this in mind, the team decided to make lesson plans in the eMuseum browsable by educational standards, historical time frame, subject, and lesson title (see Figure 6.3). This allows teachers to find out immediately if a lesson plan will help their lesson meet state and national standards.

Create Browsable Video Clips

The NLB eMuseum contains an online archive of video oral history interviews with people who were involved in the Negro Leagues. The entire collection of interviews is available and searchable by keyword

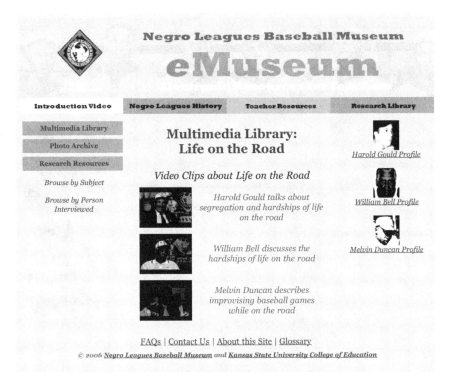

Figure 6.4.   Browsable video clips in the NLB eMuseum.

using a software system called Virage. Since most of the interviews are an hour long, we decided to break down some of the interviews into short clips that could be used by teachers in their classrooms. Members of the NLB eMuseum team watched the video interviews and identified segments that could be used as clips in the classroom. Each clip was given a subject heading and short description. Teachers can browse these clips by subject or by the name of the person being interviewed (see Figure 6.4).

When including video online, best practice is to include:

1. The format of the file. If the file is a Windows Media File, Real Media, or QuickTime, let the user know.

2. The length of the clip. Before committing to watching an online video, a user wants to know if watching the clip will take 30 seconds, 3 minutes, or 60 minutes.

3. A link to a Web site where the user can download the necessary software to watch the video. If they do not have Real Media and the video using that application, they will need to visit real.com to download the necessary software.

4. Captions for the video in case a user is hearing impaired. A written transcript can also be provided.

The eMuseum team tried to match the video oral history clips with existing lesson plans to enhance the lesson content, but these attempts were not successful. The video clips and the lesson plans had been created independent of each other and, as a result, we found it extremely difficult to find video clips that fit in with the content of the lesson plans. This experience taught us that if we want to use the oral history video clips in a lesson plan, then the lesson plan should be created around the content in the video clip.

Make Searching User Friendly

The NLB eMuseum uses software called Virage to digitize and store video oral histories. One feature of this particular software is that it allows users to search the videos with keywords. For instance, a student looking for interviews discussing racism could type "racism" in the Virage search box and receive a list of video clips in which the speaker uses the term racism. Purchasing and implementing a commercial content media manager like Virage is cost-prohibitive for many organizations. A less expensive way to let students and researchers search the text of oral history interviews is to have the interviews transcribed. Transcribed video and audio sources make it easy for researchers to save time because they can search the script for keywords. Transcription also makes primary sources like oral interviews accessible to diverse learners who have difficulty following information presented in a video or audio format.

Most of an eMuseum's visitors are used to using search engines like Google to search for information. A search engine can be used to search the entire eMuseum site. This allows users to search at the same time for curriculum materials, primary and secondary resources, and digital collections available in the eMuseum. To provide a search function for the eMuseum site, an option is to use a remote search engine. Remote, or hosted, search engines are not installed on your server, but are hosted on the server of the company providing the search service. The search engine's host site indexes your Web site and stores that information on their server. There are many commercially hosted Web site searches available. An alternative to using a hosted search engine is to use an open source program to host your own search engine. Open source software is free and allows participants to use the software and contribute to the improvement of the software. Technical support for open source software is generated from other users and developers online.

Examples of Remote Search Engine Web sites

- Atomz
  http://www.atomz.com
- FreeFind
  http://www.freefind.com
- Google Site Search
  http://www.google.com/services/websearch.html
- Master
  http://www.master.com/
- PicoSearch
  http://www.picosearch.com
- Zoom Search Engine
  http://www.wrensoft.com/zoom

- For more information see *Hosted Search Engines for Nonprofit Web sites,* from Alder Consulting (http://alderconsulting.com/searches.html)
- *A Comparison of Free Search Engine Software by Yiling Chen* (http://searchtools.com/analysis/free-search-engine-comparison.html)
  Adding a Search Engine is Easier than You Think, by Yann Toledano (http://www.techsoup.org/learningcenter/web-building/page4899.cfm)

THE NEED FOR METADATA

Not all museums that make their collections available online have been successful in meeting the information seeking needs of their online audiences. Traditionally, museums are concerned about conserving, curating, and exhibiting works in permanent collections and special exhibits. Often, when museums approach a digitization project, the majority of resources go to activities strictly related to creating digital images of collection objects, while activities such as creating additional descriptive content, building access points based on data standards and controlled vocabularies, and identifying audience needs and behaviors are put to the side to be addressed at a later date. The number of museums with Web sites is large, but the number of museums that integrate information management techniques into their Web site is relatively small. Information management techniques include using metadata standards and controlled vocabulary to describe pieces of the collection. Metadata is the structured information used to describe information resources or objects. Metadata can be categorized as descriptive, structural, and administrative (see Table 6.1). Controlled vocabulary consists of the terms used to create subject headings to use in searching a database.

> ***Example of Descriptive Metadata for a***
> ***NLB eMuseum Oral History***
>
> - **Title:** Henry Presswood
> - **Publisher:** Negro Leagues Baseball Museum
> - **Duration:** 00:50:09.00
>   **Series Title:** Negro Leagues Baseball Oral History Project
>   **Date of Interview:** 2004-07-19
> - **Keywords:** Henry Presswood, baseball, Negro Leagues, folklore, Satchel Paige

Without metadata, browsing and searching digital collections can be difficult, if not impossible, for users. Since metadata creation and implementation are resource-intensive processes, it is important to balance costs and benefits in developing a metadata strategy, taking into consideration the needs of current and future users and collection managers.

Table 6.1.   Description of Three Types of Metadata

Categories of Metadata	Description
Descriptive	Information that describes the content of the item, such as title, author, publisher, subject, and physical dimensions.
Structural	Information about the internal structure of resources including page, section, chapter numbering, indexes, and table of contents. For example, structural metadata might include identifying an oral history video interview with Buck O'Neil as Part V in the Negro Leagues Baseball Oral History Project.
Administrative	Information used to manage the object or control access to it. This may include information on how the object was scanned, its storage format, copyright, and licensing information, and information necessary for the long-term preservation of the digital objects.

There are established metadata standards suitable for use in an eMuseum such as Dublin Core and Metadata Object Description Schema (MODS). It is not uncommon to start out with the key elements of an established metadata standard and then alter them to meet the needs of the collection being described. The simple Dublin Core Metadata Element Set (DCMES) consists of the following 15 metadata elements:

1. Title
2. Creator
3. Subject
4. Description
5. Publisher
6. Contributor
7. Date
8. Type
9. Format
10. Identifier
11. Source
12. Language
13. Relation
14. Coverage
15. Rights

For more information about Dublin Core and MODS go to:

- *Dublin Core Metadata Initiatives* (http://www .dublincore.org)
- *Dublin Core Metadata Best Practices* by the CDP Metadata Working Group (http://www.bcr.org/cdp/ best/dublin-core-bp.pdf)
- *Metadata Object Description Schema* (MODS) (http:// www.loc.gov/standards/mods)

Assigning metadata is a complex task involving more than simply inserting descriptions in assigned fields. Developing metadata may require developing a standardized vocabulary and providing administrative metadata related to an item's accessioning, preservation, and collection use. Structured metadata conforms to a predictable standardize structure. Metadata that is highly structured provides more ways for users to manipulate and search items. For a good overview about using metadata see *Introduction to Metadata: Pathways to Digital Information* by Tony Gill, Anne J. Gilliland, Mary S. Woodley (http://www.getty.edu/research/conducting_research/standards/intrometadata/index.html).

When it comes to digitally preserving an object, the object and its metadata should be backed up and have the ability to be transitioned from one format to another as technology and standards change. Another reason why working with universities, libraries, and other organizations familiar with putting material online is a good idea is because they are already thinking on these terms.

> *For more information about digital preservation see:*
>
> • Digital Preservation by the Library of Congress (http://www.digitalpreservation.gov/)
> • Digital Preservation Tutorial on the Cornell University Library Web site (http://www.library .cornell.edu/iris/tutorial/dpm/eng_index.html)

REACHING DIVERSE LEARNERS

When the NLB eMuseum was developed, the development team included a teacher who is the director of special education for her school district. Thanks to her insightful perspective, we were able to use the eMuseum to address some of the needs of diverse learners by making certain that our curriculum materials made accommodations for diverse learners. The term "diverse learner" refers to differences in ability, interests, background knowledge, learning style, culture, and language that are represented in a classroom. Each lesson plan in the NLB eMuseum includes resources for diverse learners (RFDLs). Many of the RFDLs include technological resources that are freely available online to facilitate the education of learners with special needs. These RFDLs consist of alternative lesson activities and assessments for each lesson plan. In addition to providing RFDLs, the site has a Teacher's Toolkit that presents teachers with ideas and recommended resources from the Internet that can be used to accommodate their students' learning needs (see Figure 6.5). By using the Teacher's Toolkit, teachers can learn things such as how to develop their own podcasts, find tools for creating and modifying text, and implement

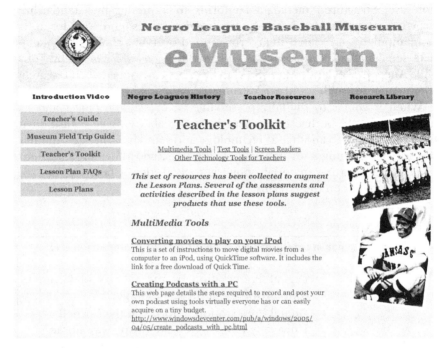

Figure 6.5.   NLB eMuseum Teacher's Toolkit.

free screen readers for their students. Like the rest of the eMuseum, the Teacher's Toolkit continues to grow and change as technology and students' needs change.

WEB ACCESSIBILITY

Web accessibility refers to making Web site content usable to people with disabilities. In other words, Web accessibility means people with disabilities can perceive, understand, navigate, and interact with and contribute to a Web site. Web accessibility addresses visual impairments (e.g., blindness, low vision, color blindness), motor impairments (e.g., Parkinson's Disease, cerebral palsy, stroke), cognitive/intellectual disabilities (e.g., learning disabilities, cognitive disabilities), hearing impairments, and seizures. For example, to make an audio file Web accessible, a text equivalent of the audio in the form of a transcript should be provided. A text equivalent should also be created for images and graphical buttons. This can be accomplished easily by including short descriptive text within the

For more information about Web Accessibility, visit these Web sites:

- *Step-by-Step Usability Guide* from the U.S. Department of Health & Human Services (http://usability.gov/)
- *Web Accessibility Initiative Guidelines and Techniques* (http://www.w3.org/WAI/guid-tech)

image or button's code. These are just a couple examples of making a Web site web accessible.

A key principle of Web accessibility involves designing Web sites and software that are flexible enough to meet different user needs, preferences, and situations. This flexibility also benefits people without disabilities. Additional situations where users benefit from Web accessibility include people with a slow Internet connection, "temporary disabilities" such as a broken arm, changing abilities due to aging, and varied learning styles. Some people are auditory learners and enjoy a text-reader even though they do not "need" it.

Tools for checking the eMuseum's Web accessibility:

- Wave 4.0 Accessibility Tool (http://wave.webaim.org)
- Vischeck (http://www.vischeck.com/vischeck)

WEB 2.0—MUSEUM 2.0

The original World Wide Web, sometimes referred to as Web 1.0, consisted of a system of interlinked Web sites. The capabilities of Web 1.0 have been surpassed and the next generation of the Web is being established. This second generation of new, Web-based capabilities is referred to as Web 2.0. Tim O'Reilly defines Web 2.0 as "a set of economic, social, and technology trends that collectively form the basis for the next generation of the Internet—a more mature, distinctive medium characterized by user participation, openness, and network effects" (O'Reilly, 2005). With Web 2.0, online community spaces are created through the input of content from that community's users, emphasizing collaboration and sharing.

Technologies such as weblogs, social bookmarking, wikis, podcasts, and RSS (Really Simple Syndication) feeds are the tools that make these interactive and interconnected communities possible. Table 6.2 compares the characteristics of Web 1.0 with those of Web 2.0. Selected Web 2.0 characteristics are explained further in this chapter.

Web 2.0 has significance for all educational institutions, including museums and libraries. As museums strive to meet the needs of their users, museums need to think about how they can define themselves in this new medium. Museums need to be where visitors are technologically. A report from Pew Internet & American Life indicates that 80% of online teens and adults under the age 28 visit blogs and 40% report they have created their own blogs (2005). In addition to being where users are technologically, Web 2.0 technologies, described later in this chapter, can offer more meaningful learning experiences for online visitors.

Did you know?
Pew Internet & American Life reports that 87% of online users have at one time used the Internet to carry out research on a scientific topic or concept and 40 million adults use the Internet as their primary source of news and information about science (Horrigan, 2006).

SOCIAL BOOKMARKING, WIKIS, BLOGS, AND PODCASTS

Social Bookmarking

Social bookmarking is a Web-based way to share Internet bookmarks. An Internet bookmark is a stored location for quick retrieval at a later date. Web browsers provide bookmarks that contain the addresses (URLs) of favorite or frequently used sites. In a social bookmarking system, users store lists of Internet resources they find useful. These lists are either accessible to the public or to a specific network. People with similar interests can view the links by category, tags, or even randomly. The Powerhouse Museum in Sydney, Australia has been finding ways to take advantage of social bookmarking. The museum's Preservation Department uses the social bookmarking Web site del.icio.us to share bookmarks with people from across departments and outside of the museum (see http://del.icio.us/phmpreservation). Users of social bookmarking sites like del.icio.us categorize their resources by the use of informally assigned, user-defined keywords or tags, sometimes referred to as folksonomy.

Table 6.2.   Comparison of Web 1.0 and Web 2.0 characteristics

Web 1.0 Characteristics	Web 2.0 Characteristics
• Reading	• Writing
• Individuals	• Communities
• HTML	• XML
• Personal Web page	• Blog
• Web portals	• RSS
• Directories (taxonomy)	• Tags (Folksonomy)
• Going to a Web site for information	• RSS feeds
• Wired connections	• Wireless
• Netscape, Internet Explorer	• Google, Firefox
• Professional	• Amateur
• Britannia Online	• Wikipedia
• Content management systems	• Wikis
• Homepage	• Mashup

Social bookmarking Web sites:

- Reddit: http://reddit.com
- Digg: http://digg.com
- De.lic.ious: http://del.icio.us

Did you know?
Folksonomy is a form of metadata generated by *users* and attached to content.

Wikis

Wikis are Web pages that allow users to collaborate by easily adding and editing content. Single pages in a wiki are referred to as "wiki pages," while the entire body of pages, which are usually interconnected by hyperlinks, are "the wiki." A wiki is actually a very simple, easy-to-use user-maintained database for creating, browsing, and searching information. A well-known example of a wiki is Wikipedia (http://en.wikipedia.org). Wikis can provide an interactive way for museum staff to interact with each other and their patrons. The Mint Museum Library uses a wiki to share exhibition information and resources, and to provide a place for curators, educators, docents, and others to share their expertise and knowledge (see Figure 6.6).

Interested in starting your own wiki?
WikiMatrix lets compare wiki platforms to find one that best suits your needs (http://www.wikimatrix.org).

Kansas State University Libraries uses wikis for internal communication purposes. Many of the departments and working teams in the libraries have their own wikis. For example, there is a team in the library working on an electronic portfolio (ePortfolio) project. The library's ePortfolio Team uses a wiki to communicate and keep track of their progress (see Figure 6.7).

Blogs (Web Logs)

A blog is a Web site where entries are made in journal style and displayed in reverse chronological order. Blogs are often used to provide commentary on a particular subject, such as news or politics. Blogs combine text, images, and links to other blogs and Web pages and allow readers to leave comments, making the blog an interactive form of communication. Museums and libraries are increasingly using blogs to communicate with colleagues and the public. To see how other museums are using blogs, go to the Web site *Museum Blogs*, which is a directory of museum and museum-related blogs (http://www.museumblogs.org/).

Podcasting

Podcasting is the preparation and distribution of audio files to the computers of subscribers using RSS. These audio files can be uploaded to digital music or multimedia players such as an iPod. Once users have downloaded a podcast onto their digital music player, they can listen to the podcast whenever they want. Some museums are using podcasting to create audio tours of their exhibits. The Kansas State Historical Society has podcasts of their curator talking about different objects in their collections (see Figure 6.8).

REFERENCES

Alder Consulting. (2003). *Hosted search engines for nonprofit websites*. Retrieved March 20, 2009, from http://alderconsulting.com/searches.html

Atomz. (2009). Retrieved March 20, 2009, from http://www.atomz.com

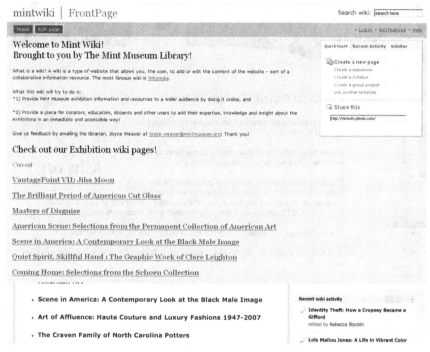

Figure 6.6.   Mint Museums library wiki.

Figure 6.7.   K-State Libraries ePortfolio wiki.

Figure 6.8.   Kansas State Historical Society podcasts.

Audacity. (2009). Retrieved March 20, 2009, from http://audacity.sourceforge.net/download

Bloglines. (2009). Retrieved March 20, 2009, from http://www.bloglines.com

CDP Metadata Working Group. (2006). *Dublin Core Metadata best practices.* Retrieved March 20, 2009, from http://www.bcr.org/cdp/best/dublin-core-bp.pdf

Chen, Y. (2006). *A comparison of free search engine software.* Retrieved March 20, 2009, from http://searchtools.com/analysis/free-search-engine-comparison.html

Cornell University Library. (2007). *Digital preservation tutorial.* Retrieved Retrieved March 20, 2009, from http://www.library.cornell.edu/iris/tutorial/dpm/eng_eindex.html

De.lic.ious. (2009). Retrieved March 20, 2009, from http://del.icio.us

Digg. (2009). Retrieved March 20, 2009 from http://digg.com

Dublin Core Metadata Initiatives. (2009). Retrieved March 20, 2009, from http://www.dublincore.org

Easy Podcast. (2008). Retrieved March 20, 2009, from http://www.easypodcast.com

FreeFind. (2008). Retrieved March 20, 2009, from http://www.freefind.com

Google Site Search. (2009). Retrieved March 20, 2009 at http://www.google.com/sitesearch/

What is RSS?
Really Simple Syndication or Rich Site Summary, commonly known as RSS, is a family of Web-feed formats used to publish frequently updated digital content, such as blogs, news feeds, or podcasts. Users of RSS content use programs called feed "readers" or "aggregators." A user subscribes to a feed by supplying to his or her reader a link to the feed. The reader can then check the user's subscribed feeds to see if any of those feeds have new content since the last time checked, and if so, retrieve that content and present the content to the user. Examples of feed readers include Bloglines (http://www.bloglines.com), Netvibes (http://www.netvibes.com), and Mozilla Firefox which has RSS integrated into its browser (http://www.mozilla.com/firefox).

To find more information about feed readers, see:
Dave Winer's site at
http://www.reallysimplesyndication.com/

Software for getting started with podcasting:

- **Audacity**
  Free, cross-platform, open source software for recording and editing sounds (http://audacity.sourceforge.net/download/)
- Easy Podcast
  A cross-platform GUI tool for easy podcast publication (http://www.easypodcast.com/)

Horrigan, J. (2006, November 20). The Internet as a resource for news and information about science. *Pew Internet & American Life Project*. Retrieved March 20, 2009, from http://www.pewinternet.org/~/media//Files/Reports/2006/PIP_Exploratorium_Science.pdf.pdf

Ideum. (2009). *Museum blogs*. Retrieved March 20, 2009, from http://www.museumblogs.org

Kansas State Historical Society. (2008). *Cool things podcast*. Retrieved May 21, 2008, from http://www.kshs.org/audiotours/coolthings/index.htm

Kansas State University Libraries. (2007). *Kansas State University Libraries Wiki*. Retrieved March 20, 2009, from http://docs.ksulib.org

Library of Congress. (2008). *Digital preservation*. Retrieved March 20, 2009 http://www.digitalpreservation.gov

Library of Congress. (2009). *Metadata Object Description Schema (MODS)*. Retrieved March 20, 2009, from http://www.loc.gov/standards/mods

Mint Museum Library. (2007). *Mintwiki*. Retrieved May 25, 2008, from http://mintwiki.pbwiki.com

Master. (2003). Retrieved March 20, 2009, from http://www.master.com

Mozzilla Firefox. (2009). Retrieved March 20, 2009, from http://www.mozilla.com/firefox

Negro Leagues Baseball Museum and Kansas State University. (2007). *Negro Leagues Baseball eMuseum*. Retrieved March 20, 2009, from http://www.coe.ksu.edu/nlbemuseum

O'Reilly, T. (2005). *What is Web 2.0? Design patterns and business models for the next generation of software*. Retrieved March 20, 2009, from http://www.oreilly-net.com/pub/a/oreilly/tim/news/2005/09/30/what-is-web-20.html

PicoSearch. (2008). Retrieved March 20, 2009, from http://www.picosearch.com

Reddit. (2009). Retrieved March 20, 2009, from http://reddit.com

Toledano, Y. (2005). Adding a search engine is easier than you think. *TechSoup*. Retrieved March 20, 2009, from http://www.techsoup.org/learningcenter/webbuilding/page4899.cfm

U.S. Department of Health & Human Services. (2007). *Step-by-step usability guide*. Retrieved March 20, 2009, from http://usability.gov

Vischeck. (2007). Retrieved March 20, 2009, from http://www.wave.webaim.org

WebAIM. (2008). *Wave 4.0*. Retrieved March 20, 2009 from http://wave.webaim.org

WikiMatrix. (n.d). Retrieved March 20, 2009, from http://www.wikimatrix.org

Winer, D. (2008). *Dave Winer's RSS blog*. Retrieved March 20, 2009, http://www.reallysimplesyndication.com

World Wide Web Consortium. (2006). *Web accessibility initiative guidelines and techniques*. Retrieved March 20, 2009, from http://www.w3.org/WAI/guid-tech

WrenSoft. (2008). *Zoom search engine*. Retrieved March 20, 2009, from http://www.wrensoft.com/zoom

CHAPTER 7

FORMATIVE ASSESSMENT AND SUMMATIVE EVALUATION

Assessment of the eMuseum's content, functionality, and interface should be ongoing. Formative assessments are ongoing and can occur at any point in the life of the eMuseum. For example, a formative assessment occurs when a focus group of potential users are asked to evaluate a prototype of the eMuseum's home page before any final decisions are made about the layout and content of the page. A summative evaluation is a final, overall assessment of the eMuseum. The summative evaluation occurs once all components of the eMuseum are in place. Summative assessments of the eMuseum should be conducted regularly, but not as frequently as formative assessments. Consider conducting a summative assessment whenever new content is added to the eMuseum.

DEVELOPING THE ASSESSMENT TEAM

Assessment and evaluation should be conducted by a team that includes the eMuseum webmaster, a technical services member or Web designer responsible for developing the eMuseum's interface, a public services person who is in contact with the customers on a daily basis, a museum administrator, and one or two museum staff members who can provide a pair of fresh eyes. The assessment team should also include representatives from stakeholder groups, such as students and teachers.

Handbook on Developing Curriculum Materials for Teachers:
Lessons From Museum Education Partnerships, pp. 59–63
Copyright © 2010 by Information Age Publishing
59

GATHERING DATA FOR ASSESSMENT

There are several ways data can be gathered for assessment and evaluation including Web analytics, usability studies, and Web-based feedback forms. Assessment of the eMuseum should be an ongoing process. Some of these data gathering methods can be done by someone in-house (developing a Web-based feedback form) while other methods may require outside expertise (Web analytics), depending on the skill levels of the museum staff.

Web Analytics

Web metrics, Web analytics, and site stats are some of the terms used to describe the recording and interpreting of Web site statistics. Web metrics and statistics involve sorting through data to identify patterns (trends) to determine user behavior for analysis. Analysis of data helps determine how visitors use the eMuseum site. For example, web analytics can provide details about which Web pages are most frequently accessed on a particular Web site, giving a good sense of what audiences are interested in and which webpages may need more prominence. Additional examples of data that can be collected include:

- Clickstream analysis: Involves analysis of the route that visitors choose when navigating through the Web site. A clickstream is a list of all the pages viewed by a user, presented in the order the pages were viewed. A clickstream will show when and where a user came in to a site, all the pages viewed, the time spent on each page, and when and where they left;
- Web page significance: Significance metrics measure the "quality" and "relevance" of Web pages in response to user needs. Significance metrics rate Web pages in response to a search query and have an impact on the quality of search and retrieval on the Web;
- Referring URL: Which Web pages users visit to get to your site, such as another museum page, another page at your institution, or a search engine;
- IP (Internet Protocol) address: Indicates where users' computers are located, based on the domain names to determine if access is primarily from computers within your institution or remote;
- Browser: Information about which browsers and versions are most often used to access your site. Statistics that show the percentage of page views from various versions of browsers provide a glimpse of

how a site is experienced by a visitor and if visitors are using Macs or PCs;

- Login time and session end time: How much time from beginning to end of the visit and times of day and week when the site is used the most and the least;

- Number of unique visits or accesses to the eMuseum: How many times the site has been visited; and

- Server load or responsiveness: How quickly a user is able to access pages during peak periods of demand.

Many vendors offer Web analytic services. For more information on Web analytics and vendors, see:

- Web Analytics Report from CMS Watch (http://www.cmswatch.com/Analytics/Report)
- Omega Digital Media's Web Traffic Data Sources and Vendor Comparison (http://www.ga-experts.co .uk/web-data-sources.pdf)

Usability Studies

Web analytics entails sorting through data to identify patterns (trends), whereas usability studies involve observing people to see how they interact with the Web site. Usability testing allows testers to collect both qualitative and quantitative data as the user performs a real task or set of tasks. Usability testing can be done before committing time and resources to actually building the site by using paper prototypes or computer-based mockups. Usability testing is not a tool of validation but one of evaluation where the goal is to uncover any problems or stumbling blocks that may interfere with navigation through a Web site. Participants are observed completing one or more assigned tasks using the eMuseum Web site. These tasks should require the participant to find something on the eMuseum Web site and should be kept to a minimum of seven to 10 tasks for a 1-hour session.

Tips for Usability Research

- Develop a consent form to be signed by study participants. The form should disclose the purpose of the study, outline how the research team will ensure participant privacy, provide an escape clause giving participants permission to stop the test and leave at

---

Usability Test Consent Form

Please read and sign this form.

In this usability test for the Negro Leagues Baseball eMuseum:
- You will be asked to perform certain tasks on a website.
- We will also conduct an interview with you.
- You will be asked to fill in a questionnaire.

Participation in this usability study is voluntary. All information will remain confidential. The descriptions and findings may be used to help improve the website, but at no time will your name or other identifying information be used. You can withdraw your consent to the experiment and stop participation at any time.

If you have any questions or concerns, please contact Tara Baillargeon at 532-5760.

I have read and understood the information on this form and had all of my questions answered

_____   _____

Subject's Signature   Date

_____

Subject's Name Printed

Figure 7.1.   Example of a usability test consent form.

any time, and provide participants with contact information for members of the research team should they have any questions or concerns (see Figure 7.1).

- To ensure that participants experience the usability assessment in exactly the same way, compose a script that volunteers read before and after each test session and/or focus group. This standardized protocol was developed to combat experimenter bias where researchers unwittingly influence the behavior of their subjects.
- Use mock session to rehearse the usability test to detect errors or misleading instructions.

Web-Based Feedback Form

A simple Web-based feedback system is useful for acquiring user feedback for ongoing formative assessment. Users have the option of sending comments and questions to the eMuseum through an e-mail link, an online form, or real-time chat.

REFERENCES

CMS Watch. (2008). *Web analytics report*. Available at http://www.cmswatch.com/Analytics/report/

Dhyani, D., Ng, W. K., & Bhowmick, S. S. (2002). A survey of web metrics. *ACM Computing Surveys, 34*(4), 469-503.

Nielsen, J. (2009). *Useit: Usable information technology*. Retrieved March 20, 2009, from http://www.useit.com

Omega Digital Media. (2008). *Web traffic data sources & vendor comparisons*. Retrieved March 20, 2009, from http://www.cmswatch.com/Analytics/report

TechSoup: The technology place for non-profits. (2009). Retrieved March 20, 2009, from http://www.techsoup.org

User Interface Engineering. (2009). Retrieved March 20, 2009, from http://www.uie.com

VandeCreek, L. M. (2005). Usability analysis of Northern Illinois University Libraries' website: A case study. *OCLC Systems & Services, 21*(3), 181-192.

CHAPTER 8

MAINTENANCE AND FUNDING

Who will be responsible for maintaining and updating the eMuseum? The eMuseum will need continued maintenance and financial support. Funding is needed not only to start up the project, but to maintain the eMuseum into the future. As you consider long-term staff and technology needs, find out how much financial support is available from your own organization and if the organization is willing to offer long-term support.

GRANT SOURCES

The creation of an eMuseum involves the digitization of materials. Any large-scale digitization project benefits from external financial support to get started. Consider local, state, national, philanthropic, and collaborative sources for grant opportunities. These are sources that can help with start-up costs. These grant opportunities are not designed for long-term support, so it is crucial to think about long-term ways of sustaining the eMuseum. Here are some suggested sources for finding out about external funding opportunities:

- *Technology Grant News*, published four times a year, identifies funding sources in technology. More information and a sample issue are available online (http://www.technologygrantnews.com).
- Institute of Museum and Library Services (IMLS): Several of their grants are designed to support museum and library partnerships,

Handbook on Developing Curriculum Materials for Teachers:
Lessons From Museum Education Partnerships, pp. 65–69
Copyright © 2010 by Information Age Publishing

and services to Native American and Hawaiian populations (http://www.imls.gov).

- National Endowment for the Humanities (NEH): For information on digitization projects, look for their Digital Humanities Initiative and Preservation and Access Grants (http://www.neh.gov/grants/index.html).
- National Historical Publications and Records Commission (NHPRC): Features a grant for digitizing historical records (http://www.archives.gov/nhprc).

There may be local or state agencies available to provide funding for the eMuseum project. For example, each U.S. state has a state humanities council (http://www.statehumanities.org). These state agencies offer grant opportunities for nonprofit organizations. Consider other state agencies that are related to the subject matter of the eMuseum who may have grant opportunities.

Check if there are local resources that may be able to help fund your project. Kansas State University Libraries and the NLBM found a grant available at Kansas State University that had the potential to help us with our start-up costs. We applied for this small grant at the beginning of our library-museum partnership to fund meeting expenses and the cost of hiring a part-time worker to digitize collections. The collaborative work required to apply for a small, start-up grant was an effective way to solidify the K-State University Libraries–Negro Leagues Baseball Museum partnership and help us to clarify our goals and outcomes, regardless of whether or not we were awarded the small grant.

Before applying for start-up funding, think about how the eMuseum will be maintained and updated once the initial phase of the project is completed. An eMuseum is never a "finished" project because the site will continually need updated information about collections and events. Web 2.0 technologies such as blogs and wikis will need to be maintained, and eventually, the eMuseum may need to migrate to new platforms, depending on how technology changes in the future.

Free Resource for Finding Grant Opportunities

- Library Grants Blog
  (http://librarygrants.blogspot.com)

This is a free resource for finding grant and award opportunities suitable for libraries and museums.

How will the eMuseum be maintained in the future? Consider some of the following questions:

- How do you plan to store exhibition or archival images and where?
- What kind of backup mechanism do you have in place in case of hardware/software failure?
- What plans have you considered for data migration and refreshment? Data migration involves transferring data between storage types, formats, or computer systems and is required when organizations change computer systems or upgrade to new systems.
- What level of long-term institutional commitment have you secured for your project?
- Do you have funding resources secured for maintenance of the digitized collection into the future?
- Is staff available to keep curriculum materials up to date by checking and maintaining links?

ADDITIONAL FUND RAISING SOURCES

The search for funding can take a long time so it is important that the eMuseum's leadership encourages staff and volunteers. Look at funding models used by other nonprofit institutions offering services to the public, such as museums, zoos, and science centers. When seeking money from donors, the eMuseum should play up its strengths and not present itself to potential donors as being a poor organization. After all, few people will want to donate money to a project that is on the verge of failure. People want to give to organizations that have the ability to sustain themselves. Focusing on the strengths of the eMuseum is one effective way to make donors feel assured about giving money. Link private donations to specific donor interests by supplying donors a checklist where they can specify which area of the eMuseum they wish to support. When developing the donation checklist, be sure to provide a category that allows donors to give money "where it is needed most." Museums and libraries that are serious about fund raising should have a full-time staff member dedicated to raising money. Fund raising experts should be able to pay for themselves by making their own salary and more within 1 year.

Corporate Sponsorships

Corporations realize that providing funding for digital information projects reflects positively on themselves. Through these partnerships, museums get funding and corporations build their brand and extend their customer base by associating with a museum. Sponsorship can take the form of sponsoring a piece of equipment, a session at an event, part of the salary of a staff member, or print-based, public-relations materials. Some sponsorship might involve giving gifts in the form of business and financial planning, marketing, and subject-matter expertise. Though there is evidence that corporate money influences the content of museums' exhibits, some museums are comfortable with industry funding and believe it does not compromise their activities and strategies (Jacobson, 1993).

Special Event Support

Special events for the eMuseum's target audience such as concerts, workshops, demonstrations, seminars, silent auctions, and sports tournaments have the potential to create publicity and can generate some profits. Heritage Canada has a good resource published online called *Guide to Special Events Fundraising* by Ken Wyman. It is available at http://www.nald.ca/fulltext/heritage/ComPartnE/specev1.htm

E-Commerce

E-commerce is a method that museums are increasingly using to generate income, though few museums report making a significant amount of money from online sales. However, e-commerce may provide new ways of selling existing products, or reaching new customers and providing a better range of services. Having a clear link on the eMuseum Web site to the museums' gift shop may solicit purchases from Web site users. Also, some museums, libraries, and archives offer patrons the opportunity to purchase high-quality prints of images featured in their online collections.

Training and Consulting

There is a demand for training in developing and maintaining digital collections. If your museum staff has a member with expertise in a particular subject, technology, or user groups, then there are possibilities for offering their services on a consultancy basis. Consulting has the advantage of often being short-term and, therefore, could be used as a contract-filler (and staff retainer) between longer periods of project funding.

CONCLUSION

Small- and medium-sized museums can develop eMuseums to reach audiences beyond the museum walls. Museums can enhance their relevancy by being where users are when information is needed. By making collections, exhibits and curriculum materials available online, eMuseums are making valuable resources available to their audiences. With the implementation of Web 2.0 technologies, eMuseums are able to engage with audiences in ways that were previously unknown. Undoubtedly, small museums will face challenges related to staffing and availability of resources during the creation of an eMuseum. However, the eMuseum Development Model provides guidelines for planning, developing and evaluating eMuseums emphasizing the value of developing partnerships. As demonstrated by the K-State–Negro Leagues Baseball Museum partnership, collaborating with outside institutions and sharing expertise can alleviate some of the staffing and resource challenges faced by small museums.

REFERENCES

Federation of State Humanities Councils. (2008). Retrieved March 20, 2009 http://www.statehumanities.org

Institute of Museum and Library Services. (2008). Retrieved March 20, 2009 from, http://www.imls.gov

Jacobson, M. (1993). Museums that put corporations on display. *Business and Society Review, 86*, 24-28.

Library Grants Blog. (2009). Retrieved March 20, 2009, from http://librarygrants.blogspot.com

National Endowment for the Humanities. (2008). *Apply for a grant.* Retrieved March 20, 2009, from http://www.neh.gov/grants/index.html

National Historical Publications and Records Commission. (2008). Retrieved March 20, 2009, from http://www.archives.gov/nhprc

Technology Grant News. (2009). Retrieved March 20, 2009, from http://www.technologygrantnews.com

Wyman, K. (1998). *Guide to special events fundraising*. Retrieved March 20, 2009, from http://www.nald.ca/fulltext/heritage/ComPartnE/specev1.htm

REFERENCES

Advanced Survey. (2009). Retrieved March 20, 2009, from http://www .advancedsurvey.com

Alder Consulting. (2003). *Hosted search engines for nonprofit websites*. Retrieved March 20, 2009, from http://alderconsulting.com/searches.html

Atomz. (2009). Retrieved March 20, 2009, from http://www.atomz.com

Audacity. (2009). Retrieved March 20, 2009, from http://audacity.sourceforge.net/ download

Bailey, G. D., Bailey, G. L., & Lumley, D. (1998). *101 tips, traps, and to-dos for creating teams: A guidebook for school leaders*. Bloomington, IN: National Educational Service.

BCR Collaborative Digitization Program. (2004). *Digital toolbox*. Retrieved March 20, 2009, from http://www.bcr.org/cdp/digitaltb/index.html

Bennett, N. A., Sandore, B., & Pianfetti, E. S. (2002) Illinois digital cultural heritage community-collaborative interactions among libraries, museums and elementary schools. *D-Lib Magazine, 8*(1). Retrieved March 20, 2009, from http://www.dlib.org/dlib/january02/bennett/01bennett.html

Bergy, L. (2006). Promoting your new (or redesigned) Web site: Ten cost-effective and easy ways to generate a buzz. *TechSoup*. Retrieved March 20, 2009, from http://www.techsoup.org/learningcenter/webbuilding/page5958.cfm

Bevan, B. (2005). Starting with what we know: A CILS framework for moving from physical to virtual science learning environments. In L. Tan & R. Subramaniam (Eds.), *E-learning and virtual science centers* (pp. 68-92). Hershey, PA: Information Science.

Bloglines. (2009). Retrieved March 20, 2009, from http://www.bloglines.com

Bowen, J. (2006). *Virtual Library Museums Page*. Retrieved March 20, 2009, from http://vlmp.icom.museum

Canadian Heritage Information Network. (2002). *Capture your collection: A guide for managers*. Retrieved March 20, 2009, from http://www.chin.gc.ca/English/ Digital_Content/Managers_Guide/index.html

CDP Metadata Working Group. (2006). *Dublin Core Metadata best practices*. Retrieved March 20, 2009, from http://www.bcr.org/cdp/best/dublin-core-bp.pdf

Chen, Y. (2006). *A comparison of free search engine software*. Retrieved March 20, 2009, from http://searchtools.com/analysis/free-search-engine-comparison.html

CMS Watch. (2008). *Web analytics report*. Retrieved March 20, 2009, from http://www.cmswatch.com/Analytics/report/

Coudal Partners. (2009). *The Museum of Online Museums (MoOM)*. Retrieved March 20, 2009, from http://www.coudal.com/moom.php

Coburn, E., & Baca, M. (2004). Beyond the gallery walls: Tools and methods for leading end-users to collections information. *Bulletin of the American Society for Information Science and Technology, 30*(5), p. 14-19.

Cohen, D. J., & Rosenzweig, R. (2005). *Digital history: A guide to gathering, preserving, and presenting the past on the web*. Philadelphia: University of Pennsylvania Press.

Collaborative Digitization Project. (2006). *Toolbox*. Retrieved March 20, 2009, from http://www.bcr.org/cdp/digitaltb/index.html

De.lic.ious. (2009). Retrieved March 20, 2009, from http://del.icio.us

Dhyani, D., Ng, W. K., & Bhowmick, S. S. (2002). A survey of web metrics. *ACM Computing Surveys, 34*(4), 469-503.

Digg. (2009). Retrieved March 20, 2009 from http://digg.com

Doswell, R., Bailey, G. D., & Lumley, D. (2006). Educational partnerships: Times, traditions, and technology-teaching the Negro Leagues. In E. J. Rielly (Ed.), *Baseball in the classroom: Essays on teaching the national pastime* (pp. 33-39). Jefferson, NC: McFarland.

Dublin Core Metadata Initiatives. (2009). Retrieved March 20, 2009, from http://www.dublincore.org

Easy Podcast. (2008). Retrieved March 20, 2009, from http://www.easypodcast.com

EZquestionnaire. (2008). Retrieved March 20, 2009, from http://www.ezquestionnaire.com

Federation of State Humanities Councils. (2008). Retrieved March 20, 2009 http://www.statehumanities.org

FreeFind. (2008). Retrieved March 20, 2009, from http://www.freefind.com

Google Site Search. (2009). Retrieved March 20, 2009 at http://www.google.com/sitesearch/

Horrigan, J. (2006, November 20). The Internet as a resource for news and information about science. *Pew Internet & American Life Project*. Retrieved March 20, 2009, from http://www.pewinternet.org/~/media//Files/Reports/2006/PIP_Exploratorium_Science.pdf.pdf

Ideum. (2009). *Museum blogs*. Retrieved March 20, 2009, from http://www.museumblogs.org

Institute of Museum and Library Services. (2008). Retrieved March 20, 2009 from, http://www.imls.gov

Jacobson, M. (1993). Museums that put corporations on display. *Business and Society Review, 86*, 24-28.

Kalfatovic, M. R. (2002). *Creating a winning online exhibition: A guide for libraries, archives, and museums.* Chicago: American Library Association.

Kansas State Historical Society. (2008). *Cool things podcast.* Retrieved May 21, 2008, from http://www.kshs.org/audiotours/coolthings/index.htm

Kansas State University Libraries. (2007). *Kansas State University Libraries Wiki.* Retrieved March 20, 2009, from http://docs.ksulib.org

Lesk, M. (2005). *Understanding digital libraries.* New York: Morgan Kaufmann.

Lewis, M. (1995). Focus group interviews in qualitative research. *Action Research Electronic Reader.* Retrieved March 20, 2009, from http://www.scu.edu.au/schools/gcm/ar/arr/arow/rlewis.html

Library Grants Blog. (2009). Retrieved March 20, 2009, from http://librarygrants.blogspot.com

Library of Congress. (2008). *Digital preservation.* Retrieved March 20, 2009 http://www.digitalpreservation.gov

Library of Congress. (2009). *Metadata Object Description Schema (MODS).* Retrieved March 20, 2009, from http://www.loc.gov/standards/mods

Marty, P. F. (2008). Museum websites and museum visitors: Before and after the museum visit. *Museum Management and Curatorship, 22*(4), 337-360.

Marty, P. F., & Twidale, M.B. (2004). Lost in gallery space: A conceptual framework for analyzing the usability flaws of museum *Web sites. First Monday, 9*(9). Retrieved March 20, 2009, from http://firstmonday.org/htbin/cgiwrap/bin/ojs/index.php/fm/article/view/1171/1091

Master. (2003). Retrieved March 20, 2009, from http://www.master.com

Minerva. (2004). *Digitisation guidelines: A selected list.* Retrieved March 20, 2009, from http://www.minervaeurope.org/guidelines.htm

Mint Museum Library. (2007). *Mintwiki.* Retrieved May 25, 2008, from http://mintwiki.pbwiki.com

Mozzilla Firefox. (2009). Retrieved March 20, 2009, from http://www.mozilla.com/firefox

Museums Association. (2005). *Collections for the future: Report of a Museums Association inquiry.* Retrieved March 20, 2009, from http://www.museumassociation.org/asset_arena/text/ns/policy_collections.pdf

National Endowment for the Humanities. (2008). *Apply for a grant.* Retrieved March 20, 2009, from http://www.neh.gov/grants/index.html

National Historical Publications and Records Commission. (2008). Retrieved March 20, 2009, from http://www.archives.gov/nhprc

National Opinion Research Center. (n.d.). *What is a survey?* Retrieved March 20, 2009, from http://www.whatisasurvey.info

Negro Leagues Baseball Museum and Kansas State University. (2007). *Negro Leagues Baseball eMuseum.* Retrieved March 20, 2009, from http://www.coe.ksu.edu/nlbemuseum

Nielsen, J. (2009). *Useit: Usable information technology.* Retrieved March 20, 2009, from http://www.useit.com

North Central Regional Educational Laboratory. (2004). *Components of a vision.* Retrieved March 20, 2009, from http://www.ncrel.org/sdrs/areas/issues/educatrs/leadrshp/le1comps.htm

O'Reilly, T. (2005). *What is Web 2.0? Design patterns and business models for the next generation of software.* Retrieved March 20, 2009, from http://www.oreillynet .com/pub/a/oreilly/tim/news/2005/09/30/what-is-web-20.html

Omega Digital Media. (2008). *Web traffic data sources & vendor comparisons.* Retrieved March 20, 2009, from http://www.cmswatch.com/Analytics/report

PicoSearch. (2008). Retrieved March 20, 2009, from http://www.picosearch.com

Plosker, G. (2005, March/April). Revisiting library funding: What really works? *Online, 29*(2), 48-51.

Puglia, S. (1999). The costs of digital imaging projects. *RLG DigiNews 3*(5). Retrieved March 20, 2009, from http://worldcat.org/arcviewer/1/OCC/2007/ 08/08/0000070511/viewer/file422.html

Reddit. (2009). Retrieved March 20, 2009, from http://reddit.com

Schonlau, M., Fricker, R. D., and Elliott, M. N. (2003). *Conducting research surveys via e-mail and the web.* Retrieved March 20, 2009, from http://www.rand.org/ pubs/monograph_reports/MR1480/index.html

Search Engine Watch. (2009). Retrieved March 20, 2009, from http:// searchenginewatch.com

Smithsonian National Museum of American History. (2006). *The price of freedom: Exhibition.* Retrieved March 20, 2009, from http://americanhistory.si.edu /militaryhistory/exhibition/flash.html

Survey Monkey. (2008). Retrieved March 20, 2009, from http://www.surveymonkey .com

SurveyKey. (2008). Retrieved March 20, 2009, from http://www.surveykey.com

Technology Grant News. (2009). Retrieved March 20, 2009, from http://www .technologygrantnews.com

TechSoup: The technology place for non-profits. (2009). Retrieved March 20, 2009, from http://www.techsoup.org

Toledano, Y. (2005). Adding a search engine is easier than you think. *TechSoup.* Retrieved March 20, 2009, from http://www.techsoup.org/learningcenter /webbuilding/page4899.cfm

U.S. Department of Health & Human Services. (2007). *Step-by-step usability guide.* Retrieved March 20, 2009, from http://usability.gov

User Interface Engineering. (2009). Retrieved March 20, 2009, from http://www .uie.com

United States President's Research Committee on Social Trends. (1934). *Recent social trends in the United States: Report of the President's Research Committee on Social Trends.* New York: McGraw Hill.

University of Greenwich, School of Architecture and Construction. (2008). *Website architecture.* Retrieved March 20, 2009, from http://www.websitearchitecture .co.uk

VandeCreek, L. M. (2005). Usability analysis of Northern Illinois University Libraries' website: A case study. *OCLC Systems & Services, 21*(3), 181-192.

Vischeck. (2007). Retrieved March 20, 2009, from http://www.wave.webaim.org

WebAIM. (2008). *Wave 4.0.* Retrieved March 20, 2009 from http://wave .webaim.org

WikiMatrix. (n.d). Retrieved March 20, 2009, from http://www.wikimatrix.org

Winer, D. (2008). *Dave Winer's RSS blog*. Retrieved March 20, 2009, http://www.reallysimplesyndication.com

World Wide Web Consortium. (2006). *Web accessibility initiative guidelines and techniques*. Retrieved March 20, 2009, from http://www.w3.org/WAI/guid-tech

WrenSoft. (2008). *Zoom search engine*. Retrieved March 20, 2009, from http://www.wrensoft.com/zoom

Wyman, K. (1998). *Guide to special events fundraising*. Retrieved March 20, 2009, from http://www.nald.ca/fulltext/heritage/ComPartnE/specev1.htm

APPENDIX

Recommended Web Sites
by Chapter and Subject

Chapter 3

Focus Groups:

- Lewis, M. *Focus group interviews in qualitative research.* http://www.scu.edu/au/schools/gcm/ar/arr/arow/rlewis.html

Surveys:

- AdvancedSurvey. http://wwwadvancedsurvey.com
- EZquestionnaire. http://www.ezquestionnaire.com
- National Opinion Research Center. *What is a survey?* http://www.whatisasurvey.info
- Schonlau, M., Fricker, R. D., & Elliott, M. N. *Conducting research surveys via e-mail and the web.* http://www.rand.org/pubs/monography_reports/MR1480/index.html
- SurveyKey. http://www.surveykey.com
- Survey Monkey. http://www.surveymonkey.com

Handbook on Developing Curriculum Materials for Teachers: Lessons From Museum Education Partnerships, pp. 77–80
Copyright © 2010 by Information Age Publishing

Website Promotion:

- Bergey, L. *Promoting your new (or redesigned) web site: Ten cost-effective and easy ways to generate a buzz.* http://www.techsoup.org /learningcenter/webbuilding/page5958.cfm
- Search Engine Watch. http://searchenginewatch.com

Chapter 5

Directories of Museum Websites:

- The Museum of Online Museums (MoOM). http://www.coudal.com/ moom.php
- Virtual Library Museum Page. http://vlmp.icom.museum

Selecting Objects:

- Canadian Heritage Information Network. *Capture your collection: A guide for managers.* http://www.chin.gc.ca/English/Digital_Content/ Managers_Guide/index.html
- Minerva. *Digitisation guidelines: A selected list.* http://www .minervaeurope.org/guidelines.htm

Digitization:

- The Collaborative Digitization Program. *Digital toolbox.* http:// www.bcr.org/cdp/best/digital-imaging-bp.pdf

Web Site Design:

- University of Greenwich. *Website architecture.* http://www .websitearchitecture.co.uk

Chapter 6

Web Site Search Engines:

- Alder Consulting. *Hosted search engines for nonprofit websites.* http:// alderconsulting .com/searches.html
- Atomz. http://www.atomz.com
- Chen, Y. *A comparison of free search engine software.* http://search-tools.com/analysis/free-searchengine-comparison.html
- FreeFind. http://www.freefind.com
- Google Site Search. http://www.google.com/services/websearch.html

- Master. http://www.master.com
- PicoSearch. http://www.picosearch.com
- Toledano, Y. *Adding a search engine is easier than you think*. http://www.techsoup.org/learningcenter/webbuilding/page4899.cfm
- Zoom Search Engine. http://www.wrensoft.com/zoom

Metadata:

- Dublin Core Metadata Initiatives. http://www.dublincore.org
- CDP Metadata Working Group. *Dublin Core Metadata best practices*. http://www.bcr.org/cdp/best/dublin-core-bp.pdf
- Gill, T., Gilliland, A. J., & Woodley, M. S. *Introduction to metadata: Pathways to digital information.* http://www.getty.edu/research/conducting_research/standards/intrometadata/index.html
- Library of Congress. *Metadata object description Schema (MODS)*. http://www.loc.gov/standards/mods

Digital Preservation:

- Library of Congress. *Digital preservation*. http://www.digitalpreservation.gov
- Cornell University Libraries. *Digital preservation tutorial*. http://www.library.cornell.edu/iris/tutorial/dpm/eng_index.html

Web Site Accessibility:

- U.S. Department of Health & Human Services. *Step-by-step usability guide*. http://usability.gov
- Wave 4.0 Accessibility Tool. http://wave.webaim.org
- Web Accessibility Initiative. *WAI guidelines and techniques*. http://www.w3.org/WAI/guid-tech
- Vischeck. http://www.vischeck.com/vischeck

Social Bookmarking Web Sites:

- Reddit. http://reddit.com
- Digg. http://digg.com
- De.lic.ious. http://del.icio.us

Wikis:

- WikiMatrix. http://www.wikimatrix.org

Blogs and RSS:

- Bloglines. http://www.bloglines.com

- Mozilla Firefox (RSS integrated browser). http://www.mozilla.com/firefox
- Museum Blogs. http://www.museumblogs.org
- Netvibes http://www.netvibes.com
- Dave Winer's Really Simple Syndication. http://wwwreallysimple-syndication.com

Podcasting:
Audacity. http://audacity.sourceforge.net
Easy Podcast. http://www.easypodcast.com

Chapter 7

Web Analytics:
- CMS Watch. *Web analytics report*. http://www.cmswatch.com/Analytics/Report
- Omega Digital Media. *Web traffic data sources and vendor comparison*. http://www.ga-experts.co.uk/web-data-sources.pdf

Online Usability:
- Useit.com. http://www.useit.com
- User Interface Engineering. http://www.uie.com

Chapter 8

Grant Sources:
- Institute of Museum and Library Services (IMLS). http://www.imls.gov
- Library Grants Blog. http://librarygrants.blogspot.com
- National Endowment for the Humanities (NEH). http://www.neh.gov/grants/index.html
- National Historical Publication and Records Commission (NHPRC). http://www.archives.gov/nhprc
- State Humanities Council. http://www.statehumanities.org
- Technology Grant News. http://www.technologygrantnews.com

Special Event Support:
Wyman, K. *Guide to special events fundraising*. http://www.nald.ca/fulltext/heritage/ComPartnE/specev1.htm

SECTION II

Museum and Public School Partnerships

A Step-by-Step Guide for Creating Standards-Based Curriculum Materials in High School Social Studies

by

Cari D. Barragree
Kansas State University

Ann Elliott
Auburn Washburn Unified School District

Tara Baillargeon
Kansas State University

Gerald D. Bailey
Kansas State University

CONTENTS

INTRODUCTION

The idea of museum and public school partnerships is not new. However, the nature of the museum and public school partnership has shifted since the call for increased accountability and the strengthening of the curriculum in public schools. The shift was brought about primarily from the No Child Left Behind Act of 2001. The No Child Left Behind Act redefined the federal role in K-12 education and aimed to improve the academic achievement of all students in the United States.

Partnerships between museums and public schools are striving to achieve excellence with equity and for a higher percentage of students meeting the curriculum standards. Museums and public schools are interdependent when they partner to create standards-based curriculum materials. Without the help of each other, museums and public schools could be competing for the same resources. Instead, through a partnership, museums and public schools experience mutual success and increased resources.

The success of the partnership's curriculum materials has the potential to increase the success of schools through improved academic performance, and the success of the museum through improved attendance and greater public awareness of services at the museum. The success of the partnership results in more resources being allocated or made available to museums and schools which in turn repeats the cycle of success.

A museum and public school partnership has the ability to make almost any subject more relevant to students' lives, increase students'

Handbook on Developing Curriculum Materials for Teachers:
Lessons From Museum Education Partnerships, pp. 85–91
Copyright © 2010 by Information Age Publishing
85

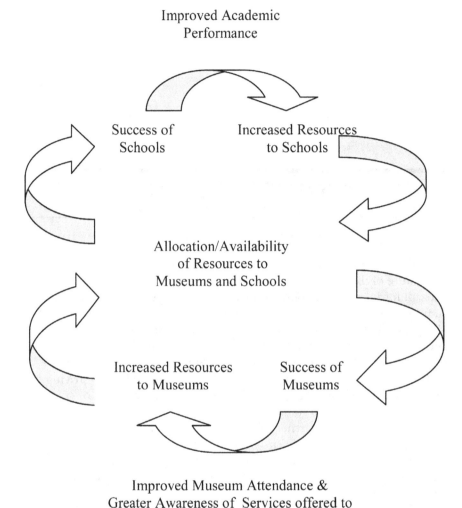

Improved Academic
Performance

Success of
Schools

Increased Resources
to Schools

Allocation/Availability
of Resources to
Museums and Schools

Increased Resources
to Museums

Success of
Museums

Improved Museum Attendance &
Greater Awareness of Services offered to
the Community

Figure 1.   Effective partnerships chart.

interests, and make learning more effective. Museums of all types and sizes offer educational programs that support public school curriculum standards at all grade levels. However, most of those materials have been for elementary-level students. In fact, fourth-grade curriculum materials are the most abundantly created by museum and public school partnerships.

Advantages for a museum and public school partnership are twofold: (1) To enrich the education of students, and (2) to ensure that learning objectives and curriculum standards have been met. Some of the curriculum materials created thus far by museum and public school partnerships are standards based, but usually do not focus on motivating students to learn. Even fewer curriculum materials focus on high school students and the subject of social studies.

There are limited resources for high school educators and even fewer museum and public school partnerships are creating motivational standards-based curriculum materials in high school social studies. Therefore, museums and public schools need to partner to develop motivational standards-based curriculum materials in high school social studies.

The intention of this guide is to provide museum and public school educators the information, resources, and strategies necessary to successfully form a partnership and to create standards-based curriculum materials in high school social studies.

HOW TO USE THIS GUIDE

The guide is written for museum and public school educators. This includes museum curators, education directors, teachers, curriculum and technology coordinators, administrators, volunteers, and others who work in a partnership to create motivational standards-based curriculum in high school social studies. The purpose of the guide is to provide museum and public school educators with step-by-step instructions on how to partner and create motivational standards-based curriculum material in high school social studies. However, the materials and examples in the guide can be adapted for a number of other types of partnerships, grade levels, and subject areas.

The guide is organized into six stages. Each stage examines an important element in the planning process of museum and public school partnerships creating motivational standards-based curriculum materials in high school social studies.

The six stages are:

- **Stage 1—Creating a Partnership:** This section provides information on varying aspects of creating and sustaining a museum and public school partnership.
- **Stage 2—Preparing a Plan:** This section details why creating a plan is important for museum and public school partnerships and how to best facilitate the development of the plan through establishing a

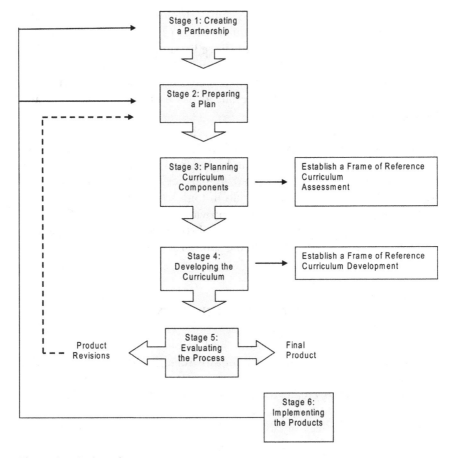

Figure 2.   Action plan.

planning committee and creating a timeline for completion of the plan.

- **Stage 3—Planning Curriculum Components:** This section discusses how to establish a frame of reference, curriculum considerations, product examples, and keys to assessing the partnership's products as the products relate to the plan components.

- **Stage 4—Developing the Curriculum:** This section also addresses how to establish a frame of reference, curriculum considerations, product examples, and keys to assessing the partnership products but focuses on how these areas relate to the steps in the curriculum process.

- **Stage 5—Evaluating the Process:** This section provides examples for museum and public school partnerships to utilize when evaluating the effectiveness of the partnership and the quality of the partnership's curriculum materials.
- **Stage 6—Implementing the Products:** This section explains two important aspects of implementing the plan: (a) how to reach the target audience, and (b) how to promote the partnership's products.

There are certain products that may need revision after Stage 5. In that case, the partnership should return back to Stage 2 and follow the stages until a desired product is finalized. Stages 3 and 4 will require the most time from the partnership as these two stages are the most detailed stages of the plan and are the stages in which the curriculum materials are actually created.

APPENDIXES

Appendix A is the Missouri Department of Elementary and Secondary Education: Social Studies Grade-Level Expectations. Appendix B is the list of The Show-Me Standards from Missouri. The glossary of terms follows in Appendix C with definitions and terminology of the bolded words found in the guide. This information can be used throughout the guide. Appendix D contains a categorical listing of further resources for the partnership which are useful throughout the entire planning and implementation process.

GUIDE PROCESS

Each stage of the guide should be read in order. The stages provide the foundation for understanding how to form a partnership to create standards-based curriculum materials in high school social studies. Stages 3 and 4 are specifically for partnership-planning committee members because these stages describe "how-to" aspects of creating motivational standards-based curriculum materials in high school social studies. Stage 5 provides help for partnership members to organize and evaluate quality of the curriculum materials created through the partnership. Partnership members can move on to Stage 6: Implementing the Products, once positive feedback has been received about the quality of the curriculum materials.

There are symbols throughout the guide. These symbols signify additional information that can be used by partnership members. The symbols include:

The light bulb indicates a great idea or tip.

The magnifying glass signifies additional information or clarification of an idea.

The question mark indicates an important question museum and public school educators should think more about.

The book refers to a print resource, such as a book, journal article, or magazine article. Complete references for print resources are located in the reference section of the guide.

The computer mouse represents an electronic resource such as a webpage, e-book, online journal article, or online magazine article. Complete references for electronic resources are located in the reference section of the guide. (All resources were active at the time of publication. Some may not work at a later date).

an **RFDL** is … Words in **bold print** in the text are defined in the glossary in Appendix C. (Only the first instance of each word will be in bold print.)

Throughout the guide, products created from the Negro Leagues Baseball Museum (NLBM) and Kansas State University (KSU) partnership are included as partnership product examples. The NLBM-KSU partnership developed standards-based curriculum materials for high school social studies educators. The high school level curriculum materials produced through the NLBM-KSU partnership incorporated state and national standards, utilized NLBM content in social studies, and infused technology into the curriculum materials for a motivational approach.

CHAPTER 1

STAGE 1

Creating a Partnership

INTRODUCTION

This stage of the planning process is the most crucial for the **museum** and **public school partnership**. Although there is not one formula or check-list to follow to create an effective partnership, completion of tasks in this stage are imperative to the success of the partnership. This section is not meant to be prescriptive, but rather a starting point for museum and public schools that wish to begin planning a mutually successful and effective partnership.

WHY IS A PARTNERSHIP IMPORTANT?

Museums and public schools benefit when a partnership is created. When museums link their resources and knowledge with public schools and other community organizations, the participants' experiences become richer, deeper, and more engaging. Since 1991, museums reported that the number of students, **educators**, and public schools they serve has continued to grow (Institute of Museum and Library Services [IMLS], 2002, p. 1).

Handbook on Developing Curriculum Materials for Teachers:
Lessons From Museum Education Partnerships, pp. 93–101
Copyright © 2010 by Information Age Publishing
93

A museum and public school partnership is important because the partnership:

- Can educate more people;
- Works toward educating more diverse populations and increasing the academic excellence of **high school** students in the United States;
- Can find ways to make connections to the lives of high school students;
- Can strengthen high school students' basic skills, and increase students' knowledge, comprehension, and understanding;
- Plays a critical role in the development of motivational **standards-based curriculum** materials for high school **social studies**;
- Incorporates **curriculum standards** and basics to help meet the goal of educating others to achieve more;
- Creates motivational **curriculum materials** that meet the increased expectations of national education and **state standards**, and changing **technology**;
- Has a mutual concern about an existing problem(s) within their organizations;
- Has the assistance of both museum and public school educators working together toward a common goal; and
- Can achieve mutual goals in a practical manner that meets state and local needs.

Review the following resources to learn about the increased expectations of state, national, and **social studies** education **standards**.

- Daley, R. (2003, May). *No geographer left behind: A policy guide to geography education and the No Child Left Behind Act.*
- Ravitch, Diane. (2005, November 7). *Every state left behind.*
- Saxe, D. (1998). *State history standards: An appraisal of history standards in 37 states and the District of Columbia.*

WHO SHOULD BE INVOLVED IN THE PARTNERSHIP?

A museum and public school partnership does not have to start with a large number of members. The partnership could start with:

Table 1.1.   Effective Partnerships Chart

Type of Partner	Partners Name and Contact Information	Role in Creation and Implementation	Role in Supporting the Creation and Implementation
Museum personnel			
High school educators or administrators			
Public school districts			
Postsecondary institutions			
Government agencies, community groups, etc.			

- One to two museum educators, curators, or docents, and
- One to two public school educators, **curriculum coordinators**, or **administrators.**

Use the Effective Partnerships Chart (Table 1.1) to guide partnership member selections, obtain contact information, and clarify members' role(s) in the partnership. A facilitator should be identified to keep the process moving forward and to ensure the partnership stays on track toward achieving its goals.

 Partnership members should have administrative commitment before beginning the partnership process.

Once the word spreads about the partnership's efforts to achieve common goals, participation will increase. Form an educator advisory board to help spread the word about the partnership's mission, how the partnership and the **curriculum material**s fit into the school's existing **curricu-**

lum, and how the curriculum materials meet national and **state standards** while motivating **high school** students. It does not matter when a member wants to join the partnership, welcome them! Involve as many educators and administrators from the public school as possible.

 Who, in additional to subject area educators, should be included in the partnership? Librarians, technology coordinators, special education teachers, etc.

WHAT ARE THE STEPS IN CREATING AN EFFECTIVE PARTNERSHIP?

There is no established philosophical framework for museum and public school partnerships to utilize for guidance when trying to sustain a partnership, and many museum and public school partnerships exist in relative isolation from one another. So how is an effective partnership formed?

Basic guidelines for developing a museum and public school partnership include:

- First and foremost, put time and energy into building trust.
- Second, **museum personnel** need to listen to public school educators' needs and wants. Talking and listening in small groups and informal conversations is best in the beginning.
- Third, all partnership members need to be part of the decision-making process. Ensure each member has an active role in the partnership.
- Fourth, ensure partnership members benefit from the relationship. For example:
    o Curriculum materials for classroom use
    o Increased attendance at museum functions
    o Graduate credit
    o Educator release-time
    o Substitute teacher stipends

Table 1.2.   Action Plan

Action Step	Person Responsible	Completion Date
Obtain early commitment from appropriate school and museum administrators.		
Establish early, direct involvement between museum and school staff.		
Understand the school's need in relation to curriculum and state and local education reform standards.		
Create a shared vision for the partnership, and set clear expectations for what both partners hope to achieve.		
Recognize and accommodate different organizational structures of museums and schools.		
Set realistic, concrete goals for the partnership through careful planning.		
Allocate enough human and financial resources.		
Define roles and responsibilities.		
Promote dialogue and open communication.		
Provide real benefits that teachers can use.		
Encourage flexibility, creativity, and experimentation.		
Seek parent and community involvement.		

Source: Adapted from Hirzy (1996).

- Fifth, identify available resources, strengths and weaknesses, and build on the strengths and successes. Start slowly and realistically, and recognize limitations.
- Finally, create an action plan (see Table 1.2).

Partnership members need to understand the museum's mission and the school's philosophy before proceeding to the **Needs Assessment**.

Conduct the Needs Assessment. A needs assessment will help determine if the museum and public school have a mutual concern about an existing problem(s) within their organizations. Without a mutual concern, the partnership would only benefit one organization. For a partnership to be effective both organizations need to benefit.

Use the following questions adapted from *Museum School Partnerships: Plan and Programs Sourcebook #4* by Alberta Sebolt (1981) to guide the development of the partnership's needs assessment.

1. **Identification of Needs and Options:**

   - What are the needs of the partnership?
   - Define the mutual concern or problems the partnership wants to address.
   - What are the stages the partnership should follow?

Analyze the elements of the partnership.

   - What are the partnership's options?
   - What are the partnership's goals?
   - Develop a course of action.
   - Analyze the resources available.
   - Estimate the amount of time needed for planning.

   - Who is the target audience?
   - What timeframe do we want/need the products completed by?
   - What products do we need to create to meet the partnership's needs?

2. **Development of the Partnership:**

   - What is the reason for forming the partnership?
   - List the important reasons for the partnership. Design and write a 50-100 word rationale for the partnership.
   - Address museum and school objectives.
   - What are the major ideas the partnership wishes to develop?
   - Identify major ideas the partnership hopes to develop.
   - As a result of this partnership we will ...
   - What do partnership members expect to learn/create?
   - How will partnership members assist each other?
   - List the activities and strategies the partnership will use to meet to accomplish the partnership goals, formal meetings, teacher in-service time, e-mail communications, and so forth.

3. **Implementation of the Partnership:**

   - What are the roles of the museum and school staff?
   - What are the materials needed to accomplish the tasks?
   - List the available resources and make plans for those which are not readily available.

4. **Revision of the Plan:**

  - How will the partnership know if the program is effective?
  - Develop a system of evaluation.
  - Use the information to revise the plan.

5. **Planning for the Future:**

  - How will the partnership continue the program?

The partnership needs to plan to nurture the relationship or the relationship may not continue. The partnership needs to plan to let people know about the program in order to build support to sustain involvement.

 If the goals are not what the partnership originally expected, change the goals to reflect the current needs of the museum and the public school.

WHY DO PARTNERSHIPS FAIL?

In planning for the future of the partnership avoid the major causes of partnership failure:

1. Lack of funding;
2. Fit of the museum and the public school is wrong; and
3. Lack of familiarization time (American Association of Museums, 1995).

The number one reason most museum and public school partnerships dissolve is lack of funding. However, staff changes, competition for resources, and the fluctuating relationship between the museum and the school contribute to the dissolution of museum and public school partnerships. In addition, the view in some museums that education is just a revenue maker and is part of the museum marketing department, not the education department, can speed up the decline of the partnership.

To avoid a lack of funding identify sources of funding from the beginning. Sources of funding could include federal funds, donated time, or

Table 1.3. Sustainability Chart

Type of Support Provided (Examples)	Individual(s) Responsible Person(s) or Job Title(s)	Plan for Providing This Support
Ongoing curricular support		
Benefits to partnership members		
Professional development		
Support provided during school hours		
Support provided outside of school hours		
Support provided during museum hours		
Support provided outside museum hours		

Source: Barragee (2005c, Summer).

direct cash payments from partners. Because time and expertise are free sources of funding it is critical to establish trust and familiarization amongst partnership members.

Time can be the hardest resource to glean from partnership members. In order to gain time commitments from partnership members, museums need to recognize public schools' busy schedules and public schools need to understand museums' role in education.

Creating stronger bonds among partnership members at the beginning of the partnership creates a better chance for long-term commitments from members as the partnership matures. To do this, more familiarization time is needed. Familiarization time engages members in team building exercises and provides time for partners to become familiarized with each other's programs, facilities, staff, and needs.

Use the sustainability chart (Table 1.3) adapted from the California Department of Education (2001) to define the partnerships role over the next 3 to 5 years.

Learn more about developing successful partnerships through these resources:

- American Association of Museums. (1984). **Museums for a new century. A report of the commission on museums for a new century.**

- Bevan, B. (2003). **Urban network: Museums embracing communities.** *Windows onto worlds.*

- Center for Museum Education. (1981). **Museum school partnerships: Plans & programs sourcebook #4.**

- Hirzy, E. (Ed.). (1996). **True needs, true partners: Museums transforming schools.**

- Institute of Museum and Library Services (IMLS). (2004). **Charting the landscape, mapping new paths: Museums, libraries, and K-12 learning.**

- Sheppard, B. (1993). **Building museum & school partnerships.**

- Tushnet, N. (1993). **Guide to developing educational partnerships.**

- **American Association of Museums (AAM).** www.aam.org

- **Institute of Museum and Library Services.** www.imls.org

CHAPTER 2

STAGE 2

Preparing a Plan

INTRODUCTION

Stage 2 outlines the logistics of the museum and public school partnership and identifies and articulates the plan for forming the partnership to create **standards-based curriculum** materials in high school social studies. Do not try to skip stages 1 or 2 in the partnership process as each stage has a specific focus and adds essential elements to the partnership process.

WHO SHOULD BE INVOLVED IN THE PLANNING PROCESS?

Assess who is already involved in the partnership and what his/her area(s) of expertise include.

Handbook on Developing Curriculum Materials for Teachers:
Lessons From Museum Education Partnerships, pp. 103–113
Copyright © 2010 by Information Age Publishing
All rights of reproduction in any form reserved.

- What area(s) of expertise is still needed?
- What key personnel are not yet represented?
- Who wants to be included and has been overlooked?

Begin filling in the management chart (Table 2.1) to define the leadership structure and time commitment anticipated for the partnership when creating and implementing motivational standards-based curriculum materials in high school social studies.

With current partnership members, make a list of potential members who meet the missing criteria. Try to list more than one person in each area and then decide and how potential partnership members should be contacted. Many public schools are looking for staff development ideas outside their organization. Consider advertising the partnership in local

Table 2.1. Management Chart

Individual(s)/Person(s) Responsible	*Responsibilities (Samples)*	*Estimated Time*
	Provide overall leadership and coordination.	
	Coordinate potential partnership member contacts and sustainability.	
	Manage and coordinate understanding of museum content and the museum's mission.	
	Manage and coordinate selection and definition of **lesson plan** components.	
	Manage and coordinate lesson plan development.	
	Manage and coordinate understanding of and creation of RFDLs.	
	Manage project budget and benefits to partnership members.	
	Coordinate ongoing partner involvement.	

school district newsletters, staff bulletin boards and **Web sites**, professional organizations, educational workshops and conferences, newspapers, television, and radio stations.

 Educators know more about their students and curriculum than anyone else. Museums needed to include public school educators from various areas and utilize the educators' expertise and experience.

HOW SHOULD CONTACTS BE MADE TO ESTABLISH MEMBERS OF THE PLANNING COMMITTEE?

People trust people they know and respect. Be sure partnership members are acquainted with potential members, and if possible, know the potential member well before any kind of contact is made. If partnership members are excited about the partnership that enthusiasm will come through in the initial contact made with potential members.

 No partnership member should be cold calling (contacting a stranger) potential members.

Sometimes a partnership member may not feel well-versed enough about the role a potential member may take within the partnership. In this case, the partnership member should go ahead and make initial contact with the new potential member anyway.

 Speak from the heart and tell the truth when making initial contacts. If you don't know much about the museum content or school's standards, say so. Do convey excitement about the partnership's plans and how the plans will benefit the potential member.

If a potential member is interested, then someone else from the partnership should contact them to provide further details about the partnership and their possible role(s). The contact should be ended by inviting the potential member to the next partnership meeting.

 If the potential member is known well by the partnership member, an offer to provide transportation to and from the meeting is typically welcomed.

HOW DO I RETAIN OR REPLACE PLANNING COMMITTEE MEMBERS?

The first step in retaining partnership members is to make sure the structure and goals of the partnership are a good fit for both organizations and that information is shared freely. Every partnership will have problems and encounter its own unique struggles, but the way the problems and struggles are overcome by the partnership is more important to retaining partnership members. In addition to rewarding challenges and positive outcomes, partnership members want benefits. Providing benefits can help motivate partnership members and encourage others to become partnership members.

Partnership members may want monetary benefits for being involved in the partnership. However, most museums and public schools operate on a limited budget and recent budget cuts have made budgets even tighter. There are benefits that can be offered to members that are worthwhile, but have little or no monetary value. For example:

- release time for educators to attend partnership meetings/events;
- graduate credit from a local college or inservice credit for participation;
- educators receive free copies of curriculum materials, museum tour or program for their classes, and/or invitations to special museum functions; and
- public recognition in newspapers, school board meetings, radio, television, and the like.

Each partnership should consult the members to decide what benefits are achievable and best meet the partnership's needs.

To replace partnership members, get referrals from current members and then return to the previous step of how to contact partnership members. Contact local organizations such as public schools, colleges and universities, and professional organizations to provide information about the opportunities the partnership has to offer. Some organizations may let the partnership post advertisements, set up a booth, or speak to interested groups.

Who or what organization(s) that are not involved could benefit from the partnership?

HOW OFTEN SHOULD MEMBERS MEET?

Ensure that meeting dates and times are scheduled regularly. Weekly, biweekly, or at least monthly meetings work best, but the frequency of meetings may fluctuate depending on the current partnership priority. Take advantage of public school **inservice** and planning days, and scheduled breaks such as spring break and summer vacation to meet with educators. Sending email reminders about meeting dates can also increase member attendance at meetings or events.

WHAT IS THE BEST TIME FOR MEMBERS TO MEET?

Consult with partnership members to see what time best works for members to meet. Museums should consider that educators' work days often extend beyond the first and last school bell of the day. Most educators have additional duties such as supervision, committee meetings, and coaching throughout the year. Try scheduling the first meeting around 5:00 or 6:00 P.M. and providing a light dinner. Schedule meetings when educators are "fresh" on weekends; have a Saturday breakfast or luncheon.

Provide food or snacks of some sort and a beverage (even water) at every meeting to entice members to attend.

At the first meeting determine what the best time is for partnership members to meet in the future and set a meeting schedule.

WHAT MEDIUM WORKS BEST FOR MEMBERS TO MEET?

Another question to address at the first meeting is: Do partnership members want to meet face-to-face every time or through some other medium?

In today's **technology**-hyper world members may decide meeting face-to-face is not an efficient or effective use of their time or budget. Partnership members may want to "meet" via conference calls, through email, or even by **web** conferencing. Guidelines need to be developed before implementing virtual meetings.

 Not everyone may be comfortable with email or virtual meetings, so decisions about the type of medium should be dependent on members' technology skill level.

WHAT IS THE TIMELINE FOR THE COMPLETION OF THE PLAN?

The timeline for completion of the partnership's plan will vary depending on the size of the project, the number of members in the partnership, the frequency of meetings, and budgetary considerations. However, preparing the plan should take no longer than four or five meeting dates.

HOW SHOULD THE PLAN BE DEVELOPED?

Each partnership's plan will be different due to the varying mutual concerns and goals of the partnership. Follow these three steps.

- **Step 1**: Obtain agreement from partnership members about the product(s) to be produced.
- **Step 2**: Review and coordinate any existing plans (i.e., action plan, needs assessment, budget forms, etc.).
- **Step 3**: Complete the implementation timeline chart incorporating the coordinated plan.

Table 2.2   Implementation Timeline

Start Date (M/Y)	Completion Date (M/Y)		Activity or Benchmark	Target Audience	Person Responsible	Component
	Projected	Actual				

Source: Reprinted by permission, California Department of Education, CDE Press, 1430 N. Street, Suite 3207, Sacramento, CA 95814.

The implementation timeline (Table 2.2) provides space for partnership **benchmarks** and specific components to be included in the form. By completing the implementation timeline the partnership should have a clear understanding of how and when the plan begins and ends, and what will be accomplished by the partnership and by whom.

Use the evaluation **rubric** starting on the next page to assess the partnership's primary and secondary relationships. The rubric asks six questions, the first three relate to the partnership's primary relationships and the last three relate to the partnership's secondary relationships.

Table 2.3.   Evaluation Rubric

Primary Relationships			*Secondary Relationships*		
1	*2*	*3*	*4*	*5*	*6*
Partnership Members to the Partnership	*Institution(s) to the Partnership*	*External Stakeholders to the Partnership*	*Institutions to External Stakeholders*	*Institution(s) to Partnership Members*	*Partnership to External Stakeholders*

A. Who was served or engaged?

B. Did the partnership fulfill the mission, values, or needs (as applicable)?

C. Who was involved in the project development and implementation and how?

D. How did the partnership change relationships and perceptions?

E. What lessons were learned and what was/will be their impact?

F. How were partnership results communicated?

Primary Relationships		
1	*2*	*3*
Partnership Members to the Partnership	*Institution(s) to the Partnership*	*External Stakeholders to the Partnership*

A. Who was served or engaged?

Who composed the audience served (document quantity, age, gender, race, educational background, geography, etc.)?	Who was involved within your institution, including staff and others?	What external stakeholders were involved and at what level?
		External stakeholders include collaborators, cooperators, partners, funders, government, etc.
Were primary goals identified and assessed?		

B. Did the partnership fulfill the mission, values, or needs (as applicable)?

Were the partnership's goals met?	Did the partnership advance or impact the vision, mission, values, and/or needs, of your institution? If so, how?	Did the partnership advance the vision, mission, values, and/or needs of the external stakeholders? If so, how?
Did the partnership meet partnership members' needs?		
Were the needs of the museum(s) and school(s) met?		

C. Who was involved in the project development and implementation and how?

Were partnership members involved in the development of the partnership? If so, how did you select and involve them?	Outside the partnership staff, were other colleagues at your institution involved in the development of the partnership? If so, how did you select and involve them (administrators, peers, board members, etc.)?	Were external stakeholders involved in the development of the partnership? If so, how did you select and involve them?
Did you shape the partnership based on partnership members' input? If so how? Was it ongoing?	Did you shape the partnership based on the input of other colleagues at your institution? If so, how? Was their input ongoing?	Did you shape the partnership based on the input of external stakeholders? If so how? Was their input ongoing?

Methods for Measurement

Measure content and attitude change among partnership members (use surveys, focus groups, document baseline content and attitude).	Measure institutional change through awareness and support surveys (through focus groups).	Measure stakeholders' expectation (through questionnaires and interviews).
Measure the responsiveness of program participants' performance/input (through evaluation tests and surveys—include functions of age, gender, and ethnicity as appropriate).	Measure institutional support of the partnership (through anecdotal reports and questionnaires; document baseline of performance expectations).	Measure stakeholders' impact on the program (anecdotal reports; document stakeholders' baseline for attitudes and expectations).

(Table continues on next page)

Table 2.2. (Continued)

Secondary Relationships		
4	*5*	*6*
Institutions to External Stakeholders	*Institution(s) to Partnership Members*	*Partnership to External Stakeholders*

D. How did the partnership change relationships and perceptions?

Did stakeholders' perceptions of the institution change as a result of the partnership? If so, how?	Did the partnership members perceptions of the institutions change as a result of the partnership? If so, how?	Did the partnership members perceptions of the stakeholders change as a result of the partnership? If so, how?
Did the institution's perception of the stakeholders change as a result of the partnership? If so, how?	Did the institution's perception of the partnership members change as a result of the partnership? If so, how?	Did the stakeholders' perception of the partnership members change as a result of the partnership? If so, how?
Did the program cause increase communication between external stakeholders and the institution? If so, how?	Did the partnership cause increased communication between partnership members and the institution? If so, how?	Did the partnership cause increased communication between external stakeholders and the partnership members? If so, how?

E. What lessons were learned and what was/will be their impact?

What did you learn about the relationship between the museum and stakeholders during the partnership implementation?	What did you learn about the relationship between your institution and partnership members during the partnership implementation?	What did you learn about the relationship between stakeholders and partnership members during the partnership implementation?
How will lessons learned from the partnership impact future relationships between the museum, schools, and stakeholders?	How will lessons learned from the partnership impact future relationships between your institution and partnership members?	How will lessons learned from the partnership impact future relationships between stakeholders and partnership members?

F. How were partnership results communicated?

Did members of your institution outside of partnership staff communicate appropriate invitations to stakeholders to participate in the partnership? If so, who invited whom and how?

Did members of your institution outside of partnership staff communicate appropriate invitations to participate in the partnership? If so, who invited whom and how?

Did external stakeholders use the partnership to reach prospective partnership participants (e.g., educators, administrators, museum personnel, community members). If so, who reached whom and how?

Did external stakeholders communicate their enthusiasm or concerns for the partnership to members of your institution outside of partnership staff? If so, who communicated what to whom and how?

Did partnership members have opportunities to communicate their enthusiasm or concerns for the partnership to members outside the partnership staff? If so, who communicated what to whom and how?

Did program participants share their enthusiasm or concerns about the partnership with external stakeholders or others (e.g. newspapers, other local media, etc.). If so, who communicated what to whom and how?

Methods for Measurement

Measure change in relationship between institution and stakeholders (identify number of board members, contributions, document baseline of the relationship).

Measure institutional awareness of partnership members (number of new members, programs/venues).

Measure change in stakeholder relationship with partnership members (more projects, increased involvement).

Measure change in partnership members utilization of institution (document baseline participation levels).

Measure change in attitude/behavior of partnership members toward stakeholder (determined by nature of stakeholder).

Source: Adapted from Spitz and Thom (2003).

CHAPTER 3

STAGE 3

Planning Curriculum Components

INTRODUCTION

Curriculum materials created through the partnership need to address specific teaching needs of public school educators to be successful.

 Institute of Museum and Library Services. (2002). **True needs, true partners: Museums serving schools 2002 survey highlights.**

ESTABLISH A FRAME OF REFERENCE

Subject Area and Grade Levels

The first step in establishing a **frame of reference** is to decide the subject area and grade level(s) of the curriculum materials.

Handbook on Developing Curriculum Materials for Teachers: Lessons From Museum Education Partnerships, pp. 115–140

- What grade level(s) need motivational standards-based curriculum materials?
- Why are these curriculum materials needed?
- What type of curriculum materials are needed most?
- What subject area(s) in that grade level lack standards-based motivational curriculum materials for students?
- Why is there a lack of motivational standards-based curriculum materials in this area?

High school students are usually the most difficult audience for museums and public schools to reach. Therefore, most curriculum materials created by museum and public school partnerships are for elementary age students, particularly for the fourth grade. In addition, motivational curriculum materials for high school students are needed in subject areas not evaluated by state tests, such as social studies. In 2002, educators indicated the integration of social studies into **museum education**al programs as an area of continued need and 62% of museums said their ability to meet standards of **learning** was a strong to moderate influence in schools deciding to utilize the museum's resources (Institute of Museum and Library Services, 2002, pp. 10-11).

Historical Timeframe

The next step is to determine the historical timeframe of the curriculum materials. The historical timeframe identifies and organizes significant historical eras in the school district's high school social studies curriculum. This allows partnership members to establish a common historical timeframe for U.S. history taught in the public schools and through the museum's content.

The partnership then creates a historical timeframe based on the local public high school's social studies curriculum.

Obtaining any textbooks and other supplemental materials, educators in the district use to teach social studies, are ideal to use when planning the historical timeframe.

Included herein is an example of a historical timeframe created by the **Negro Leagues Baseball Museum** and Kansas State University partnership based on one school district's curriculum materials for high school social studies.

UNIT PLANNING FOR U.S. HISTORY

- **Unit 1**: 1861-1880s—Civil War and Reconstruction—War; Black Codes; Jim Crow laws; 13th, 14th, and 15th Amendments
- **Unit 2**: 1860-1890s—New Frontiers—Westward Movement; Industrialism; Populism; and the Monroe Doctrine
- **Unit 3**: 1890-1914—Progressive Reforms—Labor; Women's Rights; Urban Growth; *Plessey v. Ferguson*; Booker T. Washington; and W.E.B. DuBois
- **Unit 4**: 1898-1917—Expansionism and World War I—Panama Canal; Europe's War through American Involvement in World War I; Mobilization; Segregated Forces; War and Civil Liberties; President Wilson and the changing world
- **Unit 5**: 1920s—Postwar—Labor; African American Movement North to the Urban Centers; Consumer Well-being; Transportation; Jazz Age; the Negro Renaissance; the Scopes Trial; Religion; and Prohibition
- **Unit 6**: 1930-1940s—The Great Depression and New Deal—Stock Crash; Causes of Depression; President Hoover's Response; Bonus Army; Dust Bowl; Tenant Farmers; the New Deal; and the Impact of New Deal
- **Unit 7**: 1941-1946—World War II—European War through U.S. Fighting; Atomic Bomb and Aftermath; and the Civil Rights Movement
- **Unit 8**: 1945-1950s—Cold War—Truman Doctrine; Integration of Military; Korean War; Atomic Age; Space; Cuban Missile Crisis; Postwar Economy; Jackie Robinson; and the McCarthy Era Red Hunt
- **Unit 9**: 1954-1960s—Civil Rights Struggle—Segregation; NAACP; *Brown v. Board of Education;* Little Rock, Arkansas; Rosa Parks; Martin Luther King, Jr.; SNCC; Freedom Riders; Sit-ins and Demonstrations; and Malcolm X (Chandler & Molt, 2005).

The historical timeframe is organized into units of study, similar to the organization of the district's high school social studies curriculum **guide**.

Organize the historical timeframe in a way that meets the partnership's needs.

After creating a historical timeframe, using the district's high school social studies curriculum and museum content, the partnership identifies and organizes the historical timeframe into critically important areas.

Using the **Negro Leagues Baseball** historical timeframe cited earlier and museum content, six historically significant eras in high school social studies curriculum are identified:

1. 1860-1880: Slavery, War, and the Growth of Baseball;
2. 1880-1900: American Reconstruction and Early Black Professional Baseball;
3. 1900-1920: America's Century and Independent Black Baseball;
4. 1920-1945: The Birth of the Negro Leagues, its Rise and Fall;
5. 1945-1960: Integration and the "Barrier Breakers"; and
6. 1960-Present: The Negro Leagues Legacy and Civil Rights.

By incorporating the museum's content, into historical eras in social studies, it is easier for educators to implement the motivational standards-based curriculum materials into the classroom's existing social studies curriculum. For example, a lesson plan titled, "Negro League Baseball's Impact on Segregation and Integration" is set in the fifth historical era of 1945-1960 called Integration and the "Barrier Breakers." This lesson can be used as a platform for teaching larger social studies concepts during 1945-1960 such as the Civil Rights era, Jim Crow laws, the Civil Rights Act, and important historical figures.

Copyright Laws

When creating the curriculum materials, ensure copyright laws are not being infringed upon. Designate a copyright expert, preferably someone with ample experience in research, law, and/or educational copyright law. The copyright expert researches educational copyright law and then creates a copyright law guide for partnership members. Partnership members refer to the copyright law guide when they have questions about copyright use when creating and citing curriculum materials for the partnership. Having a copyright expert allows partnership members to contact one person and receive a definitive answer to copyright questions. This avoids differing answers and eliminates confusion about copyright law.

The copyright law guide for the partnership should cover general information about copyright law and include topics that relate specifically to creating, citing, and using curriculum materials. An example of a copyright laws guide was created by the NLBM-KSU partnership.

COPYRIGHT LAWS GUIDE

Use of Copyrighted Images in Lesson Planning Materials

1. Copyright Basics.
2. Using Copyrighted Images.
3. Fair Use.
4. Getting Permission from the Copyright Holder.
5. Important Reminders from the Conference on Fair Use (Nov., 1998).

1. Copyright Basics

Four basic categories of rights are created by copyright protection. The author of a copyrighted work has the exclusive rights to:

1. Reproduce, or make copies of the work.
2. Prepare derivative works based on his or her work (such as writing a sequel or making a movie of a book).
3. Distribute copies of the work to the public.
4. Publicly display the work.

2. Using Copyrighted Images

Because a copyright owner is not required to include notice of copyright on his or her work in order to protect it, you cannot know by looking at an item that it is not copyrighted just because it does not have the © on it.

Using copyrighted images is problematic if you do not have the owner's permission because:

1. By including the image on a Web page, a copy is being made (Basic Rights #1).

2. The image is distributed to the public via the Web (Basic Rights #2).

3. By putting it within a context other than that which the copyright owner intended, a derivative work has probably been created with the photo (Basic Rights #3).

What to do? Either seek permission from the copyright owner or do not use the image at all.

3. Fair Use

*Is copying an image to use on a nonprofit, educational, **Webpage** allowed under the fair use doctrine?*

The short answer is: There are no guarantees of what will be covered by fair use, despite many misconceptions that any nonprofit use is okay.

Aren't all educational uses considered to be fair use?

No. Fair use is determined by the application of four criteria to any and every case in which a defendant claims his or her use is fair. Nonprofit institutions, libraries, and educational institutions get no break per se. Many uses by the groups will be fair, but only because their uses tend to be more likely than many to meet the requirements of fair use. It is important to understand that there are no guarantees under the fair use doctrine. Decisions of fair use are made on an individual, case-by-case basis.

The four criteria include:

1. Purpose and Character of the Use.

   (a) Whether the use is commercial or for a nonprofit educational purpose and

   (b) Whether the use is transformative (use that changes the original work in some way, as opposed to flat-out copying it. Altering with new expression, meaning or message is more likely to be fair).

2. Nature of the Copyrighted Work.

   (a) Whether the work is factual or creative. The work being copied must be original and show a "modicum of creativity" to be protected by copyright.

3. Amount and Substantiality of the Portion Used in Comparison to the Work as a Whole.

   (a) The smaller the portion of the work used, the more likely the use will be considered fair. However, even taking proportionately tiny portions of a work may constitute infringement if the portion taken is important enough to the work as a whole.

4. Effect on the Potential Marketplace.

    (a) How great was the effect of use on the potential market for or value of the work? If the copyright owner's ability to sell his or her work is impaired significantly, so it the incentive basis for copyright protection.

Take the Fair Use Test!
http://www.utsystem.edu/ogc/intellectualproperty/copypol2.htm#test

4. Getting Permission From the Copyright Holder

Contact the copyright holder by phone or e-mail and then follow up with a letter to officially document your agreement. Here are links to sample permission letters that can be adapted to suit your need:

- University of Texas System Office of Intellectual Property: http://www.utsystem.edu/ogc/intellectualproperty/permmm.htm
- Library Law: http://www.librarylaw.com/perm.htm
- Consortium for Educational Technology in University Systems: http://www.cetus.org/fair7.html

Tip: When you ask for permission directly from the copyright owner, tell them what you plan to do with the work. If a statement of permission is made with the work, look at it to see exactly what it is giving permission for. If it is only to copy, contact the copyright owner and ask specifically for permission to put it on your Web page, lesson plan, etc.

5. Important Reminders From the Conference on Fair Use (November 1998)

http://www.uspto.gov/web/offices/dcom/olia/confu/confurep.pdf

6.1 Cautions in Downloading Material from the Internet

Educators and students are advised to exercise caution in using digital material downloaded from the Internet in producing their own educational multimedia projects, because there is a mix of works protected by copyright and works in the public domain on the network. Access to works on the Internet does not automatically mean that these can be reproduced and reused without permission or royalty payment and, furthermore, some copyrighted works may have been posted to the Internet without authorization of the copyright holder.

6.2 Attribution and Acknowledgement

Educators and students are reminded to credit the sources and display the copyright notice and copyright ownership information if this is shown in the original source, for all works incorporated as part of educational multimedia projects prepared by educators and students, including those prepared under fair use. Crediting the source must adequately identify the source of the work, giving a full bibliographic description where available (including author, title, publisher, and place and date of publication). The copyright ownership information includes the copyright notice (©, year of first publication and name of the copyright holder).

6.3 Notice of Use Restrictions

Educators and students are advised that they must include on the opening screen of their multimedia project and any accompanying print material a notice that certain materials are included under the fair use exemption of the U.S. Copyright Law and have been prepared according to the educational multimedia fair use guidelines and are restricted from further use.

6.4 Future Uses Beyond Fair Use

Educators and students are advised to note that if there is a possibility that their own educational multimedia project incorporating copyrighted works under fair use could later result in broader dissemination, whether or not as commercial product, it is strongly recommended that they take steps to obtain permissions during the development process for all copyrighted portions rather than waiting until after completion of the project.

6.5 Integrity of Copyrighted Works: Alterations

Educators and students may make alterations in the portions of the copyrighted works they incorporate as part of an educational multimedia project only if the alterations support specific instructional objectives. Educators and students are advised to note that alterations have been made.

SOURCES

The Conference on Fair Use: Fair Use Guidelines for Multimedia. (1998, November). Retrieved August 23, 2006, from http://www.uspto.gov/web/offices/dcom/olia/confu/confurep.pdf

Hoffman, G. M. (2001). *Copyright in cyberspace: Questions and answers for librarians.* New York: Neal-Schuman.

Russell, C. (2004). *Complete copyright: An everyday guide for librarians.* Chicago: American Library Association.

Baillargeon, T. (2005, October). *Copyright laws guide.* Unpublished document, Kansas State University, Manhattan, Kansas.

Add additional questions from partnership members to the copyright laws guide as they occur.

CURRICULUM

Determine Curriculum Standards

Curriculum standards are a permanent part of the curriculum in public education and must be included in museum and public school partnerships' motivational standards-based curriculum materials to be successful. The first steps in determining what standards to include in the curriculum materials have already been completed by the partnership. The subject area is social studies and the grade level is high school. Therefore, standards for high school social studies at the national and state levels need to be included in the curriculum materials.

 Contact and recruit curriculum coordinators now, if they are not already involved in the partnership.

National Council for the Social Studies Standards

The **National Council for the Social Studies (NCSS)** has identified 10 themes for K-12 schools to use as organizing strands in the social studies curriculum at each grade level.

The 10 NCSS themes in *Expectations of Excellence: Curriculum Standards for Social Studies* (1994) are:

"Social studies programs should include experiences that provide for the study of:

   i.   Culture
  ii.   Time, Continuity, and Change
 iii.   People, Places, and Environment
 iv.   Individual Development and Identity
  v.   Individuals, Groups, and Institutions

    vi.   Power, Authority, and Governance

   vii.   Production, Distribution, and Consumption

  viii.   Science, Technology, and Society

   ix.   Global Connections

    x.   Civic Ideals and Practices" (pp. ix-xii).

NCSS: www.ncss.org

For an NCSS limited online version or to order a copy of *Expectations of Excellence* go to: http://www.socialstudies.org/standards/

State Standards

The partnership should also include state social studies standards when creating the curriculum materials. Though the **No Child Left Behind** Act of 2001 did not require state assessment systems to test social studies, social studies remains an integral part of the public school curricula and most states have some type of social studies standards for their state. For example, the Missouri State Board of Education approved *The Show-Me Standards* for social studies on January 18, 1996. *The Show-Me Standards* (Missouri Department of Elementary and Secondary Education, 1996) included seven standards that "students in Missouri public schools will acquire a solid foundation which includes knowledge of:

1. Principles expressed in the documents shaping constitutional democracy in the United States;
2. Continuity and change in the history of Missouri, the United States and the world;
3. Principles and processes of governance systems;
4. Economic concepts (including productivity and the market system) and principles (including the laws of supply and demand);
5. The major elements of geographical study and analysis (such as location, place, movement, regions) and their relationships to changes in society and environment;
6. Relationships of the individual groups to institutions and cultural traditions; and
7. The use of tools of social science inquiry (such as surveys, statistics, maps, documents)" (p. 1).

The Missouri Show-Me Standards. Social Studies

Missouri State Department of Elementary and Secondary Education: http://dese.mo.gov/standards/ss.html

In October of 2004, the Missouri Department of Elementary and Secondary Education published *Social Studies Grade-Level Expectations*. Two high school examples listed in the *Social Studies Grade-Level Expectations* document were, "principles of constitutional democracy in the United States, and understanding the relevance and connection of constitutional practice" (pp. 32-33).

The next step in planning motivational standards-based curriculum materials is to cross-reference the national and state standards. It is important to cross-reference the standards so a correlation between the national and state social studies standards can be established and clarified before incorporating other standards into the curriculum materials.

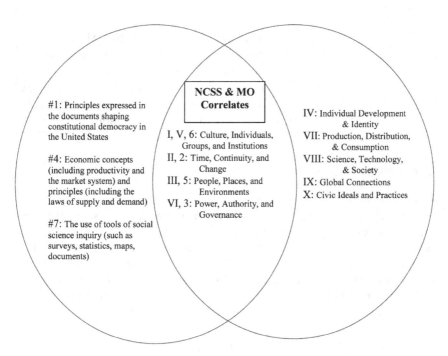

Figure 3.1.   National and state social studies standards correlate graph.

Once the national and state standards are identified in the content area, museum and public school educators should consider if any other standards need to be included in the curriculum materials.

International Society for Technology Education Standards

Since **technology-infused** curricula has a motivational effect on high school students, technology standards need to be included in the planning stages of creating the partnership's curriculum materials. The **International Society for Technology Education (ISTE)** has six broad categories of **National Educational Technology Standards (NETS)** for K-12 students. Educators use these standards as guidelines for planning technology-infused activities that motivate high school students to achieve academic success and life skills.

ISTE also has technology standards for educators, called *NETS for Teachers*. NETS for teachers are designed to assists educators in understanding what teachers should know and be able to do with technology. Teacher technology proficiency is the key to implementing technology-infused curriculum materials in high school social studies.

ISTE: www.iste.org

- **ISTE: Technology Foundations for All Students. Student Standards Grades 9-12**: http://cnets.iste.org /students/s_profile-912.html
- **ISTE NETS for Teachers**. Educational technology standards and performance indicators for all teachers: http://cnets.iste.org/teachers/t_stands.html

Curriculum Framework

The Purpose of Curriculum Framework

The primary purpose of **curriculum framework** is to establish **learning outcomes** expected of all students. Curriculum framework provides educators a frame for teaching and building curriculum in their subject area and grade level, in this case high school social studies. "The framework helps teachers to develop specific programs and judge the effectiveness of their teaching by the outcomes students achieve" (Government of Western Australia, n.d.). Curriculum framework is not:

- Required by law for district use;
- Detailed lesson plans or curricula;

- Items on which all students must be tested;
- Directives for uniform programs or textbook adoption;
- Mandates for inclusion of particular teaching methods or programs;
- A format that all district curriculum guides must follow; and
- A curriculum or syllabus for social studies educators (Missouri Department of Elementary and Secondary Education, 2004).

Organization of the Framework

The example curriculum framework is organized into four columns. The first column shows the correlation between the NCSS, MO, and ISTE standards. The NCSS standards are indicated by a roman numeral(s) followed by the ISTE standards and then the Missouri state *Show-Me Standards*. The second column lists the grade level focus of the curriculum framework. The third column lists the Missouri grade level expectations for high school social studies. The fourth column lists possible curriculum ideas for a specific topic, in this case Negro Leagues Baseball.

Table 3.1 Curriculum Framework (9-12 Grade Level)

National and State Standards Correlation	Missouri Grade Level Expectations	Negro League Baseball Possible Topics
NCSS: I, V, VI, X ISTE: 1, 2 MO: 1, 3, 6	B2-1, Government: Examine the relevance and connection of constitutional principles in the following: • U.S. Constitution • key Supreme Court decisions (e.g., *Marbury v. Madison*, *McCulloch v. Maryland*, *Miranda v. Arizona*, *Plessy v. Ferguson*, *Brown v. Topeka Board of Education*)	• *Brown v. Topeka Board of Education* • Integration • Black American Rights under Constitution
NCSS: I, II, V, VI ISTE: 1, 2 MO: 2, 3, 6	B2-2a, U.S. History: Analyze the evolution of American democracy, its ideas, institutions and political processes from colonial days to the present including: • Civil War and Reconstruction • struggle for Civil Rights • expanding role of government	• Civil Rights • Reconstruction Era • Governmental laws and policies
NCSS: I, II, V, VI ISTE: 1, 2 MO: 2, 3, 6	B2-2a, Government: Analyze the evolution of American democracy, its ideas, institutions and political processes from colonial days to the present, including: • American Revolution • Constitution and amendments • Civil War and Reconstruction • struggle for civil rights • expanding role of government	• North vs. South • Constitutional Rights • Civil Rights • Reconstruction Era • Governmental laws and policies
NCSS: I, II, V, VIII ISTE: 1, 2, 3 MO: 2, 6, 7	E5-2a, U.S. History: Describe the changing character of American society and culture (i.e., arts and literature, education and philosophy, religion and values, and science and technology)	• Overcoming societal, religious, economic, and political barriers • Negro Renaissance • *Brown v. Topeka Board of Education*
NCSS: I, II, III, V, VIII ISTE: 1, 3, 4 MO: 2, 5, 6, 7	F6-2a, U.S. History: Analyze Missouri history as it relates to major developments of United States history, including: • exploration and settlement • mid 1800s (conflict and war) • urbanization, industrialization, postindustrial societies	• Great Depression • Civil Rights • Black American rights, voting, owning land and businesses

Standards	Description	Content
NCSS: VI, X ISTE: 1, 2, 3, 4 MO: 1, 3	A1-3, U.S. History: Explain the importance of the following principles of government: • limited government • majority rule and minority rights • constitution and civil rights • checks and balances • merits of the above principles	• Civil Rights • Abolition • Stereotypes
NCSS: VI ISTE: 1, 2, 3 MO: 3	A1-3, Government: Describe the purposes and structure of laws and government (with emphasis on the federal and state governments) Explain the importance of the following principles • limited government • majority rule and minority rights • constitution and civil rights • checks and balances • merits of the above principles	• Jim Crow laws • Civil Rights Acts • *Brown v. Topeka Board of Education* • *Plessy v. Ferguson*
NCSS: VI, VII ISTE: 1, 2, 3 MO: 3, 4	B2-4, U.S. History: Apply the following major economic concepts in the context of the historical period studied: • scarcity • opportunity cost • factors of production (human resources, natural resources and capital resources) • supply and demand (shortages and surpluses) • gross domestic product (GDP) • savings and investment • business cycle • profit • government regulation and deregulation • budgeting • income • unemployment and full employment • inflation and deflation	• Great Depression • White businesses not serving Black Americans • Black American business ownership • Black American unemployment • Salaries • Cost of goods • NL player salaries

(Table continues on next page)

Table 3.1   (Continued)

National and State Standards Correlation	Missouri Grade Level Expectations	Negro League Baseball Possibile Topics
NCSS: III, IX ISTE: 1, 3, 4, 5 MO: 5, 6	C3-5, U.S. History: Locate major cities of Missouri, the United States, and world; states of the United States and many of the world's nations' the world's continents and oceans; and major topographic features of the United States and world Communicate locations of places by creating maps and by describing their absolute locations and relative locations	• Barnstorming NL team location • Major events in U.S. and N.L. history
NCSS: II, III ISTE: 1, 3, 5 MO: 2, 5	G7-5, U.S. History: List and explain criteria that give regions their identities in different periods of United States history Explain how parts of a region relate to each other and to the region as a whole (e.g., states to nation) Explain how regions relate to one another (e.g., river-drainage regions) Explain how and why regions change	• North vs. South • NL team game locations • Barnstorming • Abolition
NCSS: I, V, IX ISTE: 1, 2, 3, 5 MO: 6	A1-6: Compare and contrast the major ideas and beliefs of different cultures	• NL teams • Game locations • Barnstorming • Slavery/abolition • North vs. South
NCSS: I, II, V ISTE: 1, 2, 3, 6 MO: 2, 6	B2-6: Summarize how the roles of class, ethnic, racial, gender and age groups have changed in society including the causes and effects	• Prejudice/racism • Bus boycott • Jim Crow laws • Black Americans in baseball

NCSS: I, VI ISTE: 1, 2 MO: 3, 6	C3-6: Describe the major social institutions (family, education, religion, economy of government) and how they fulfill human need	• Family • Community • Education • Religion
NCSS: IV, V ISTE: 1, 2, 3, 6 MO: 6	D4-6: Identify the consequences that can occur when: • institutions fail to meet the needs of individuals and groups • individuals fail to carry out their personal responsibilities	• Demonstrations • March on Washington • Demise of the NL • Jim Crow laws • Dr. Martin Luther King, Jr. • ALB and ML team membership
NCSS: I, IX, X ISTE: 1, 2, 3, 5, 6 MO: 6	E5-6: Determine the causes, consequences and possible resolutions of cultural conflicts	• Stereotypes • Demonstrations • Passage of law
NCSS: VIII ISTE: 1, 3, 5, 6 MO: 7	A1-7: Develop a research plan and identify appropriate resources for investigating social studies topics	• Education about others • Historical documents
NCSS: VIII ISTE: 1, 3, 6 MO: 7	B2-7: Distinguish between and analyze primary sources and secondary sources	• Historical documents • Journals, letters • Photographs • Interviews

(Table continues on next page)

Table 3.1 (Continued)

National and State Standards Correlation	Missouri Grade Level Expectations	Negro League Baseball Possibile Topics
NCSS: VIII, X ISTE: 1, 3, 6 MO: 6, 7	C3-7: Distinguish between fact and opinion and analyze sources to recognize bias and points of view	• Stereotypes • Jim Crow laws • Segregation • Integration
NCSS: VIII ISTE: 1, 3, 4, 6 MO: 7	D4-7: Interpret maps, statistics, charts, diagrams, graphs, timelines, pictures, political cartoons, audiovisual materials, continua, written resources, art, and arti-facts	• Major events in NL and U.S. history • NLB Museum
NCSS: VIII ISTE: 1, 3, 4, 6 MO: 7	E5-7: Create maps, charts, diagrams, graphs, timelines and political cartoons to assist in analyzing and visualizing concepts in social studies	• NL vs. ML salaries • NLB players, owners, and teams

Source: Barragree (2005, July).

TIPS FOR CREATING A CURRICULUM FRAMEWORK

1. Start by researching other curriculum frameworks online and in pertinent publications. Check to see if the state has created a social studies curriculum framework. Many states have already created a state curriculum framework for social studies and post them online.
2. Decide on a simple format to organize the framework.
3. Complete one section of the framework at a time and do not be afraid to revise and/or rework the existing framework format to meet the partnership's evolving needs.
4. Complete the last column of possible topics in the curriculum framework as a team. The list will be a more complete and accurate listing of common topics the school and museum content cover.
5. Create the curriculum framework and add a rationale explaining the purpose and organization of the framework. The rationale helps demonstrate the standards-based focus of the curriculum materials to outside constituents and new partnership members.
6. Ask all members to provide suggestions and changes to the curriculum framework and then finalize a copy of the framework for distribution.

Michigan Curriculum Framework. Michigan Department of Education: http://www.michigan.gov/documents/MichiganCurriculumFramework_8172_7.pdf

Massachusetts History & Social Sciences Curriculum Framework. Massachusetts Department of Education: http://www.doe.mass.edu/frameworks/hss/final.doc

Type and Kind of Curriculum Materials

The challenge is for museum and public school partnerships to create standards-based curriculum materials that high school students want to learn, believe are beneficial and meaningful to them, and are designed to challenge them at their level. Before determining the kind of motivational standards-based curriculum materials to create in high school social studies, decide what type of curriculum materials need to be created.

- What motivates high school students to learn?

- What do high school students want in a social studies curriculum?

What Motivates High School Students to Learn?

High school students dislike social studies because:

1. Of attrition in attitudes as they progress in school.
2. Of negative perceptions as social studies relates to future occupations.
3. Social studies lacks relevancy.
4. Other subjects are preferred.
5. Social studies is boring.

- Ellis, A., Fouts, J., & Glenn, A. (1991). *Teaching and learning secondary social studies.*

- Scherer, M. (2002, Summer). *Do students care about learning?*

Understanding the Keys to Motivation to Learn.

McCombs, B. Mid-Continent Research for Education and Learning: http://www.mcrel.org/PDFConversion/ Noteworthy/Learners_Learning_Schooling /barbaram.asp

The number one influence on high school **student motivation** is the social studies educator. Studies suggest that educator interest and classroom environment may be more influential regarding students' positive attitudes toward social studies than the method of instruction. Everything educators do in the classroom has a positive or negative motivational impact on high school students.

The National Research Council (2004) indicated that studies suggest practices promoting student motivation are less likely to be employed by educators at the secondary level than the elementary level (p. 58). High school student attitudes wane throughout high school as educators employ less motivational strategies in their classroom. Every educator's motivation declines when they are told what to teach, when to teach, and how to evaluate student performance. Many educators do not realize the same is true for students. Corbin (1997) noted that museums and public school educators that fail to recognize and implement changes to the social studies curriculum for high school students probably lead to a decline in students' positive perceptions in social studies. So what do high school students want in a social studies curriculum?

National Research Council. (2004). *Engaging schools: Fostering high school students' motivation to learn.*

What High School Students Want in a Social Studies Curriculum

High school students want specific items incorporated into the social studies curriculum. Numerous authors have indicated high school social studies students want:

1. Curriculum relevant to their own lives.
2. Varied **instructional strategies**, educators rely too heavily upon lecturing, videos, and worksheets.
3. To actively engage in learning how to problem solve and apply new knowledge to real problems.
4. Collaboration among peers.
5. An environment where students are not afraid to take risks or make mistakes.
6. An environment that students see as full of vivid and valuable choices.
7. An engaging, not watered-down curriculum.

Partnerships need to ensure the curriculum materials created are challenging, relevant to students' lives, have variety, and engage the student.

The partnership should rely on what public school educators identify as potential curriculum material needs. Possible curriculum material needs might include: sponge activities, lesson plans, test preparation activities, and other supplemental materials. The most commonly needed and created curriculum materials in a museum and public school partnership have been lesson plans because high school educators are lacking the motivational standards-based curriculum materials that meet students' needs.

 The guide from this point forward refers to lesson plans when using the term curriculum materials.

Curriculum Topics

The partnership needs to identify what topics the motivational standards-based lesson plans cover. The lesson plan topics can be created in list form, organized by differing academic disciplines, or subdivided into smaller categories. By identifying and organizing lesson plan topics before creating lesson plans, partnership members can agree on what topics are most important. Another benefit is partnership members can assign lesson plan topics to particular members based on the members' expertise, background knowledge, and/or interest level.

 Allowing members of the partnership to choose the lesson plan topics they want to use to create the lesson plans increases the lesson planner's motivation and ensures not all lesson plans will be created on the same topic.

Step 1: Create a **graphic organizer** illustrating the organization of lesson plan topics based on museum content, and identified lesson plan topics.

Step 2: Identify lesson plan topics and decide the overarching focus of the lesson plans. Technology is an essential component of the lesson planning process and is therefore included as the overarching focus of the NLBM-KSU partnership's lesson plans.

Step 3: Pair lesson plans in U.S. history and African American history through the previously created historical timeframe. This helps partnership members clarify areas of interest in lesson planning. Assigning a significant era to each lesson plan from the beginning has the added benefit of being able to easily organize lesson plans chronologically. For example:

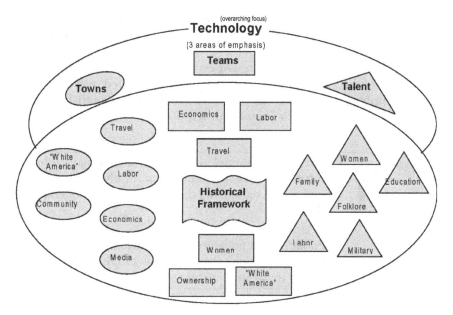

Figure 3.2.   Lesson plan topic graphic organizer.

Member #1 might be assigned/choose the timeframe of 1920-1945, Member #2 might be assigned/choose the timeframe of 1945-1960 to create a lesson plan.

Step 4: Decide on areas of emphasis to focus lesson planning efforts. In the lesson plan topic graphic organizer there are three areas of lesson plan emphasis for Negro Leagues Baseball: *Towns, Teams,* and *Talent.*

Step 5: Each of the three areas of emphasis contains lesson plan topics that are most likely to be found in that area. For instance, under *Talent* there are six lesson plan topics associated with this area of emphasis:

1. Women;
2. Family;
3. Education;
4. Folklore;
5. Labor; and
6. Military.

At this point, partnership members can determine the timeframe, area(s) of emphasis, and a number of lesson plan topics to begin creating motivational standards-based lesson plans. For example, Member #1 could write a technology-infused (overarching focus) lesson plan about teams (area of emphasis) traveling (lesson plan topic) from 1920-1945 (timeframe).

Note the lesson plan topics are not exclusive to one area of emphasis. For instance, the lesson plan topic Travel is also associated with the *Towns* area of emphasis. Therefore, the topic of Travel is listed in both *Teams* and *Towns* as a possible topic for lesson plan creation.

- Museum personnel should take the primary role in submitting areas of emphasis, a variety of lesson plan topics, and organizing the topics into areas of emphasis.

- Public school personnel can contribute by suggesting lesson plan topics that are lacking in the current high school social studies curriculum.

ASSESSMENT

Assessment should be a consistent and continual piece of the partnership process. Before moving on to Stage 4, partnership members need to assess the progress of their plan to ensure that all plan components have been completed. Use the *Frame of Reference Checklist* to assess if the partnership has successfully established a frame of reference.

Use the *Planning Curriculum Components Checklist* to assess the partnership's progress on the completion of planning curriculum components.

Table 3.2.   Frame of Reference Checklist

Frame of Reference Component	Yes	No	Actions to be Taken
Subject area and grade level(s) for curriculum materials have been decided.			
A clear historical timeline has been established.			
The historical timeline has been broken down into specific eras.			
A copyright laws guide has been created and distributed to partnership members.			
National and state curriculum standards have been identified for the subject area and grade level(s).			
All the desired standards are incorporated into the curriculum materials plan components.			
A curriculum framework and rationale have been created.			
The standards and the curriculum framework are presented in a concise and user-friendly manner.			
The type and kind of curriculum materials to be created has been decided.			
Lesson plan topics have been selected and organized graphically.			
Does the timeframe for completing the curriculum materials need to be revised?			

Source: Barragree (2006a).

Table 3.3.   Planning Curriculum Components Checklist

Component	Yes	No	Actions to be Taken
Subject area and grade level(s) for curriculum materials have been decided.			
A clear historical timeline has been established.			
The historical timeline has been broken down into specific eras.			
A copyright laws guide has been created and distributed to partnership members.			
National and state curriculum standards have been identified for the subject area and grade level(s).			
All the desired standards are incorporated into the curriculum materials plan components.			
A curriculum framework and rationale have been created.			
The standards and the curriculum framework are presented in a concise and user-friendly manner.			
The type and kind of curriculum materials to be created has been decided.			
Lesson plan topics have been selected and organized graphically.			
Does the timeframe for completing the curriculum materials need to be revised?			

Source: Barragree (2006b).

CHAPTER 4

STAGE 4

Developing the Curriculum

INTRODUCTION

Educators must establish a frame of reference utilizing museum content to be able to contribute effectively to the creation of curriculum materials for a successful partnership.

ESTABLISH A FRAME OF REFERENCE

Research Lesson Plan Components

First, conduct research to determine what components to include in the lesson plans. For example, the PBS Web site (www.pbs.org) provides lesson plans with a consistent format and set lesson plan components which are extremely important in lesson plan development. Inconsistencies will create frustration for educators that use the lesson plans. Members of the partnership should collaboratively decide which components to include and consistently use in the lesson plans.

Handbook on Developing Curriculum Materials for Teachers:
Lessons From Museum Education Partnerships, pp. 141–202
Copyright © 2010 by Information Age Publishing

Quality lesson plans have these elements in common:

- Clearly stated standards and objectives;
- Opportunities to address varied **learning styles**;
- Practice of skills/concepts;
- Materials and resources needed;
- Some form of assessment

Some partnership members may need more information about curriculum frameworks, assessments, and rubrics. Partnership members with expertise in a particular area(s) should serve as resources for other team members.

Some beneficial Web sites include:

The Getty Museum: http://www.getty.edu/

NEA Jazz in the Schools. National Endowment for the Arts: http://www.neajazzintheschools.org/home.php

BrainPOP: http://www.brainpop.com/

Creating Curriculum and Delivering It: Air War College: http://www.au.af.mil/au/awc/awcgate/awceauth .htm#lessonplans

Research Museum and Public School Curriculum Materials

Next, educators need to research the museum, museum content, and schedule a tour of the museum. A tour of the museum enables educators to learn a lot of background information about the museum's content in a short amount of time.

Research other museums including **virtual museums** and online related topics, and read books and watch films related to the museum's content. There are numerous virtual museums available online for viewing. Some virtual museums, such as the Getty Museum, include examples of curriculum materials. Try the following Web sites for more information on virtual museums.

Virtual Library Museums Pages: International Council of Museums: http://icom.museum/vlmp/

Eternal Egypt: Center for Documentation of Cultural and Natural Heritage, Egypt: http://www.eternale-gypt.org/EternalEgyptWebsiteWeb/HomeServlet

Once again, relying on partnership members' areas of expertise is beneficial in researching curriculum materials. It is helpful if partnership members create a list of recommended resources for each other. Knowing what content is deemed important allows partnership members to create a **common content language** when creating motivational standards-based curriculum in high school social studies.

The NLBM-KSU partnership obtained a list of recommended resources from the NLBM curator, Ray Doswell. Educators saved a lot of time by not having to sift through thousands of documents to find the best resources and helped educators quickly establish a frame of reference about relevant historical time periods and Negro Leagues baseball.

Mr. Doswell's list is provided as an example (titles listed in bold lettering are considered essential resources and titles in italics are available for purchase at the NLBM bookstore).

NEGRO LEAGUES BASEBALL: IMPORTANT BOOKS AND FILM

I. ADVANCED STUDY:

* *Negro League Baseball: The Rise and Ruin of a Black Institution* by **Neil Lanctot**

General Narrative History
* ***The Negro Leagues* by James Riley**
* *Black Diamonds* by McKissack & McKissack
* *Only the Ball was White* by Robert Peterson

Photographs/Reference
* **The Negro Baseball Leagues: A Photographic History by Phil Dixon**
* *Negro League Baseball* by Earnest Withers
* *Jackie Robinson: An Intimate Portrait* by Rachel Robinson

General Research/References/Statistics

- **The Biographical Encyclopedia of the Negro Baseball Leagues by James Riley**
- *The Negro Leagues Book* edited by Dick Clark and Larry Lester
- *Complete Book of Baseball's Negro Leagues* by John Holway
- *Crossing the Line: Black Major Leaguers, 1947-1959*, edited by Larry Moffi and Jonathan Krondstadt

II. PRIMARY SOURCES:

- *Sol White's History of Colored Baseball* (1903), edited by Jerry Malloy
- *The Jackie Robinson Reader* by Jules Tygiel

Regional Studies

- **Every Other Sunday (Birmingham Black Barons) by Chris Fullerton**
- *Sandlot Season* (Pittsburgh) by Rob Ruck
- **The Kansas City Monarchs: Champions of Black Baseball by Janet Bruce**
- *The Kansas City Monarchs, 1920-1938 featuring Wilber "Bullet" Rogan*, by Phil Dixon
- *Beyond the Shadow of the Senators* (Washington, D.C.) by Brad Snyder
- *Brushing Back Jim Crow* (integration of the South Atlantic League) by Bruce Adelson
- *Turkey Stearnes and the Detroit Stars* by Norman Bak

Biography/Autobiography

- **I Was Right on Time by John "Buck" O'Neil**
- **Jackie Robinson by Arnold Ramparsand**
- *The Best Pitcher in Baseball: The Life of Rube Foster, Negro League Giant* by Robert C. Cottrell
- *Maybe I'll Pitch Forever* by Leroy "Satchel" Paige
- *Josh Gibson* by Mark Ribowsky
- *I Never Had it Made* by Jackie Robinson
- *It's Good to be Alive* by Roy Campanella
- *Baseball Great Experiment* by Jules Tygiel

Fiction
- *Bingo Long's Traveling All-Stars and Motor Kings* by William Brashler
- *Finding Buck McHenry* by Alfred Slote
- *Shadowball* by Peter Rutkoff
- *Hanging Curve* by Troy Soos

III. FILM:

Documentary Film
- *Baseball: A Film by Ken Burns—5th Inning, Shadowball* (1995)
- *There Was Always Sun Shining Someplace* (1993)
- *Only the Ball Was White* (1992)

Feature Film/Television Film
- *Bingo Long's Traveling All-Stars and Motor Kings* (1979)
- ***Don't Look Back: The Life of Satchel Paige* (1981)**
- *Soul of the Game* (1998)
- *Finding Buck McHenry* (2000)

Source: Doswell (2005).

Another idea to assist in establishing a frame of reference for educators is for the partnership to create a distributable fact packet based on museum content. A fact packet might include one page about each of the following:

1. The history of the museum subject(s), such as the Negro Leagues.
2. A list of key people, dates, and the role(s) they played during this time.
3. Barriers/challenges that were overcome.
4. Contributions to society, honors/awards, inventions, and so on.

The fact packet can include any number of items that may assist partnership members in establishing a frame of reference. The fact packet should be informative, creative, and tailored to specific museum content.

Subscribe to Relevant Organizations and Publications

Broaden members' frame of reference even more by subscribing to professional organizations and electronic journals that relate to the museum's content and current educational practices. Subscriptions to many online journals and professional associations are free or available with a paid membership.

Before paying for an organization membership, check to see if any partnership members already belong to the organization and if materials can be legally copied and distributed to other partnership members.

Partnership members may want to subscribe to the following resources.

Museum resources

- American Association of Museums (AAM): http://www.aam-us.org/index.cfm
- The Institute of Museum and Library Services (IMLS): http://www.imls.gov/index.shtm

Technology resources:

- eSchool News: http://www.eschoolnews.com/
- Infobits: http://www.unc.edu/cit/infobits/

Search engines and alerts can also be utilized by members, for example, **Google alerts** can be set to be received on a regular basis for the latest news on topics of focus such as high school social studies, high school student motivation, museum+lesson planning, and so on.

Not all resources are reliable or reputable. Check the source of online resources carefully.

CURRICULUM DEVELOPMENT

Lesson Plan Prototype

Once the lesson plan components are identified and agreed upon by the partnership members, the lesson plan components need to be included in a blank lesson plan format. A blank lesson plan format can assist partnership members that need help in the lesson planning process.

Blank Lesson Plan Format

Title

Key Features of Powerful Teaching and Learning: (National Council for the Social Studies. "A Vision of Powerful Teaching and Learning in the Social Studies: Building Social Understanding and Civic Efficacy." http://www.socialstudies.org/positions/powerful/)

Grade Level:
Subject:
Standards:
NCSS Standards:
ISTE Standards:
Missouri Standards:
Time allotment:

Meaningful:

Integrated:

Value-based:

Challenging:

Active:

Purpose and Objectives: (include appropriate number of objectives)
1.
2.
3.
Primary Resources:
Procedures & Activities:
Assessment:
Alternate Assessment:
Conclusion:
Extension and Enrichment:
Online Resources:
Secondary Resources:

Source: Barragree (2005a, Summer).

Lesson Plan Components and Definitions

Once the lesson plan components have been decided, the components are defined collaboratively before beginning the lesson planning process. Defining the lesson plan components should not be difficult or time consuming. Use definitions from educational resources to help define each component. By defining the lesson plan components, it is easier for partnership members to begin lesson planning and clarifies what should be included in each lesson plan. An example of lesson plan component definitions is shown.

LESSON PLAN COMPONENT DEFINITIONS

Title: Lesson title

Grade Level & Subject: Grade appropriate level(s), and subject

Standards: List of correlating national, state, and ISTE standards

Key Features of Powerful Teaching and Learning: NCSS' five components of ideal social studies instruction—meaningful, integrative, value-based, challenging, and active learning. Not all five keys must be present in each lesson plan.

Purpose: Brief explanation of the lesson purpose and student activities

Objectives: Knowledge and skills the student will obtain and be able to demonstrate from the lesson

Time Allotment: The amount of time generally needed to complete the lesson

Primary Resources: Any instructor materials needed to complete the lesson plan effectively

Procedures & Activities: Detailed lesson plan procedures and activities

Conclusion: A review of essential lesson objectives and student learning

Assessment: Educator's evaluation of student learning

Alternate Assessment: Another mode of assessing student learning

Extension and Enrichment: Ideas for further teaching, researching, or student interest

Online Resources: Electronic student resources

Secondary Resources: Any materials created or needed to support the educator's procedures and activities portion of the lesson plan

Source:　Barragree (2005b, Summer).

The definitions of the components are short, concise, and written clearly so lesson plan creators understand the function of each component in the lesson plan. Use the Checklist of Lesson Plan Components to determine if all the components necessary are included in the motivational standards-based curriculum materials in high school social studies.

CHECKLIST OF LESSON PLAN COMPONENTS

Lesson Plan Components

___ Title
___ Grade Level
___ Subject
___ Standards
___ Time Allotment
___ Key Features of Powerful Teaching and Learning
___ Purpose & Objectives
___ Primary Resources
___ Procedures & Activities
___ Assessment
___ Alternate Assessment
___ Conclusion
___ Extension & Enrichment
___ Online Resources
___ Secondary Resources
___ RFDLs
___ Technology is Integrated

Supplemental Materials

___ Student Rubrics
___ Educator Rubrics
___ Student Handouts
___ Educator Key Sheets
___ Powerpoint Presentations or Other Media
___ Additional RFDLs

Source: Barragree (2006a, November).

Step-by-Step Lesson Planning

Learning to lesson plan is a skill. Lesson planning takes practice and patience, especially at first. By creating lesson plans, the partnership begins to "own" the content. Therefore, to assist beginning lesson planners, create a step-by-step graph of how to create a lesson plan. Using the step-by-step graph, members that have limited or no prior lesson planning experience are able to create high quality curriculum materials without much difficulty. Thorough preplanning and continued communication among members makes it easier for all lesson plan developers to create motivational standards-based lesson plans regardless of their previous experience.

 Veterans to lesson planning will also benefit from the graphs easy to follow format.

A step-by-step lesson planning graph is shown as an example in Figure 4.1.

The first three steps in lesson planning, (1) determining the subject area and grade level, (2) selecting a topic, and (3) researching the topic have already been completed in earlier stages. Next, add a purpose and objectives to the lesson plan.

Add purpose and objectives: The purpose of the lesson plan should be stated in one or two succinct sentences and clearly state the overarching goal of the lesson. The purpose is sometimes called a rationale.

Objectives are the goals of the lesson plan. Objectives' characteristics include:

- Are written clearly.
- Are specific.
- Include 3-4 per lesson plan, but the number can fluctuate.
- States a specific skill/concept that students should understand and be able to do.
- Are measurable.
- Support the curriculum standards of the lesson.

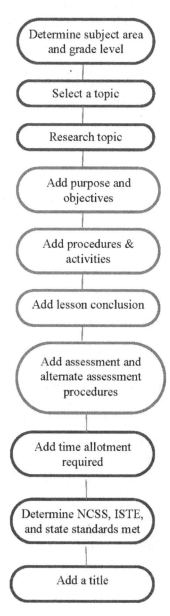

Figure 4.1.   Lesson planning.

Add procedures & activities: Procedures should describe what the educators do and what instructional techniques are to be used during the lesson. Procedures need to be highly detailed and clear so educators easily understand how to teach the skills/concepts of the lesson plan.

 Can a public school educator outside the partnership clearly understand the written procedures of the lesson?

Include activities that reinforce and relate directly to the objectives of the lesson plan.

Activities:

- Are not busy work.
- Are grade-level appropriate.
- Challenge students.
- Include opportunities for student choice.

- What supporting documents do educators and students need to complete the lesson plan? Student handouts, assessment rubrics, a key for educator use, enrichment opportunities for students, etc.
- What primary and secondary resources, hard copy and online, are needed?
- What materials are needed?

 Rubistar: Create rubrics for your lesson plan projects: http://rubistar.4teachers.org/index.php

Create any supporting documents, add the primary and secondary resources, and add any materials needed to the lesson plan. List only the materials and resources actually being used in the lesson.

Web sites often change content and/or are no longer accessible, so it is best not to base an entire lesson plan on one Web site.

Add lesson conclusion: The conclusion is a wrap-up or summary of the lesson. The conclusion should restate the lesson plan objectives and review student understanding of the skills/concepts of the lesson plan. The conclusion is typically brief, approximately 5-15 minutes of the lesson plan.

Add assessment and alternate assessment procedures: The assessment and alternate assessment determine the criteria for educators to evaluate students' progress toward the lesson plan objectives. Assessments should be measurable and describe the expectations students should have achieved through the lesson plan objectives. Alternate assessments are designed to provide alternative opportunities for students with varying **learning styles** to demonstrate their knowledge of the lesson plan objectives in an, often times, nontraditional way.

Add time allotment required: The time allotment is decided toward the end of the lesson planning process because the time required can vary greatly depending on the number of objectives to be achieved, type and number of activities, and assessment methods.

Provide educators with a variety of choices for different lengths of lesson plans.

Determine NCSS, ISTE, and state standards: Once the lesson plan is completed determine which curriculum standards are included in the content of the lesson. List the standards in a conspicuous place in the lesson plan so educators can easily find and reference the standards.

Add a title: Every lesson plan needs a title. Lesson plans change and take on form as they are written. The title should be determined after the lesson plan is completed. Titles should capture the essence of the lesson plan, be creative and intriguing, and catch the attention of educators and students. A good title will spark interest in further exploration of a lesson plan. For example, a lesson titled *What is Oral History and Folklore?* could be titled *Blogging Baseball*. The second title catches students' attention by using a technology (blogging) they are familiar with and typically do not get to use in the school setting and by using the term *baseball* as a hook to interest baseball fans.

The partnership may want to explore other methods of creating lesson plans. Examine the following sources for alternate ways to create lesson plans.

Lesson Planning, Lesson Plan Formats and Lesson Plan Ideas. Kizlik, B.

Lesson Planning Procedures. Faculty Development at Honolulu Community College: http://honolulu.hawaii .edu/intranet/committees/FacDevCom/guidebk/teachtip/ lesspln1.htm

---

A Lesson Plan Explanation

Next, an explanation of how to use the motivational standards-based high school social studies lesson plans is created. The explanation of how to use the lesson plans helps lesson plan creators and other constituents understand the partnership's philosophy behind the lesson plans. An example of a lesson plan explanation looks like this:

LESSON PLANNING FOR THE NLBM

Introduction

Untold stories of NLB wives, children, relatives, and friends, as well as, the economic, social and political impact the NLB had on U.S. history and the world will be the focus of the lesson plans. The charge is to create lesson plans that are **interactive** and multimedia-based, designed for middle school to high school level students, and concentrate on social studies standards while incorporating the content of the untold and oft overlooked NLB.

An Overview

The lesson plan components are a comprehensive list of required parts for each NLBM lesson plan. Then the lesson plan is scored by educators outside the partnership using the lesson plan rubric. The lesson plan definitions further explain the lesson plan components and assist in clarifying the components for curriculum developers. Once each NLBM lesson plan includes all the defined lesson plan components, then the lesson plans are scored using the lesson plan rubric. The lesson plan components should each score a four rating and in the Exemplary category on the rubric before the lesson plan is accepted for the NLBM project. There are several crucial components to creating a quality lesson plan for the NLBM, they include:

Standards

Each lesson plan includes the National Council for the Social Studies (NCSS) standards, International Society for Technology in Education (ISTE) standards, and specific social studies state standards. "Because educational standards are being developed both in social studies and in many of the individual disciplines that contribute to social studies, one might ask: what is the relationship among these various sets of standards? The answer is that the social studies standards address overall curriculum design and comprehensive student performance expectations, while the individual discipline standards (civics and government, economics, geography, and history) provide focused and enhanced content detail" (NCSS: http://www.socialstudies.org/standards/execsummary/). The goal of NLBM lesson plans is to integrate new technologies into national and state social studies curriculum, culminating in technologically and civically-minded students.

Key Features

The NCSS key features are one aspect of ideal social studies teaching and learning. Not all five key features are included in each lesson plan. The goal of including the key features is to guide teachers understanding of why the lesson's content is important to student learning, and not merely miscellaneous information which lacks the ability to focus student learning.

Procedures

Procedures are instructional methods and activities which "should be planned to encourage students to connect what they are learning to their prior knowledge and experience, to think critically and creatively about what they are learning, and to use it in authentic application situations. Learning activities should be introduced and developed so as to make them minds-on activities that engage students with important ideas, not just hands-on activities that may or may not have educational value" (NCSS: http://www.socialstudies.org/positions/powerful/). The procedures and activities include the use of technology, communication, research, and problem-solving and decision-making tools. It is imperative to remember while lesson planning: social studies, as a subject, drives curriculum content while technological means enhance the effectiveness of the content.

Assessment

"The assessment mechanisms focus on the degree to which major social understanding and civic efficacy goals are accomplished, rather than on measuring the acquisition of miscellaneous information or command of generic skills" (NCSS: http://www.socialstudies.org/positions/powerful/). This is accomplished by combining new technologies-pod casting, video games, MP3s, and other interactive platforms with traditional technologies such as film, television, and the internet; to advance students' knowledge of American history and civics (The Corporation for Public Broadcasting. American Civics and History: A Request for Proposals).

Source: NLBM-KSU Partnership. (Fall, 2005b).

The introduction and overview sections are particularly helpful to educators when they begin to utilize the motivational standards-based lesson plans for high school social studies in their classroom. The overview details how the lesson plans are assessed by outside educators before being accepted as a part of the museum's published curriculum materials.

A Completed Lesson Plan

A complete lesson plan includes all the identified lesson plan components. The lesson plan is detailed, clearly written, and relates directly to the curriculum standards. The lesson plan includes all materials, resources, and information a high school social studies educator needs to accomplish the lesson plan objectives while motivating high school students to learn. An example lesson plan created by the NLBM-KSU partnership follows:

LESSON PLAN EXAMPLE

Blogging Baseball

Key Features of Powerful Teaching and Learning: (National Council for the Social Studies. "A Vision of Powerful Teaching and Learning in the Social Studies: Building Social Understanding and Civic Efficacy." http://www.socialstudies.org/positions/powerful/)

Grade Level: 9-12

Subject: Social Studies

Standards:

NCSS Standards: I, III, V, VIII, IX

ISTE Standards: 1, 2, 3, 4, 5

Missouri Standards: 5, 6, 7

Time allotment: 3-4, sixty minute time periods

Meaningful: Students will know the difference and importance of oral tradition and folklore in the Negro Leagues and reflect upon their findings.

Challenging: Students must work cooperatively and individually with technology to understand the lessons key concepts and promote student discussion through a class blog.

Active: Students work in groups to find pertinent information, and post reflections and findings on the class blog.

Purpose/Rationale/Introduction:

Students will understand the differences between the terms oral tradition and folklore as it relates to the history of Negro Leagues baseball players. Through research and class blogging students will express and reflect upon the knowledge they gained regarding the Negro Leagues players and how oral tradition and folklore is important.

Objectives:

1. Students will be able to define the terms oral tradition and folk-lore.
2. Students will understand the difference between oral tradition and folklore and factual information.
3. Students will research and post their oral traditions, folklore, and findings on Negro League players to a class blog.

Materials:

Internet access, Negro League resources listed and other reputable resources, and the provided student handout

Primary Resources:

Black Diamond by P. McKissack and F. McKissack
Only the Ball was White by Robert Peterson
Webster's Dictionary online-www.websters.com

Procedures & Activities:

Day 1-2: Divide students into groups and ask them to define oral tradition, folklore, and fact. Discuss with students the difference between these three terms and have them take notes on the student handout. Then divide students into groups assigning students 1-3 players per group to research. Students may want to pay particular attention to Chapter Five in the McKissack book and utilize the indexes of both books to find specific information on the players listed on the student handout.

Day 3-4: Students finish researching the players in their groups. Students will then log on to the classroom blog for a "discussion" between other classes. Distribute the blog expectations to students and discuss the blog expectations as a class. For the first blog students should post, as a group, a thought based on their research. After the initial blog students can post their thoughts as a group or individually during class time, or individually as a homework assignment.

Note: Teachers need to allow time for students to check and respond to the blog if students are blogging during class, this might be a great sponge activity at the beginning of class. Be sure to assign a minimum number of blog responses per student for credit. Teachers may need to post questions or responses in order to "steer" the blog or prompt dialogue when the blog is stalled.

Possible questions to prompt the blog would be:

1. What did students learn that had never blogged before?

2. What did they learn about NL players, oral traditions, folklore, and factual information?

3. Why are oral traditions and folklore important to culture and society?

4. What other examples of oral traditions or folklore do you know?

5. Does your family and/or culture have oral traditions or folklore you would like to share?

Conclusion:

After 7-10 days of blogging (could be longer if students are motivated by the discussion on the blog), hold a class discussion about the blog and what new or surprising information students learned from blogging with other students in other classes.

Assessment:

Monitor the class blog during the next 7-10 days. Use the assessment rubric to determine if students met the student blog expectations or not.

Alternate Assessment (optional):

Students will form groups and write their own version of an oral tradition or folklore tale based upon what they have read about Negro League baseball and Black American history or based upon their own personal experiences. These stories could be posted on the classroom Web site or posted on the class blog.

Extension and Enrichment (optional):

Students research another culture's oral traditions and folklore further through technology and hard copy forms. Students then post their findings, at least one of the oral traditions or folklore tales they learned about another culture to the class Web site or blog.

Online Resources:

www.websters.com
http://www.blogger.com/start

Secondary Resources:

BLOGGING BASEBALL

Student Handout

1. Define oral tradition:

2. Define folklore:

3. Define fact:

4. Describe the differences between oral tradition, folklore, and fact.

5. In the space provided research and take notes on the following Negro League players. List at least one example of oral tradition *or* folklore and one fact for each player.

"Cool Papa" Bell:
Fact:

Oral Tradition/Folklore:

Satchel Paige:
Fact:

Oral Tradition/Folklore:

Dick Redding:
Fact:

Oral Tradition/Folklore:

Oscar Charelston:
Fact:

Oral Tradition/Folklore:

Joe Rogan:
Fact:

Oral Tradition/Folklore:

Josh Gibson:
Fact:

Oral Tradition/Folklore:

Charlie Grant:
Fact:

Oral Tradition/Folklore:

John Henry Lloyd:
Fact:

Oral Tradition/Folklore:

BLOGGING QUESTIONS AND DIRECTIONS

Q: What is a blog?

A: A web log (or blog) is a web-based space for writing where all the writing and editing of information is managed through a web browser and is immediately and publicly available on the Internet. A blog site is managed by an individual who compiles lists of links to personally interesting material, interspersed with information and editorial. A blog gives students their own voice on the web. A blog is a place to collect and share things that a student find interesting—whether political commentary, a personal diary, or links to Web sites you want to remember. The fastest way to understand blogging is to try blogging out.

Q: Why would students want to use a blog?

A: Students like to check where other students "are at" and want to see what other students are learning, but also to gauge their own progress compared to others. Blogs are able to integrate the personal aspect of a traditional learning journal that documents a student's thoughts and ideas about a topic(s) with the publishing capability of the web. The blog is a way of documenting learning and collecting information for self-analysis and reflection.

Q: How can I use a blog with students?

A: In this case students will use the blog to organize their thoughts and findings on oral traditions, folklore, Negro Leagues baseball, NL players, and other cultures' oral traditions and folklore. The blogging experience is about not only putting thoughts on the web, but hearing back from and connecting with other students and like-minded people. Where students are able to observe others' learning through reading each other's learning journal blogs.

Q: How simple is it to create a blog?

A: You can create your own free and private classroom blog on blogger. To get started on Blogger, click on www.blogger.com/start, you can choose to make your blog public or private. Security as a teacher is important - so you can restrict access to a certain group of people, such as students.

Q: How can I set up a class blog?

1. Click on "Set up Blog Now";
2. Enter some basic information-name, email address, etc. (they don't share info.);
3. Choose a pre-made template for your blog or make your own if you like;

4. Under "Settings" click on members and add member (student) email addresses. An invite email is sent to each member and they must accept in order to begin blogging. This allows you to see who has accessed the blog;

5. Under "settings" click on archive, select the frequency you want to archive the blog postings;

6. Under "settings" click on comments, under who can comment, set comments to only members of this blog. Now, only members (students) you have allowed can comment on this page;

7. After you make all the changes you want under "settings", be sure to click on the republish button to update your changes; and

8. To begin blogging, click on "Posting" and blog.

Note: eBlogger allows for lots of control. Go to the "Settings" page and you can modify things like time stamps, who can comment, etc. You can take the blog out of public view, but the best way is to limit the blogging capability only to approved members of the blog. You can add members (students) by adding in their email addresses, and that makes the blog a private blog. You can even create a mirror blog for parents to read and respond as well.

STUDENT BLOGGING EXPECTATIONS

Do:

1. Post to the blog _____ number of times for full credit.

2. Blogs should not display personal information directly like last names, addresses, phone numbers, etc.

3. Write your thoughts about what you are learning, what you understand and don't understand, why what you are learning is meaningful or not.

4. Strive to improve your writing and take risks with expressing your ideas and bouncing those ideas off of other students in other classes.

5. Convince others that you are thinking and learning (and improving your writing).

6. Make connections to your learning by exploring what other students have written about on the blog.

7. Contribute your ideas, express your opinion, but back your comments up with well thought out reasons and resources.

8. Ask questions that will make a reader think and want to comment on your posting.

Don't:

9. Do not plagiarize or use profanity.
10. Do not use the blog to negatively criticize others thoughts, ideas, or findings.

Blogging Directions:

You will receive an invite letter via your email address, then:

1. Click on the link.
2. Click on create an account.
3. Click on a link to the class blog.
4. Click on the link to the blog.
5. Click on the "View Blog" tab.

To post on the Blog:

1. Click on the Post tab.
2. Select the "Create" link.
3. Type a message in the message box.
4. Click "Republish Entire Blog".
5. View the blog and check to see if your post is there.

Source: http://anne.teachesme.com/2005/11/08#a4515

BLOGGING BASEBALL RUBRIC

Name: _____   HR: _____

Post frequency	Frequencies of the postings meet or exceed class requirements.	Excellent - 2 Satisfactory - 1 Unsatisfactory - 0
Timeliness	Correct numbers of posts have been submitted and were completed on time.	Excellent - 2 Satisfactory - 1 Unsatisfactory - 0
Knowledge	Student demonstrated knowledge of the subject matter through their postings.	Excellent - 2 Satisfactory - 1 Unsatisfactory - 0
Ideas and content	Student has expressed original ideas about the content related to the subject.	Excellent - 2 Satisfactory - 1 Unsatisfactory - 0
Writing quality	Posting are well written, ideas are clearly communicated through the blog, and punctuation and grammar are correct.	Excellent - 2 Satisfactory - 1 Unsatisfactory - 0

TOTAL: _____

Comments:_____
_____
_____
_____
_____

Source: NLBM-KSU Partnership (Spring, 2006a).

A Philosophy and FAQ Sheet

The purpose of creating a philosophy and **FAQ (frequently asked questions)** sheet is to outline the partnership's objectives for users of the lesson plans. The philosophy and FAQ sheet also assists educators in understanding the mission of the lesson plans before implementing them in the classroom. An explanation of how the lesson plans are organized and how they can be used in the classroom is also included to assist educators.

The second part of the document, the FAQ's, consists of a list of most frequently asked questions regarding a particular subject. The purpose of the FAQ is to answer the most commonly asked questions about the partnerships objectives and the implementation of lesson plans before educators begin using the lesson plans in the classroom.

PHILOSOPHY AND FAQ SHEET

A Teachers Guide to Utilizing Negro Leagues Lesson Plans Effectively In the Classroom

Mission Statement:

Negro Leagues Baseball lesson plans are a platform for teaching a rich and varied historical content. The lessons are interactive, multimedia-based and designed for middle school to high school level students. The lessons effectively incorporate National Council for the Social Studies (NCSS) standards, specific state social studies standards, and the International Society for Technology in Education (ISTE) standards. The curricular focus of the lessons demonstrates how themes and issues reflected in studying African American baseball are rooted in U.S. history and social studies. These themes include, but are not limited to, economic, social and political studies, family history and genealogy, education, military history, and civil rights. These themes can be explored by examining individuals (talent), organizations (teams), and communities (towns) involved with African American Baseball. This material synthesizes the most reliable primary and secondary source materials on the subject in a useful format for educators. The lessons are organized according to six critically important U.S. historical eras, they are:

1. 1860-1880: Slavery, War, and the growth of Baseball
2. 1880-1900: American Reconstruction and early Black professional baseball
3. 1900-1920: America's Century and Independent Black baseball
4. 1920-1945: The Birth of the Negro Leagues, its Rise and Fall
5. 1945-1960: Integration and the "Barrier Breakers"
6. 1960-Present: Negro Leagues Legacy and the Civil Rights

By incorporating African American baseball lessons into important historical eras, it is easy for teachers to implement lessons into the classroom's already existing curriculum units. For example, a lesson titled, "Negro League Baseball's Impact on Segregation and Integration" could be utilized as a platform for teaching larger concepts of the Civil Rights era such as Jim Crow laws, the Civil Rights Act, important historical figures during this time, and so on. The ideal aim is for teachers to use African American baseball content throughout the year, not just during Black History Month or other limited occasions.

Frequently Asked Questions:

How does African American baseball and history fit with what I am already teaching?

Since most students have a general idea of history from previous classes, it is important that the lesson content is different than what is found in traditional textbooks and historical lessons. Negro League baseball and Black history can be used as a platform to teach important historical information throughout the year by utilizing the six historical timeframes and the platform approach when teaching social studies/history curriculum. A deeper level of historical knowledge and student engagement can be achieved through teaching all levels of learners through this approach.

How can I use this information?

The lesson plans are created by teachers for teachers, utilizing experts in Negro Leagues history. Flexible, ready-to-use lesson plans include everything teachers may need, such as assessment rubrics, pre-made worksheets, note-taking guides, extension and enrichment ideas, and *resources for diverse learners* to save time and frustration. Teachers are encouraged to use all or part of the lesson, or use the information as a springboard for existing lesson plans. The lessons can be utilized with an entire class, in small groups, or individual students if you like.

How do the lessons motivate students?

Students learn material that has meaning to them and information that is new and different. Therefore, the more interesting the lesson, the higher the students' level of engagement will be. The themes of baseball and African American accomplishments in history are highly engaging, and provide powerful platforms from which to approach other historical lessons. Almost all students have a connection to baseball either through their own experiences at home, with state and national team favorites, or participation in the sport. The multisensory, technology-infused approach catches and holds the students' interest.

Are the lessons easy to use?

Each lesson plan is designed to be comprehensive, effective and user friendly for teachers. The lessons are designed so teachers can download and use them without having to make any changes to meet the required curriculum guidelines in their school, district, or state.

Why should I use these lesson plans instead of others?

The provided lesson plans include target grade level, time allotment needed, related national and state standards, why the lesson content is important, a rationale, objectives, primary and secondary resources, online resources, detailed procedures and activities, a conclusion, assessment options, extension and enrichment, and rubrics, handouts, and technology instructions as needed.

What about students who need accommodations/modifications?

Each lesson plan contains ideas and resources for diverse learners. These resources include text written at a lower *readability level*, graphic organizers, note-taking guides and alternative assignments. The *"Big Ideas"* of each lesson plan are outlined so that teachers may sift curricular standards to meet the needs of students with different *learning objectives*. For more information click on the Resources for Diverse Learners link included with each lesson plan.

My technology skills are not very good can I still use the lessons in my classroom?

Yes, even though the lesson plans include technology skills, step-by-step directions are provided for the teacher and the students throughout the lesson plans.

Is the purchase of more technology equipment or software required?

No. Lesson plans make use of free technology such as the internet and freeware (software that is free to all users). All that is needed are computers with internet access. In addition, many lessons ask students to work in groups when using technology skills so having a limited number of computers would not greatly affect the quality of the lessons. To assist teachers, a technology toolbox has been provided for technical/instructional support. The technology toolbox contains media players, directions, and downloadable materials to assist you in using technology in the classroom.

Do I have to take my class to tour the Negro Leagues Baseball Museum in order to use the lesson plans effectively?

No, but the museum is a wonderful way to increase student motivation and further their understanding of how the Negro Leagues content connects throughout United States history. If a visit is planned, teachers can request a curriculum guide from the Negro Leagues Baseball Museum containing guiding questions to use with their students when visiting the museum. Students can also walk on the Negro Leagues field at the museum with life-size statues of some of the Negro League players. The NLBM also has a state-of-the-art traveling museum for large groups which can be arranged through the museum. More information can be found at www.nlbm.com or 1-888-221-NLBM.

What other resources are available to help teachers implement these lessons in their classrooms?

Each lesson is designed to meet national and state history/social studies standards, which are provided in each lesson plan. However, since each district's guidelines may vary, we encourage you to obtain your school district's curriculum guide to ensure the lessons you teach meet the district guidelines.

Note: Unfortunately, not all resources are reputable or fact-based, so a list of quality Web sites, books, films, and other resources for use with students has been provided. This list is not exhaustive, but can offer a place for teachers and students to research and find information.

Be sure students are using proper search engines when performing internet searches, try:

- Google: www.google.com
- Yahoo: www.yahoo.com
- Ask Jeeves: www.askjeeves.com
- Dogpile: www.dogpile.com

Source: NLBM-KSU Partnership (2006b).

An Educator's Toolbox

The educator's toolbox is a set of resources collected to augment the curriculum materials created by the partnership. The purpose of the educator's toolbox is to assist educators in implementing the curriculum materials created by the partnership. The educator's toolbox is created by compiling all the strategies used in the curriculum materials that may need further explanation, training, or skill sets for educators to effectively implement the curriculum materials. In addition, helpful Web sites, software, and other resources are added to the educator's toolbox to assist educators in better helping students of differing **readiness levels** and learning styles, and to offer educators an opportunity to independently develop the technology skills needed to implement the motivational standards-based curriculum materials.

The educator's toolbox contains a variety of tools in different categories:

1. Multimedia tools.
2. Text tools.
3. Other technology tools.

The toolbox may consist of multimedia tools such as software and instructions on how to podcast, Window Moviemaker, and trial versions of programs such as FlipPublisher Enterprises. Text tools could include trial versions of ReadPlease and Microsoft Office. Other types of tools could include skill enhancement such as how to add drop down menus to Microsoft Excel and Microsoft Word tips. Project tools can include how to create interactive timelines and rubrics for assessing projects. Here is an example of what an educator's toolbox might look like.

EDUCATOR'S TOOLBOX

Multimedia Tools

- **Converting movies to play on your iPod:** This is a set of instructions to move digital movies from a computer to an iPod, using QuickTime software. A link is included for a free download of QuickTime.
- **Creating Podcasts with a PC:** This Web page details the steps required to record and post your own podcast using tools virtually everyone has or can easily acquire on a tiny budget. Go to http://www.windowsdevcenter.com/pub/a/windows/2005/04/05/create_podcasts_with_pc.html
- **Software to get you started with Pod casting:** Propaganda (Windows Trial Version) Record, assemble, and publish your own podcasts. Check out this Web site at http://www.makepropaganda.com
- **Audacity:** Free, cross-platform software for recording and editing sounds. Go to http://audacity.sourceforge.net/download/
- **Windows Movie Maker:** With Movie Maker 2.1, you can create, edit, and share your home movies right on your computer. Build your movie with a few simple steps. Delete bad shots and include only the best scenes. Then share your movie via the web, e-mail, or CD. Try http://www.microsoft.com/windowsxp/downloads/updates/moviemaker2.mspx

- **FlipPublisher Enterprise (Trial Version):** This download lets you convert your content into electronic Flipbooks. Produce digital editions of catalogs, magazines, newsletters, photo albums, books, comics, brochures, manuals, and annual reports in a format that is natural, intuitive and familiar to everyone. Flipbooks are realistic 3D electronic books with pages you can flip like a real book. Go to this Web site, http://www.flipalbum.com/download/ ?PHPSESSID=c9ea70a66ba93a0ef28fdbaa2acb49d8

- **Historic National Archives Video Footage:** Search engine company Google.com has joined efforts with the U.S. National Archives and Records Administration to put historic video footage online. Among the first videos to be digitized from the National Archives collection of 114,000 film reels and 37,000 videos are U.S. government newsreels documenting World War II, motion picture films from the 1930s, and space flight. All of the videos are public domain, so educators, historians, and filmmakers can use these clips without fear of copyright infringement. Go to http://video.google.com/nara.html for more information.

- **Microsoft Power Point (Trial Version):** Use PowerPoint 2003 to create exciting slide shows with graphics, animations, and multimedia– and make them easier to present. Use high-quality custom animations in PowerPoint 2003 to make your presentations come alive. Create animation effects such as moving multiple objects simultaneously or moving objects along a path (path animation), as well as easy sequencing for all of your animation effects. Support for additional types of files gives you enhanced capabilities to play video full screen and use playback to stop, start, or rewind your show, or to find content. Check out the Microsoft Web site at http://www.microsoft.com/office/powerpoint/prodinfo/default.mspx

- **ikeepbookmarks.com:** iKeepBookmarks.com allows you to upload and keep your bookmarks on the Web for free. You can access them at any time, from any computer. This site stores bookmarks in a personal folder so you can use your bookmarks at work and at home, use more than one computer, share pages with others, use multiple browsers. This is a great way to store research Web sites for papers and projects. In the lesson plans that require students to do research on the web, setting up a folder on ikeepbookmarks.com would allow them to maintain sets of *hotlinks* that pertain to specific projects. Go to http://ikeepbookmarks.com

- **Inspiration (Trial Version):** There are two versions of this software; one is designed for students K-5, and one for 6-12 graders. However, the K-5 version is a good place to start for educators who are learning the software. There are free 30 day trial downloads on the Web site so one may try both. The power of this software is the interactive features. A worksheet created in Inspiration allows the educator to make all graphics and text read out loud. This is a powerful tool for *diverse learners* as they access the content in multi-sensory ways. Students can also use the software to create graphic organizers and writing tools. This is a supportive resource for writing papers, preparing presentations and organizing one's thoughts for any project. Go to http://www.inspiration.com/freetrial/index .cfm for more information.

TEXT TOOLS

- **Microsoft Word Tips 1:** Microsoft Word has the capability to determine the reading level of a selection of text. This PDF file outlines how to set that feature for any *Microsoft Word* document. This can be very helpful as educators may need to re-write a piece of text at a lower readability level in order to customize the reading level for their students (Adobe Acrobat Reader required).

  Another powerful feature of Microsoft Word is the AutoSummarize tool. This allows the either the educator or the reader to highlight key ideas and main points in a piece of text. The feature offers several options regarding how the highlighted material is displayed and comes as a standard tool within Microsoft Word. For more information about these tools, go to the Help function in Microsoft Word.

- **Microsoft Word Tips 2:** This PDF file outlines other features of Microsoft Word which educators and students may find useful as they work with text. They include: AutoCorrect, Clicking, Creating Screenshots, AutoFormat, and Customizing toolbars (Adobe Acrobat Reader required). For more information about these tools, go to the Help function in Microsoft Word.

- **Insert Hidden Support Within a Word Document:** This Web page will guide educators through a process to insert hidden instructions in a Microsoft Word document. This technique can provide educator support to students. Go to http://www.microsoft.com/education/ HiddenText.mspx for further assistance.

- **Adding Drop Down Menus to Microsoft Excel:** When using a Microsoft Excel spreadsheet to create a worksheet or a finished product, using multiple choice options in drop down menus can provide some directions and structure to the learner's experience.

- **Create an Interactive Timeline Using Microsoft Excel:** Using a spreadsheet to create a timeline allows students to fill in cells to designate time periods. Text can be entered sideways to mark the events being represented. Students can enter text inside a drawing, or add drawings. This Web site gives educators step-by-step instructions on this process. http://www.microsoft.com/Education/create-timeline.mspx?pf=true

- **Microsoft Office (Trial Version):** Download a trial version of Microsoft Office 2003, free for 60 days. This software contains Microsoft Word (word processing), Microsoft Excel (spreadsheet), Microsoft Access (database) and Microsoft Powerpoint (presentation software). The trial version is available at http://microsoft.order-10.com/OfficeStandardEdition/welcome.aspx?id=officedl7

- **ReadPlease (Trial Version):** This Web page includes a step-by-step set of instruction on how to download a 30-day trial version of *ReadPlease 2003*. This product will create an icon on the computer desktop that can convert text to speech by copying and pasting text into the window. Go to http://www.readplease.com/ This Web site also contains a download link to a 30-day trial version of Reading-Bar 2, a universal text reader that will read any Web site text out loud. The universal text reader stays in the browser and is available as a feature when one is using the Internet. Download this trial version at http://www.readplease.com/english/readingbar.php

- **ReadMark (Trial Version):** This Web page provides a description and link to download a 30-day trial version of *ReadMark*. This product creates a movable marker on the screen that can be moved by using a computer mouse or arrow keys on top of a document, webpage, or any other image, and can be used as a place holder for reading on a computer screen. Try: http://www.geocities.com/three-hillssoftware/readmark.html

- **Vocabulary Made Fun:** This Web site contains tools to work with vocabulary words. The Web site includes tools to make crossword puzzles, hangman, word searches, and so on. Go to http://www.vocabulary.co.il/

Other Technology Tools

Rubric Resources:

- **teAchnology Rubric Generators:** This Web site provides links to various rubrics and rubric generators. http://www.teach-nology.com/web_tools/rubrics/

- **Rubric Template:** This tool provides a structure to create a grading template. The rubric template allows the educator to detail criteria on a scale from one to four components.

- **4Teachers.org: Integrating Technology-Teacher Resources:** 4Teachers.org works to help you integrate technology into your classroom by offering FREE online tools and resources. This site helps educators locate and create ready-to-use web lessons, quizzes, rubrics and classroom calendars. There are also tools for student use. Discover valuable professional development resources addressing issues such as equity, technology planning and at-risk or special-needs students. For more information check out the Web site at http://www.4teachers.org/

Source: NLBM-KSU Partnership (2006).

There are a number of other tools and tool categories that could be added to the educator's toolbox. The toolbox is meant to be added to as lesson plans are created and new tools are discovered.

Why Is an Educator's Toolbox Important?

An educator's toolbox is important because educators have varying levels of technology proficiency and may need assistance in learning how to integrate new technologies into the social studies curriculum and to teach the technology skills included in the lesson plans to students.

Ask high school students for assistance when learning a new technology, most are eager to assist educators with technology if given the opportunity.

The toolbox is like a suit tailored for educators for the purpose of implementing the partnership's lesson plans. The toolbox offers an independent way to learn about and master new technology skills without having to attend costly conferences or time consuming staff development sessions.

Educators can also use the tools in the toolbox in everyday curriculum and technology applications.

RFDLS (RESOURCES FOR DIVERSE LEARNERS)

What are RFDLs?

RFDLs are defined as common **modifications** included in lesson plans that allow educators to diversify their teaching methods for varying student readiness levels. Ann Elliott, Director of Special Education for the Auburn-Washburn school district in Topeka, Kansas explains, "Some of the modifications might be outlined for students with disabilities in their Individual Education Plan (**IEP**), and some modifications may be useful for all students. Educators will find these modifications offer ideas to personalize the learning experience for their own classes" (Elliott, personal communication, September 3, 2006). There are a number of ways that curriculum can be modified for students, some methods include:

- Layered curriculum.
- Differentiated learning.
- Universal design for learning.
- The planning pyramid.

The planning pyramid is one of the easiest methods for educators to understand and use in curriculum planning. The Planning Pyramid represents a framework for planning in content area classrooms. The Planning Pyramid is designed to be a flexible tool to help teachers plan for inclusionary instruction and to enable content coverage in general education classrooms for students with diverse learning needs (Schumm, Vaughn, & Leavell, 1994). The Planning Pyramid allows a teacher to identify what information needs to be taught and to pay attention to individual students' needs to determine how the information will be taught (Vaughn, Bos, & Schumm, 2000). This information and more on methods for modifying the curriculum are available from:

 Layered Curriculum as a Means to Access the General Curriculum: A Comparison to Differentiated Instruction, Universal Design for Learning and the Planning Pyramid: http://help4teachers.com/AdrianPaper.htm

The Planning Pyramid illustrates that all students can learn, but not all students will learn everything taught within the lesson.

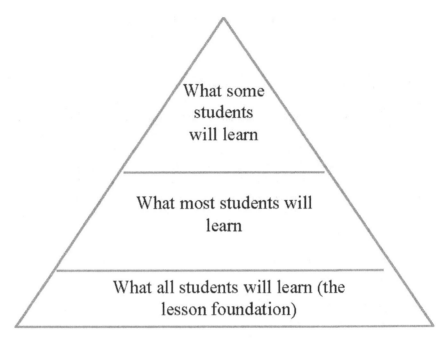

Figure 4.2.   The planing pyramid.

Kathy Nunley uses layered curriculum units to designate different layers of the Planning Pyramid. An example of a layered curriculum unit is from Kathy Nunley's Web site based on Negro Leagues Baseball:

Negro Leagues Baseball

You must complete the required number of points in each section and defend each submission individually and orally, before moving on to the next section. *A maximum of two assignments per person will be accepted per day so manage your time accordingly.*

C Level Assignments *(A maximum of 40 points can be earned at this level).*	*Points* *Possible*	*Points* *Earned*	*Teacher's* *Signature*
Write a one-page paper on one of the following players: Fleetwood Walker, Satchel Paige, Josh Gibson, or "Cool Papa Bell".	5		
Listen to the taped selection of *Black Diamond* by McKissack and McKissack and write a one-page summary of the information.	5		

Go to the following Web site and listen to interviews with NLB players and relatives, orally tell or write a one-page paper on what NLB was like during this time.	5
Draw five NLB player trading cards; include a drawing of the player, position played, and team(s) played for, team logo, and career starting and ending dates.	5
Write a diary entry from a NLB player's perspective for four days; include a description of at least one game.	5
Listen to music from Ella Fitzgerald or Duke Ellington. Tell or write the meaning of one of their songs.	5
Read the article at: http://www.infoplease.com/spot/ negroleague1.html and create a timeline from the information.	5
Watch one of the Negro Leagues videos and tell or write about the conditions NLB players endured and how they were treated by Whites and society as a whole.	5
Recreate a typical NLB stadium using whatever materials you want.	5
Draw signs (one point per sign) depicting "separate but equal" facilities and/or treatment.	5
What are Jim Crow laws? Describe, draw, or write a summary.	5
Define segregation, integration, discrimination, racism, and slavery (one point per word).	5
Tell, draw, or write one paragraph answering this question: Does slavery still exists today, and if so, why?	5
Reenact a situation in which you or someone you know was discriminated against, and explain why you think it was discrimination.	5
Define Negro Renaissance and name three important contributors of the time.	5
Write a poem or a song that reflects upon NLB.	5
Draw a cartoon depicting any NLB team(s), player(s), or owner(s).	5
Create an artists sketch of a woman involved in the NLB, be sure to color and label the sketch for full credit.	5

B Level Assignments: (Choose one for 20 points)	*Points Possible*	*Points Earned*	*Teacher's Signature*
Research NLB innovations. How did they contribute to the success of NLB? What, if any, other innovations could have helped save NLB? How would these have helped? What else could have been done to prolong NLB? Write a 3-4 page paper.	20		

	Points Possible	Points Earned	Teacher's Signature
Listen to Ted Williams' Hall of Fame induction speech. Write a 3-4 page paper detailing if you agree with his proposal to induct NLB players into the Hall of Fame, and support your position with historical information.	20		
What was the major turning point in NLB? Why? Write a 3-4 page paper and support your position with historical information.	20		

A Level Assignments: *Choose one for 30 points*	*Points Possible*	*Points Earned*	*Teacher's Signature*
Research Black women in NLB, choose one woman to write a six page historically based story about NLB from her perspective.	30		
Create an interactive timeline showing the history of NLB from its inception to its demise. Then post your timeline to a classroom Web site. See me for the directions on how to create an interactive timeline.	30		
Research court cases dealing with segregation and/or discrimination and/or integration. Write a summary of at least 3 cases. Choose one case, and write a trial transcript of what you think occurred in court include both the defending and prosecuting points of view.	30		

You can view more layered curriculum units at Dr. Kathy Nunley's Web site for educators at http://help4teachers.com

Universal Design for Learning by Nancy Safer: http://www.teachervision.fen.com

Dr. Kathy Nunley's Web site for Educators: http://help4teachers.com

Nunley, K. (1998-2006). **Layered Curriculum**. http://help4teachers.com

Tomlinson, C. (2000a). **Differentiated instruction: Can it work?**

Why are RFDLs Important?

Today educators are faced with a highly diversified classroom from students with disabilities to students that are challenged culturally and/or linguistically. Elliott states,

> Educators have been challenged to meet the needs of a variety of learners. Increasingly, educators face a classroom of students that may include those with a lower readiness level to learn, those from other cultures and those who may speak other languages. All of this diversity brings richness to the learning environment when teachers can plan lessons that reach students in many ways. (personal communication, September 3, 2006)

In order to meet the needs of a diverse population, modifications to the general curriculum are necessary. Teaching to the middle, the majority of students at an average readiness level, is no longer acceptable. Educators often fail to meet the needs of diverse learners in their classrooms because they feel modifications are not necessary or water-down the curriculum. Modifications are necessary, and if created and implemented properly do not water-down the curriculum. One way to meet the needs of diverse students is to create and include RFDLs in curriculum materials.

How do I Create RFDLs?

The best way to learn to create RFDLs is to research different strategies and consult with experienced special education administrators and teachers, and other social studies educators that have created and implemented RFDLs in their classrooms. The partnership may already have members that are familiar with and are experienced with RFDLs. Rely on their expertise to help educate other partnership members and guide the development of RFDLs for the lesson plans.

Some of the techniques used to create RFDL modifications include:

1. **Curriculum Sifting:** Prioritizing the critical learning objective(s) of the lesson and determining what "Big Ideas" should be the focus of the learning activity. This activity is very effective when a student's IEP requires shortened assignments.
2. **Lesson Tiering:** Developing multiple learning activities for the same lesson plan, with various levels of complexity, autonomy and difficulty. Tiering content is useful for student groups in which readiness levels are varied.

3. **Graphic Organizers:** Creating a note-taking guide, study sheet, or assignment that captures the lesson objective(s) in a visual manner. Graphic organizers are attractive to students who are not motivated, those that have behavioral challenges such as opposition, poor study habits and who resist authority. Students who have difficulty with executive functioning, organization, attention to task and cognitive stamina also benefit from graphic organizers.

4. **Hurdle Help**: Simple accommodations that provide additional support to students so they can complete the task more independently. Strategies might include word banks, close note-taking sheets, and visual and content specific clues. Useful with students who respond to authority with refusal to work or power struggles. They also support students with learning disabilities by providing a scaffold on which they can retain and recall information.

5. **Multiple Modality Presentation:** Using visual and auditory methods to present the lesson information in order to reach students with different learning styles. Useful for all students and especially students who have sensory disabilities (audio for the visually impaired, visual or kinesthetic for the hearing impaired). Consider the difference between reading the words of Martin Luther King's speech "I Have a Dream" versus hearing the passion in his voice on an audio recording, versus seeing and hearing the energy in his face and body language as he delivers the speech.

6. **Technology:** Using automated activities and interactive learning to allow students to engage in active participation and hands-on opportunities. Useful for most learners and written into students' IEP's for students who experience specific challenges such as motor concerns that make writing difficult or impossible, learning disabilities that impair spelling and word choice, expressive and receptive speech and language barriers, and so on.

There are many other RFDL strategies that can meet the needs of a variety of learners. Various resources exist on the Web detailing other RFDL strategies, such as the ones listed here.

Adapt Lessons to Reach All Students. Teacher Vision: http://www.teachervision.fen.com/teaching-methods/special-education/3759.html?detoured=1

The Art of Teaching: Big Ideas. Teacher Vision: http://www.teachervision.fen.com/teaching-methods/special-education/3764.html

For more information about RFDLs and methods of modification consult the *Further Resources* section.

LESSON PLAN INCLUDING RFDLS

The NLB and the Law

Key Features of Powerful Teaching and Learning: (National Council for the Social Studies. "A Vision of Powerful Teaching and Learning in the Social Studies: Building Social Understanding and Civic Efficacy." http://www.socialstudies.org/positions/powerful/)

Grade Level: 9-12
Subject: Social Studies
Standards:
NCSS Standards: II, III, V, VI, X
ISTE Standards: 1, 2, 5
Missouri Standards: 1, 2, 3, 5, 6
Time allotment: Six, 60 minute time periods

Meaningful: Emphasizes how the law and historically significant events affected social and political issues of the time and in turn affected the treatment of Blacks throughout history.

Value-Based: Student groups will explore and learn about a variety of United States laws and historical events affecting the treatment of Blacks and NLB players.

Challenging: Student groups must internalize and accurately portray the United States political system, judicial system, and historical social and cultural climate during the 1800's and 1900's.

Active: Students will work cooperatively in groups to research, write, and reenact United States laws and historically significant events affecting the NLB and American society politically and socially.

Purpose/Rationale/Introduction:

This lesson will introduce students to historical law and its impact on NLB and Black Americans. After identifying and researching laws contributing to segregation or integration, student will chose one law to reenact in a historically accurate manner.

Objectives:

1. Students will be able to identify important laws and historically significant events during the existence of NLB.
2. Students will navigate the Internet and gather information about the impact the law and historical events had on Negro Leagues Baseball and Black Americans.
3. Students will be able to identify how laws passed in the United States and historical events contributed to or discouraged segregation and/or integration in society and in the Negro Leagues.
4. Students will reenact a historically accurate interpretation of one law including key historical figures and cases.

Primary Resources:

Black Diamond: The Story of the Negro Baseball Leagues, by McKissack and McKissack, access to the Negro Leagues Baseball Museum Web site, note-taking supplies, other relevant Negro Leagues resources (see the secondary resources section).

Procedures & Activities:

*   *Day 1:* Discuss what students already know about the treatment of Blacks in the 1800s, the 1900s, and today. Ask students what they know about Jim Crow laws, *Plessy vs. Ferguson*, *Brown vs. Topeka Board of Education*, and other historically significant events such as the Alabama riots, the March on Washington, etc. Distribute the student handout. Read page 33 from *Black Diamond* aloud to students. Have students take notes and discuss the impact of these laws/events on American society, Blacks, and NLB. Group students into groups of three-five; ask student groups to select a particular law and/or event they would like to research and reenact from the approved list (See secondary resources listed, or create your own approved list). Student groups begin planning and researching their selected law or event and the impact it had on American society and NLB. Groups of two from each larger group may research on the computer. Students can switch later in the day or the next day and continue to rotate until all students have had a chance to research on the computer.
*   *Day 2:* Students continue researching laws.
*   *Day 3:* Students should begin planning and writing a draft of a reenactment of the law or event they researched. The reenactment should include key historical figures politically, socially, and in

NLB. The reenactment must be as historically accurate as possible and present the political, social, and NLB perspectives either simultaneously or in short separate reenactments of the same law or event.

- *Day 4 & 5:* Student groups should finalize and begin practicing their reenactments.

Conclusion:

Discuss what students learned about the United States judicial system then and now. Question how people, places, and events affected life in the United States and the treatment of Blacks until the 1900s. Are certain groups still treated unfairly in the United States? Who? How? Why?

Assessment:

- *Day 6:* Student groups perform their reenactments for the class. See attached scoring rubric. Teachers could videotape the reenactments and post them online for students and parents to view.

Alternate Assessment:

Students complete a final research paper based on one selected law or event.

Extension and Enrichment:

Research the treatment of a group of people still being treated unfairly in the United States. Document any laws and historical events which lead up to their current treatment, and pose possible ways to raise awareness and prevent unequal treatment of the group.

Online Resources:

- A Look at Life in the Negro Leagues: http://coe.ksu.edu/nlbm/ Negro Leagues Baseball Museum: http://www.nlbm.com/
- The History of Jim Crow: http://www.jimcrowhistory.org/home.htm
- Jim Crow Laws: http://www.nps.gov/malu/documents/ jim_crow_laws.htm
- African American History: http://www.watson.org/~lisa /blackhistory/index.html
- In Pursuit of Freedom and Equality: *Brown v. Board of Education of Topeka*, http://brownvboard.org/index.htm
- African American World: Timeline, http://www.pbs.org/wnet/ aaworld/timeline.html

- Negro Leagues Legacy: http://mlb.mlb.com/NASApp/mlb/mlb/ history/mlb_negro_leagues_story.jsp?story=kaleidoscopic

Secondary Resources:

Possible list of other laws and historical events:

The Dred Scott Case	The Housing Rights Act of 1968
School Busing	The Montgomery Bus Boycott
Sit-Ins	*Milliken v. Bradley*
The Freedom Rides	A Change in the Cloture Rule
The March on Washington	The Bakke Case
Mississippi and Freedom Summer	Perfecting Civil Rights Laws
Alabama-Selma, Birmingham	The Minority Bill of Rights
Governor Faubus, Little Rock, AR	*Plessy v. Ferguson*
The Murder of Emmett Till	

A Brief History of Civil Rights in the United States of America, http:// www.africanamericans.com/CivilRightsHistoryIndex.htm

THE NLB AND THE LAW

Student Handout

1. Describe the following laws:

    • Jim Crow laws:

    • *Plessy v. Ferguson*:

    • *Brown v. Topeka Board of Education*:

2. What was/is the impact of these laws on:

    •   American society:

    • Blacks:

    • The NLB:

3.   Select a particular law or event your group wants to research and reenact from the approved list. Why did your group choose this law or event?

4.   Who were the key historical figures for this law or event?

5.   Why were they important during this time?

6.   What impact did the law or event have on American society and NLB?

THE NLB AND THE LAW:
SCORING RUBRIC

Points	0	1	2	3
Key historical figures	No historical figures depicted in the reenactment	One key historical figure depicted in the reenactment	Most key historical figures depicted, but not all	All key historical figures were depicted in the reenactment
Historically accurate	Not historically accurate, information is inaccurate and/or fictional	Little information is historically accurate, some information inaccurate or fictional	Most information is historically accurate, some details inaccurate or fictional	All information, including details are historically accurate, no fictional information
Perspectives	No perspective is given from society, politically, or from NLB	One perspective is presented: society or politically or from the NLB	Two perspectives are presented out of the three: society, politically, NLB	All three perspectives are presented: society and politically, and from NLB
Knowledge of the law or event	Students do not understand the meaning of the law or event nor know the impact	Students understand the meaning of the law or event, but do not know the impact on any of the chosen aspects	Students understand the meaning of the law or event and know the impact on at least one of the chosen aspects: society, politically, or NLB	Students understand the meaning of the law or event and know the impact on all three chosen aspects of society, politically, and NLB
Props	No use of props	Limited use of props to what is on hand, little effort to obtain props, and/or historically incorrect	Limited use of props, limited to what is on hand, some effort to obtain props, and/or historically correct	Use of props beyond what is at hand, effort is clear, and props are historically correct
Audible	Can't hear reenactment or is indistinguishable	Can hear some of the reenactment and/or is indistinguishable	Can hear most of the reenactment, a few parts indistinguishable	Can hear all of the reenactment, no parts are indistinguishable

Script	No final script was provided to the teacher, not all students have a role in the reenactment	An incomplete final script was provided to the teacher, not all students have a role in the reenactment	A complete final script was provided to the teacher, but not all students have a role in the reenactment	A complete final script was provided to the teacher, and all students have a role in the reenactment

Total Points Earned:

Comments: _____

_____

_____

_____

_____

RFDL #1

Creating Jim Crow: In-Depth Essay
by Ronald L. F. Davis, Ph. D.

The term Jim Crow is believed to have originated around 1830 when a White, *minstrel* show performer, Thomas "Daddy" Rice, blackened his face with charcoal paste or burnt cork and danced a ridiculous jig while singing the lyrics to the song, "Jump Jim Crow." Rice created this character after seeing (while traveling in the South) a crippled, elderly Black man (or some say a young Black boy) dancing and singing a song ending with these chorus words:

> *"Weel about and turn about and do jis so,*
> *Eb'ry time I weel about I jump Jim Crow."*

Some historians believe that a Mr. Crow owned the slave who inspired Rice's act—thus the reason for the Jim Crow term in the lyrics. In any case, Rice incorporated the skit into his minstrel act, and by the 1850's the "Jim Crow" character had become a standard part of the minstrel show scene in America. On the eve of the Civil War, the Jim Crow idea was one of many stereotypical images of Black inferiority in the popular culture of the day—along with *Sambos*, *Coons*, and *Zip Dandies*. The word Jim Crow became a racial slur synonymous with Black, colored, or Negro in the vocabulary of many Whites; and by the end of the century acts of racial discrimination toward Blacks were often referred to as Jim Crow laws and practices.

Although "*Jim Crow Cars*" on some Northern railroad lines—meaning segregated cars—predated the Civil War, in general the Jim Crow era in American history dates from the late 1890s, when Southern states began systematically to codify (or strengthen) in law and state constitutional provisions the subordinate position of African Americans in society. Most of these legal steps were aimed at separating the races in public spaces (public schools, parks, accommodations, and transportation) and preventing adult Black males from exercising the right to vote. In every state of the former Confederacy, the system of legalized segregation and disfranchisement was fully in place by 1910. This system of white supremacy cut across class boundaries and re-enforced a cult of "whiteness" that predated the Civil War.

Segregation and disfranchisement laws were often supported, moreover, by brutal acts of ceremonial and ritualized mob violence (*lynchings*) against Southern Blacks. Indeed, from 1889 to 1930, over 3,700 men and women were reported lynched in the United States—most of who were

Southern Blacks. Hundreds of other lynchings and acts of mob terror aimed at brutalizing Blacks occurred throughout the era but went unreported in the press. Numerous *race riots* erupted in the Jim Crow era, usually in towns and cities and almost always in defense of segregation and white supremacy. These riots engulfed the nation from Wilmington, North Carolina, to Houston, Texas; from East St. Louis and Chicago to Tulsa, Oklahoma, in the years from 1865 to 1955. The riots usually erupted in urban areas to which Southern, rural Blacks had recently migrated. In the single year of 1919, at least twenty-five incidents were recorded, with numerous deaths and hundreds of people injured. So bloody was this summer of that year that it is known as the *Red Summer of 1919*.

The so-called Jim Crow segregation laws gained significant impetus from U. S. Supreme Court rulings in the last two decades of the nineteenth century. In 1883, the Supreme Court ruled unconstitutional the *Civil Rights Act of 1875*. The 1875 law stipulated: "That all persons ... shall be entitled to full and equal enjoyment of the accommodations, advantages, facilities, and privileges of inns, public conveyances on land or water, theaters, and other places of public amusement." The Court reviewed five separate complaints involving acts of discrimination on a railroad and in public sites, including a theater in San Francisco and the Grand Opera House in New York. In declaring the federal law unconstitutional, Chief Justice Joseph Bradley held that the *Fourteenth Amendment* did not protect Black people from discrimination by private businesses and individuals but only from discrimination by states. He observed in his opinion that it was time for Blacks to assume "the rank of a mere citizen" and stop being the "special favorite of the laws." Justice *John Marshall Harlan* vigorously dissented, arguing that hotels and amusement parks and public conveyances were public services that operated under state permission and thus were subject to public control.

It was not long after the Court's decision striking down the Civil Rights Act of 1875 that Southern states began enacting sweeping segregation legislation. In 1890, Louisiana required by law that Blacks ride in separate railroad cars. In protest of the law, Blacks in the state tested the statute's constitutionality by having a light-skinned African American, Homére Plessy, board a train, whereupon he was quickly arrested for sitting in a car reserved for Whites. A local judge ruled against Plessy and in 1896 the U.S. Supreme Court upheld the lower court's ruling in *Plessy v. Ferguson*. The Court asserted that Plessy's rights were not denied him because the separate accommodations provided to Blacks were equal to those provided Whites. It also ruled that "separate but equal" accommodations did not stamp the "colored race with a badge of inferiority."

Again, Justice Harlan protested in a minority opinion: "Our Constitution is color-blind, and neither knows nor tolerates classes among citizens."

Harlan's liberal views on race did not extend to the Chinese. He wrote this biased statement in his dissent: "There is a race so different from our own that we do not permit those belonging to it to become citizens of the United States. Persons belonging to it are, with few exceptions, absolutely excluded from our country. I allude to the Chinese race. But by the statute in question, a Chinaman can ride in the same passenger coach with White citizens of the United States, while citizens of the Black race in Louisiana, many of whom, perhaps, risked their lives for the preservation of the Union, who are entitled, by law, to participate in the political control of the State and nation, who are not excluded, by law or by reason of their race, from public stations of any kind, and who have all the legal rights that belong to White citizens, are yet declared to be criminals, liable to imprisonment, if they ride in a public coach occupied by citizens of the White race."

The *Plessy* case erected a major obstacle to equal rights for Blacks, culminating a long series of Court decisions that undermined civil rights for African Americans beginning in the 1870's, most notably the *Slaughterhouse Cases, United States v. Reese, United States v. Cruikshank*, and the Civil Rights Cases of 1883. The Supreme Court provided additional support for segregation in 1899 in the case of *Cumming v. Richmond County Board of Education*. In this first case using *Plessy* as the precedent, the Court decreed that separate schools in Georgia were allowed to operate even if comparable schools for Blacks were not available; this was the first case to apply the separate-but-equal doctrine to education. In this case, a unanimous Court ruled that because Richmond County, Georgia, had only enough money to provide a high school for Whites it need not shut down the White school in the interests of separate but equal. This case opened the door for the elimination of Black schools in districts able to demonstrate (or assert) financial hardships. It also clearly indicated that the Court was more interested in enforcing the "separate" part of *Plessy* over the "equal."

With the Supreme Court's approval, Southern states quickly passed laws that restricted the equal access of Blacks to all kinds of public areas, accommodations, and conveyances. Local officials began posting "Whites Only" and "Colored" signs at water fountains, restrooms, waiting rooms, and the entrances and exits at courthouses, libraries, theaters, and public buildings. Towns and cities established curfews for Blacks, and some state laws even restricted Blacks from working in the same rooms in factories and other places of employment.

Creating White Supremacy from 1865 to 1890

The year 1890, when Mississippi wrote a disfranchisement provision into its state constitution, is often considered the beginning of legalized Jim Crow. But legal attempts to establish a system of racial segregation and disfranchisement actually began much earlier. In the first days after the Civil War, most Southern states adopted so-called *Black Codes* aimed at limiting the economic and physical freedom of the formerly enslaved. These early attempts at legally binding Southern Blacks to an inferior status were short-lived, however, due to the presence of federal troops in the former Confederate states during *Congressional Reconstruction* (1866-1876) and the passage of the *Fourteenth* and *Fifteenth Amendments*, the *Civil Rights Acts of 1866* and *1875*, and the three *Enforcement Acts* of 1870 and 1871. (The 1871 Act is usually referred to a the Ku Klux Klan Act.)

It would be mistaken, however, to think that these federal efforts effectively protected the civil rights of African Americans. Waves of violence and vigilante terrorism swept over the South in the 1860s and 1870s (the *Ku Klux Klan* and Knights of the White Camellia), as organized bands of White vigilantes terrorized Black voters who supported Republican candidates as well as many African Americans who defied (consciously or unconsciously) the "*color line*" inherited from the slave era. Such actions often accomplished in reality what could not be done in law. Depending upon the state (and the region within states—such as the *gerrymandered* Second Congressional District in North Carolina where Blacks continued to hold power until after 1900), Blacks found themselves exercising limited suffrage in the 1870s, principally because their votes were manipulated by White landlords and merchant suppliers, eliminated by vigilantism, stolen by fraud at the ballot boxes, and compromised at every turn.

When the *Compromise of 1877* allowed the Republican candidate *Rutherford B. Hayes* to assume the presidency of the nation after the disputed election of 1876, political power was essentially returned to Southern, White Democrats in nearly every state of the former Confederacy. From that point on, the federal government essentially abandoned the attempt to enforce the Fourteenth and Fifteenth Amendments in the South—although the potential for doing so was always uppermost in the minds of Southern Whites. Numerous Southern Blacks nevertheless voted in the 1870s and 1880s, but most Black office holders held power at lower levels (usually in criminal enforcement) in towns and counties, and often did so in cooperation with White Democrats (especially in Mississippi and South Carolina) who supported elected positions for acceptable Black candidates.

In this "*fusion*" arrangement of the two political parties, White leaders of the Democratic Party in the state would agree with Black political leaders, who were usually Republicans, on the number of county offices to be held by Blacks. In theory, Black voters would choose these Black candidates, but in fact only Black candidates acceptable to the White leaders were allowed to run. Any deviation from the plan was met with violence. Most Black leaders went along with such arrangements because it was the best that could be achieved for the moment.

In Mississippi, the method of controlling Black votes and regulating their economic and public lives by full-scale and openly brutal violence was known as the *First Mississippi Plan* of 1875. Whites openly resorted to violence and fraud to control the Black vote, shooting down Black voters "just like birds." This ruthless and bloody revolution devastated the Black vote in Mississippi, and fully 66% of the Blacks registered to vote in the state failed to cast ballots in the presidential election of 1880. Of those who did vote, almost 50% voted Democratic rather than face the wrath of Whites in the state. The White vigilantes made no attempt to disguise themselves as in the days of the Ku Klux Klan, and so complete was their victory that the Republican governor fled the state rather than face impeachment charges by the newly elected legislature.

When Mississippi began formally and legally to segregate and disfranchise Blacks by changing its state constitution and passing supportive legislation in the 1890s, knowing observers referred to these legal moves as the *Second Mississippi Plan*. The principal difference between the two plans is that the latter did not resort to violence in order to eliminate the Black vote. The Second Mississippi Plan did it by law. Other states followed suit to one degree or another, with only a few Black gerrymandered districts in North Carolina, Alabama, and Mississippi witnessing significant and continuing Black political autonomy up to 1900.

In addition to the violence and non-legal measures associated with the First Mississippi Plan, Southern Whites also took legal steps to subordinate Blacks to Whites prior to the wave of segregation and disfranchisement statutes that emerged in the late 1890s. For example, between 1870 and 1884, eleven Southern states legally banned *miscegenation*, or interracial marriages. In the words of historian William Cohen, these bans were the "ultimate segregation laws" in that they clearly spelled out the idea that Whites were superior to Blacks and that any mixing of the two threatened White status and the purity of the White race. School segregation laws also appeared on the books in nearly every Southern state prior to 1888, beginning with Tennessee and Arkansas in 1866. Virginia erected in 1869 a constitutional ban against Blacks and Whites attending the same schools, followed by Tennessee in 1870, Alabama and North Carolina in

1875, Texas in 1876, Georgia in 1877, and Florida in 1885. Arkansas and Mississippi passed school segregation statutes in 1873 and 1878.

While most of the laws banning racial mixing in transportation and in public accommodations were enacted after 1890, many Southern states laid the groundwork early on. They often based their statutes on transportation legislation enacted by Northern states before the Civil War. These laws created Jim Crow cars wherein Black passengers were separated from White passengers. Indeed, the word Jim Crow as a term denoting segregation first appeared in reference to these Northern railroad cars. Responding to the federal law prohibiting racial discrimination on railroads (Civil Rights Act of 1875), Tennessee passed laws in 1881 protecting hotels, railroads, restaurants, and places of amusement from legal suits charging discrimination. The state also attempted to circumvent the federal anti-segregation laws in transportation by enacting statutes in 1882 and 1883 requiring railroads to provide Blacks with "separate but equal facilities." Florida, Mississippi, and Texas jumped on the bandwagon, as did most other states by 1894.

Almost all the Southern states passed statutes restricting suffrage in the years from 1871 to 1889. Various registration laws, such as *poll taxes*, were established in Georgia in 1871 and 1877, in Virginia in 1877 and 1884, in Mississippi in 1876, in South Carolina in 1882, and in Florida in 1888. The effects were devastating. Over half the Blacks who voted in Georgia and South Carolina in 1880 vanished from the polls in 1888. The drop in Florida was 27%t. In places like Alabama, for example, where Blacks equaled almost half the population, no African Americans were sent to the legislature after 1876.

On the local level, most Southern towns and municipalities passed strict vagrancy laws to control the influx of Black migrants and homeless people who poured into these urban communities in the years after the Civil War. In Mississippi, for example, Whites passed the notorious "*Pig Law*" of 1876, designed to control vagrant Blacks loose in the community. This law made stealing a pig an act of grand larceny subject to punishment of up to 5 years in prison. Within 2 years, the number of convicts in the state penitentiary increased from under 300 people to over 1,000. It was this law in Mississippi that turned the *convict lease system* into a profitable business, whereby convicts were leased to contractors who subleased them to planters, railroads, levee contractors, and timber jobbers. Almost all of the convicts in this situation were Blacks, including women, and the conditions in the camps were horrible in the extreme. It was not uncommon to have a death rate of Blacks in the camps at between 8 to 18%. In a rare piece of journalism, the Jackson Weekly Clarion, printed in 1887 the inspection report of the state prison in Mississippi:

We found [in the hospital section] twenty-six inmates, all of whom have been lately brought there off the farms and railroads, many of them with consumption and other incurable diseases, and all bearing on their persons marks of the most inhuman and brutal treatment. Most of them have their backs cut in great wales, scars and blisters, some with the skin peeling off in pieces as the result of severe beatings.

Their feet and hands in some instances show signs of frostbite, and all of them with the stamp of manhood almost blotted out of their faces.... They are lying there dying, some of them on bare boards, so poor and emaciated that their bones almost come through their skin, many complaining for the want of food.... We actually saw live vermin crawling over their faces, and the little bedding and clothing they have is in tatters and stiff with filth.

As a fair sample of this system, on January 6, 1887, 204 convicts were leased to McDonald up to June 6, 1887, and during this six months 20 died, and 19 were discharged and escaped and 23 were returned to the walls disabled and sick, many of whom have since died.

Although federal policy and actions (Enforcement Acts of 1870 and 1871) effectively eliminated the most organized forms of White terrorism in the 1870's, they did little to assist the formerly enslaved in gaining economic security. As a result, even before the end of Reconstruction (in 1876), the vast majority of Southern Blacks had become penniless agricultural workers indebted to and controlled by White landlords and merchant suppliers. This system of land tenancy became known as *sharecropping* because Black and White landless, tenant farmers were paid a share of the crop, which they had cultivated—usually one third. In most cases, the farmer's share did not equal in value the debts owed to the local store for supplies or to the landlord for rent. *Crop lien* laws and various creditor protection laws made it nearly impossible for African-American farmers to avoid dependency and impoverishment. Merchant suppliers charged high interest rates—often as much as 40%, and local police helped make sure that indebted tenants did not avoid their debts by leaving the area. In this situation, Black sharecroppers were often pressured to vote for the White or Black candidates supported by their White landlords or merchant suppliers.

It should also be noted that White terrorism aimed at Blacks did not end with the curtailment of organized vigilantism of the sort associated with the Ku Klux Klan. Once the South had been returned to White rule (*Redemption*), the so-called redeemers (Bourbons) effectively imposed White domination over Blacks by economic means to a large extent. When those means fell short, the White community commonly resorted to terror in the late 1870s and 1880s. Indeed, attacks and violence against Blacks by Whites was part of the fabric of Southern life. The ante-bellum system of slavery was rooted in terror and violence, and the Ku Klux Klan continued the practice in the name of White supremacy after the Civil War. Historian William Cohen notes that lynching increased by 63% in the second half of the 1880s, a greater relative jump than for any other period after those years. The number of lynchings estimated for 1880-1884 was 233 compared to 381 for the next 5-year period, peaking at 611 for the years 1890 to 1894.

What about the color line, the physical separation of the races in public and private life? In most Southern states, a clear color line separated Whites and Blacks in custom if not in law prior to 1890. Historians Joel Williamson and Neil R. McMillen demonstrate that the absence of a legalized color line did not mean that one did not exist in practice or in the minds of most White Southerners. Their research in South Carolina and Mississippi supports the view that a physical color line in public places had already crystallized by 1870, and it was a barrier to racial mixing enforced by violence whenever necessary. As in slavery, the social lives of Southern Whites remained absolutely off limits to all Blacks, except when Blacks acquiesced as servants or in some other way to the superior-inferior relationship that existed in the slavery era. The same was true for the intermixing of Whites with Blacks in civil activities; Whites generally refused to participate in any events or activities that included Blacks, such as volunteer fire companies, parades, or civic gatherings. Usually, Whites shunned any and all public places where the color line was not firmly in place.

The "New" Jim Crow Racial Scene After 1890

The upsurge of new laws and the strengthening of old ones in the 1890s was essentially an extension of the old drive for White supremacy in new ways and with more effective results. Historian C. Van Woodward sees this radical move in the 1890s to be the South's "capitulation to racism" and the rejection of viable alternatives that had existed during the post-Reconstruction period. In his view of things, it was the rise of lower-class Whites to political power in the 1880s and 1890s that brought on complete disfranchisement and segregation both in law and in practice. Other scholars contend that the driving force behind legal segregation and disfranchisement were upper-class Whites in the *black belt* areas who wanted to weaken or prevent through disfranchisement the hold of lower-classes Whites on the Democratic Party or their allegiance to newer political power bases, such as the *Farmers' Alliance* or the *Populist Party*. In this view, the desire to restrict the political power of lower-class voters of both races was as much a motive in the drive for disfranchisement as was the desire to eliminate Black voters.

Clearly, the impetus behind the legalization of segregation and disfranchisement was complex, involving one or a combination of the following reasons: (1) efforts by lower-class Whites to wrest political power from merchants and large landowners (who controlled the vote of their indebted Black tenants); (2) the fear by Whites in general that a new generation of "uppity" Blacks, those born after slavery, threatened the culture and racial purity of the superior White society; (3) the desire of White elites to use Blacks as scapegoats to side-track the efforts by lower-class Whites to seize political power; (4) the efforts of so-called progressive White reformers to disfranchise those voters—White and Black—subject to manipulation because of their illiteracy or impoverishment; (5) the fear by insurgent White populists and old-line Democrats that the Black vote might prevail if Southern Whites split their votes in struggles within and outside the Democratic Party; (6) the emergence of a racially hysterical press that fueled White fear of and hatred towards Blacks by printing propaganda stories about Black crimes; (7) the appearance of the pseudo-science of eugenics that lent respectability to the racist views of Black inferiority; (8) the jingoism associated with the nation's war with Spain and its colonization of non-European people in the Philippines; and (9) the continued depiction of Blacks as lazy, stupid, and less than human in the popular minstrel shows that played in small town America as well as the side shows and circuses that enthralled White audiences with images of inherent Black inferiority.

Whatever the motivation, these new laws and constitutional provisions were aimed at the subjugation of African Americans and the dominance of the political and economic, White elite within the Democratic Party. It was the re-assertion of the earlier drive for "White supremacy." As historian Michael Perman argues, although the legalized forms of racial subordination were new in the 1890s, the substance behind the forms was essentially unchanged from what had been attempted in the Black Codes and by the Ku Klux Klan during Reconstruction.

In the 1890s, Southern states began to systematically and completely disfranchise Black males by imposing voter registration restrictions, such as *literacy tests*, poll taxes, the *grandfather clause*, and the *white primary* (only Whites could vote in the Democratic Party primary contests). Such provisions did not violate the Fifteenth Amendment because they applied to all voters regardless of race. In reality, however, the provisions were more strictly enforced on Blacks, especially in those areas dominated by lower class Whites. The so-called "understanding clause," which allowed illiterate, White voters to register if they understood specific texts in the state constitution to the satisfaction of White registrars, was widely recognized to be a loophole provision for illiterate Whites. It was crafted to protect the suffrage of those Whites who might otherwise have been excluded from voting by the literacy qualification for registering to vote. In point of fact, tens of thousands of poor White farmers were also disfranchised because of non-payment of the poll tax, for which there were no loopholes provided.

It is important to understand that these new restrictions on voting were different from earlier restrictions in that they deprived the voter of the right to vote not at the ballot box (through force, intimidation, or fraud), but at the registration place. Before ballots were even cast, the new qualifications could be selectively applied to voters who failed to pass the tests established in the state's constitution. This new method of controlling votes eliminated the need for violence against Black voters, and the restrictions were often justified on these very grounds. In December of 1898, for example, the *Richmond Times* supported the move for disfranchisement in Virginia in the following words: "If we disfranchise the great body of Negroes, let us do so openly and above board and let there be an end of all sorts of jugglery." This rationale indicates a clear motive to remove Black votes altogether and to return to the status quo that existed prior to the introduction of Black suffrage after the Civil War.

The Fifteenth Amendment to the Constitution, ratified in 1870, placed responsibility for protecting the right of suffrage with the federal government—a right which could not be "denied or abridged on the grounds of race, color, or previous condition of servitude." The states, however, retained the authority for determining qualification for voting, as long as the qualifications did not violate the Fifteenth Amendment. This meant that the former states of the Confederacy were required to rewrite their state constitutions in order to put restrictions on voting qualifications—such as literacy tests, poll taxes, understanding clauses, and criminal convictions. The rewriting or amending state constitutions denied suffrage to Blacks by law rather than by fraud. This is what was new, legally speaking, in the drive to undermine Black suffrage in the 1890s.

These new legal restrictions were backed in turn by acts of intimidation, the use of *chain gangs* and prison farms, *debt peonage*, the passage of anti-enticement laws, and a wave of brutal lynchings that dominated the Southern racial scene for the next 40 years. Indeed, between 1882 (when reliable statistics are first available) and 1968, most of the 4,863 recorded people lynched in the United States were Southern, Black men. Not surprisingly, 97% of these lynchings occurred in the former states of the Confederacy. Although violence used to subjugate Blacks was nothing new in the South (what with its racist heritage rooted in slavery), the character of the violence was something different. Prior to the 1890s, most of the violence against Blacks stopped short of the ritualized murder associated with the lynching epidemic that began in the late 1880s.

Blacks had suffered death at the hands of White vigilantes for all of their history in the nation, but nothing like the spectacle associated with public lynching had ever occurred before. After 1890, mobs usually subjected their Black victims to sadistic tortures that included burnings, dismemberment, being dragged to death behind carts and autos, and horribly prolonged suffering. When railroad companies sold tickets to attend lynchings, when Whites hawked body parts of dead victims as souvenirs, when White families brought their children to watch the torture and death of Blacks by lynching, when newspapers carried advance notices, and when White participants proudly posed for pictures of themselves with the burned corpses of lynched men and women—and then allowed the images to be reproduced on picture postcard, something fundamental had changed.

Source: http://www.jimcrowhistory.org/resources/pdf/creating2.pdf

RFDL #2: JIM CROW—8TH GRADE READING LEVEL

Sometime around the year 1830, about 175 years ago, there was a White performer named Thomas Rice. His nickname was "Daddy" Rice. He put black makeup on his face and went around the country singing and doing a silly dance. The words to his song were:

> *"Wheel about and turn about, and do just so.*
> *Every time I wheel about, I jump Jim Crow."*

Some say Daddy Rice got the idea for his act when he saw a crippled Black man singing the song. Some people who study history believe that a man named Jim Crow owned the crippled Black slave that Daddy Rice saw, and that's why his name was included in the words to the song. Daddy Rice took his Jim Crow act on the road because he was a minstrel— a roving singer. The Jim Crow character became very popular and by the time the Civil War was just beginning, the words Jim Crow came to represent the stereotype of the Black race as inferior to Whites.

Source: http://www.jimcrowhistory.org/resources/pdf/creating2.pdf

RFDL #3: THE BIG IDEAS

Segregation—What is it?

Why did segregation come to be?

The laws

- Jim Crow
- *Plessy v. Ferguson*
- *Brown v. The Topeka Board of Education*

Jim Crow

Jim Crow—Impact

- American Society
- Black People
- The NLB

Jim Crow—Important People

Plessy v. Ferguson

Plessy v. Ferguson—Impact

- American Society
- Black People
- The NLB

Plessy v. Ferguson—Important People

Brown v. The Topeka Board of Education

Brown v. The Topeka Board of Education—Impact

- American Society
- Black People
- The NLB

Brown v. *Brown v. The Topeka Board of Education*—Important People

Summary

Introduction

Segregation and the law

RFDL #4: BIG IDEAS CHART

	Description	*Setting/ Location*	*Impact on American Society*	*Impact on Black Citizens*	*Impact on NLB*	*Important Person and His/Her Role*
Jim Crow						
Plessy v. Ferguson						
Brown v. Topeka BOE						

Source: NLBM-KSU Partnership (2005).

CHAPTER 5

STAGE 5

Evaluating the Process

INTRODUCTION

A professional organization wants to ensure the products that are produced are of high quality. Therefore, the ability to assess the quality of lesson plans is important to the museum and public school partnership. There are a number of ways that products can be assessed, but using a rubric and expert feedback are ways to secure specific feedback from knowledgeable professionals.

Are the Curriculum Materials of Professional Quality?

One way to determine if the partnership's curriculum materials are of professional quality is to design a lesson plan rubric that evaluates the quality of the lesson plans. A rubric is a scoring guide that is used to evaluate the performance of a student/person or the quality of a product. The aim of a rubric is to improve the final version of the product.

To gain unbiased feedback, the lesson plans need to be evaluated by museum and education experts outside the partnership. The rubric clearly shows experts what criteria the lesson plans should be evaluated on and is less time consuming than other evaluation methods.

Handbook on Developing Curriculum Materials for Teachers:
Lessons From Museum Education Partnerships, pp. 203–210
Copyright © 2010 by Information Age Publishing

When creating a rubric use a template to guide rubric development. Use the lesson plan rubric as an example to create a rubric template.

Table 5.1.   A Lesson Plan Rubric for NLBM Lesson Plans

Scoring:	4	3	2	1
Lesson Component	*Exemplary*	*Accomplished*	*Developing*	*Emerging*
Grade level, subject: Identifies the grade appropriate level(s), and subject area.	The grade level(s) and subject area are identified and the lesson appropriateness is obvious	The grade level(s) and subject area are identified and appropriate to the lesson, appropriateness is obvious	The grade level(s) and subject area are identified, but the appropriateness is not obvious	The grade level(s) and subject area are not identified, or are not appropriate to the lesson.
Standards: Correlating national and state standards.	Standards are listed and written clearly and succinctly. There is an evident and strong curricular connection.	Standards are listed and written clearly, possible unnecessary wording. A curricular connection is present.	Standards are listed, but are unclear and/or poorly written. Some connection to curricular standards are stated	Standards are not listed, and/ or are unclear. Relationship to the curricular focus is unclear.
Time allotment: The amount of time generally needed to complete the lesson.	Time allotment is listed, realistic, and concise.	Time allotment is listed and is realistic, not concise.	Time allotment is listed, may not be realistic and/or is vague.	Time allotment is not listed.
Key Features: NCSS' five components of ideal social studies instruction—meaningful, integrative, value-based, challenging, and active learning.	NCSS components that should be listed are listed completely and clearly.	NCSS components that should be listed are listed completely, may be vague and/or wordy.	NCSS components that should be listed are listed, may be incomplete.	NCSS components that should be listed are not listed, and/or are incomplete and/or vague.
Purpose: Brief explanation of the lesson purpose and student activities.	A purpose is listed and outcome/behaviors are clearly described and written concisely.	A purpose is listed and the outcome/behaviors are clearly defined, may be wordy.	A purpose is listed, but the desired outcome/behaviors are only somewhat clear.	A purpose is not listed, and/or the desired outcome/behaviors are vague.

Objectives: Knowledge and skills the student will obtain and be able to demonstrate from the lesson.	Behavior and criteria are listed, written clearly and defined well.	Behavior and criteria are listed and are somewhat clear and defined.	Behavior and/ or criteria are listed, but are unclear or vague.	Behavior and/ or criteria are not listed or are unclear.
Primary Resources: Any instructor materials needed to complete the lesson plan effectively.	Materials are provided and clearly explained.	Materials are provided, but use of materials may be unclear.	Materials are provided, but are unorganized and/or incomplete.	Materials are not provided.
Procedures/ Activities: Detailed lesson plan procedures and activities.	Procedures are listed, sequenced, and provide clear instruction for the implementation of the lesson.	Procedures are listed and sequenced and provide some instruction for the implementation of the lesson.	Procedures are listed, but not sequenced properly and/ or instructions are vague.	Procedures are not stated, and/ or not sequenced. Instructions are missing and/or incomplete.
Assessment: Educator's evaluation of student learning.	The assessment is provided and matches the desired outcome/ behavior in the lesson purpose and objectives.	The assessment is provided, and closely matches the desired outcome/ behaviors in the lessonpurpose and objectives.	The assessment is provided but is not consistent with the desired outcome/ behaviors in the lesson purpose and objectives.	No assessment is provided, or assessment does not measure the desired outcome/ behaviors listed in the lesson purpose and objectives.
Alternate Assessment: Another mode of assessing student learning.	The assessment is provided and matches the desired outcome/ behavior in the lesson purpose.	The assessment is provided, and closely matches the desired outcome/ behaviors in the lesson purpose.	The assessment is provided but is not consistent with the desired outcome/ behaviors in the lesson purpose.	No assessment is provided, or assessment does not measure the desired outcome/ behaviors listed in the lesson purpose.
Conclusion: A review of essential lesson objectives and student learning.	Essential lesson objectives are reviewed and clearly tied to the overall curricular purpose.	Essential lesson objectives are reviewed and are tied to the overall curricular purpose, may be vague.	Essential lesson objectives are reviewed, but not tied into the overall curricular purpose.	Essential lesson objectives are not reviewed.

Extension/Enrichment: Ideas for further teaching or researching, for the student.	Activities/Ideas are listed, clearly relate to the curriculum focus, and are concise and challenging for students.	Activities/Ideas are listed, are clearly related to the curriculum focus, but may be wordy or only somewhat challenging for students.	Activities/Ideas are listed, but not clearly related to the curriculum focus and/or are not challenging for students.	Activities/Ideas are not listed, and/or are vague.
Online Resources: Online student resources.	Resources are listed, organized, and complete to teach the lesson.	Resources are listed and organized, may be incomplete to teach the lesson.	Resources are listed, but are not organized and/or are not adequate to teach the lesson.	Resources are not listed, and/or are not organized.
Secondary Resources: Any materials created or needed to support the procedures & activities portion of the lesson plan.	Resources are listed, organized, and complete to teach the lesson.	Resources are listed and organized, may be incomplete to teach the lesson.	Resources are listed, but are not organized and/or are not adequate to teach the lesson.	Resources are not listed, and/or are not organized.
Technology Integration: The level the lesson plan integrates technology into the learning process.	Technology use is not a separate curriculum focus, rather used as a means to support and reinforce the lesson purpose.	Technology use was emphasized more than the curriculum content of the lesson, and is related to the lesson purpose.	Technology is the primary focus of the lesson and somewhat related to the lesson purpose.	Technology is not used in the lesson, and/or not related clearly to the lesson purpose.

Total Score: _____

Comments: _____

_____

_____

_____

_____

_____

_____

Use these steps to complete the rubric.

1. Choose the criteria to be evaluated.
2. Fill in the concepts and criteria for evaluation.
3. Do a trial run; compare a lesson plan to the rubric criteria to see if the desired content is included in the rubric.
4. Create an introduction to the lesson plan rubric.

The introduction for the lesson plan rubric defines what, why, and how the lesson plan rubric should be used by the experts when assessing the lesson plans. For example:

AN INTRODUCTION TO THE LESSON PLAN RUBRIC

The lesson plan rubric is designed as a guide for the curricular development of lesson plans. These lesson plans are focused on Grades 9-12, in the subject area of social studies, and incorporate cutting edge technology. The rubric allows participants to design consistent, technology-based, quality lesson plans regardless of his/her previous experience in lesson plan creation. The most beneficial approach to creating a lesson plan is by combining the lesson plan rubric with the lesson plan components and definitions.

The left-hand column of the lesson plan rubric delineates the required lesson plan components and includes the definitions of those components. Each lesson plan with these components is rated on the rubric scale, numerically, one through four, and by category, Emerging Through Exemplary. A rating of 4 and Exemplary, being the goal of the lesson plans (Barragree, 2005b).

WHO CAN WE CONTACT
OUTSIDE THE PARTNERSHIP FOR FEEDBACK?

Next, drafts of the lesson plan explanation, rubric, and lesson plans should be distributed to local and surrounding area experts for feedback. Experts may include:

- Museum personnel.
- Administrators at the high school level.
- Special education educators and administrators.
- Postsecondary education faculty and staff in the technology and education departments.
- Museum and independent museum personnel.

- District and state curriculum developers or **curriculum coordinators**.
- Technology educators and administrators.

Be sure to contact and secure support from the experts before sending the curriculum materials for feedback.

Compile a lesson plan packet to distribute to future lesson plan creators that includes a:

- Lesson plan explanation.
- Blank lesson plan.
- Lesson plan rubric and rationale.
- Sample lesson plan.

HOW CAN WE ENSURE QUALITY FEEDBACK?

Tips for obtaining quality feedback include:

1. Send only one or two lesson plans with rubrics to experts at one time.
2. Send each lesson plan to more than one expert for feedback.
3. Include a deadline date for feedback.
4. Follow up with a reminder of the deadline date about 7-10 days in advance.
5. Find out if hardcopies of electronic versions of curriculum materials best suit the experts needs.
6. Allow at least 1 week per lesson plan for experts to provide feedback.

WHAT MOTIVATES EXPERTS TO RETURN FEEDBACK?

There are many reasons experts may offer feedback, among the best motivators in promoting feedback from experts are:

1. Belief in improving the quality of motivational standards-based curriculum materials in high school social studies.
2. If materials can be used in their classrooms, school districts, museums, or for staff development.

3. A benefit such as free admittance to the museum for a class or group, free workshops or staff development trainings, and so on.

4. Know at least one partnership member well and want to help by volunteering their expertise and feedback.

5. Desire to learn more about the partnership, the lesson plans, or museum content.

Feedback may not be received from every expert; however, every effort should be made to receive several experts' feedback for each lesson plan.

WHAT IS DONE WITH THE FEEDBACK?

Once feedback is received, revisions to the lesson plans should be completed. Keep track of which expert has been sent what lesson plan and any feedback that is received from that expert. Complete the Expert Feedback Chart to track experts' information, feedback, and finalization of the partnership materials.

Table 5.2.   Expert Feedback Chart

Experts Name	Contact Information	Materials Sent	Date Sent	Date Recʋd	Materials Revised (Y/N)	Materials Finalized (Y/N)

Source: Barragree (2006b, November).

Once a final draft is complete, the lesson plan should be reviewed carefully for any grammatical and spelling errors. Documents that contain poor grammar or spelling errors are not viewed as reliable or professional and should not be distributed as a final product.

CHAPTER 6

STAGE 6

Implementing the Products

INTRODUCTION

Once motivational standards-based curriculum materials in high school social studies are created, they need to be publicized. Most public school educators know precious little about the breadth and depth of museum resources that are available, and many still think of museums only for fieldtrips. Therefore, it is critical that museum and public school partnerships ensure public school educators are aware of the curriculum resources available to them through the partnership.

REACHING THE TARGET AUDIENCE

Mailings sent specifically to the target audience are one of the most direct ways to reach public school educators. Besides high school social studies educators, be sure to include a wide range of audiences at the district and building levels such as curriculum and technology coordinators, administrators, and special education coordinators and educators.

Handbook on Developing Curriculum Materials for Teachers:
Lessons From Museum Education Partnerships, pp. 211–214
Copyright © 2010 by Information Age Publishing
All rights of reproduction in any form reserved.

Other ways to directly contact high school administrators and educators include:

- Presentations at in-service days.
- Grade level meetings.
- Social studies departmental meetings.
- Parent teacher organizations.
- Board meetings.

Conference presentations are useful for introducing curriculum materials to regional and statewide educators. Look for conferences that are affiliated with professional organizations such as NCSS, ISTE, historical and museum organizations and other educational professional organizations. Prioritize conference presentations by identifying which professional organization members would be most interested in and benefit from the partnership process and curriculum materials.

Professional journals, the partnership could create and submit numerous articles, based on the partnerships' products, for publication in professional journals such as *Museum News*, *The Social Studies*, **Institute for Museum and Library Science (IMLS)**, *Educational Leadership*, etc. Publication in scholarly/peer-reviewed journals lends credibility to the partnership's efforts and curriculum materials.

Educational institutions introducing the partnership's curriculum materials through distance education courses and/or tailoring courses to meet the needs of a higher education institution in areas such as history, social studies, teacher education, secondary education, curriculum and instruction, and/or technology leadership is a way to reach a completely different set of possible users of the curriculum materials. The museum could also offer training sessions for administrators and educators on how to effectively use the curriculum materials in their classroom setting.

Electronic access is more important than ever to high school educators. Many schools are cutting or eliminating funding for fieldtrips so less and less students are visiting museums through school programs. In addition, the physical location of some public schools will limit the ability to take a fieldtrip to the museum. Having curriculum materials available electronically allows educators across the nation and the world to access and use the partnership's materials regardless of budgetary concerns or physical location.

News conferences can be an effective way to reach a broader audience and inform the larger community about curriculum materials and services the museum has to offer.

PROMOTING THE PRODUCTS

There are three primary things to keep in mind when promoting curriculum materials created by the partnership.

1. Create visually attractive materials and distribute them to the targeted audience.

 These materials should grab the attention of readers and direct them to further resources for information and/or products.

2. Get feedback from the target audience on marketing strategies.

- What does the target audience need/want in curriculum materials?

- How would they like those materials packaged or presented?

- Would they be willing to buy the curriculum materials?

- If so, what is a reasonable cost for those materials? And so on.

3. Create a marketing plan that includes strategies based on target audience feedback.

- How will the curriculum materials be publicized?

- What venues are available to the partnership for distribution and/or presentation of the curriculum materials?

- Will the curriculum materials be available for sale at the museum and electronically?

- At what cost?

- Will public school educators receive a discount on curriculum materials?

CONCLUSION

Museums and public schools are primarily educational institutions that value education. When museums and public schools partner, the partnership must be a genuine partnership based on collaboration, not isolation, or the outcome will be disappointing for both organizations. The decisions made during the partnership support the value of creating quality curriculum materials that fulfill a need for both institutions. Through the creation of motivational standards-based curriculum materials, educators can satisfy the museum's needs and the public school's needs while motivating high school social studies students to learn.

REFERENCES

Air War College. (2006). *Creating curriculum and delivering it*. Retrieved December 3, 2006, from http://www.au.af.mil/au/awc/awcgate/awceauth.htm#lessonplans

American Association of Museums. (1984). *Museums for a new century. A report of the commission on museums for a new century*. Washington, DC: Author.

American Association of Museums. (1995). *Museums in the life of a city: Strategies for community partnerships*. Washington, DC: Author.

American Association of Museums. (1999). Retrieved August 15, 2006, from http://www.aam-us.org/

American Association of Museums and the Federal Council on the Arts and Humanities. (1969). *America's museums: The Belmont report. A report to the Federal Council on the Arts and Humanities*. Washington, DC: Author.

Answers.com. (2006). Retrieved February 23, 2006, from http://www.answers.com

Association for Supervision and Curriculum Development (ASCD). (2006a). *About ASCD*. Retrieved March 29, 2006, from www.ascd.org

Baillargeon, T. (2005). *Copyright laws guide*. Unpublished document, Kansas State University at Manhattan.

Baillargeon, T., & Barragree, C. (2005). *Step-by-step lesson planning*. Unpublished document, Kansas State University at Manhattan.

Barragree, C. (2005, June). *National and state social studies standards correlate graph*. Paper presented at the Mid-America Association for Computers in Education Conference, Kansas State University at Manhattan.

Barragree, C. (2005, July). *Curriculum framework*. Unpublished document, Kansas State University at Manhattan.

Barragree, C. (2005a, Summer). *Blank lesson plan format*. Paper presented at a meeting of the Negro Leagues Baseball Museum and Kansas State University Partnership at Manhattan.

Barragree, C. (2005b, Summer). *Lesson plan components and definitions*. Paper presented at the Mid-America Association for Computers in Education Conference, Kansas State University at Manhattan.

Barragree, C. (2005c, Summer). *Sustainability Chart*. Unpublished document, Kansas State University at Manhattan.

Barragree, C. (2005, Fall). Negro Leagues baseball. In *Layered Curriculum*. Retrieved November 1, 2005, from http://help4teachers.com/carinegroleagues.html

Barragree, C. (2005a, December). *A lesson plan rubric*. Paper presented at a meeting of the Negro Leagues Baseball Museum and Kansas State University Partnership at Manhattan.

Barragree, C. (2005b, December). *An introduction to the lesson planning rubric*. Paper presented at a meeting of the Negro Leagues Baseball Museum and Kansas State University Partnership at Manhattan.

Barragree, C. (2006a, November). *Checklist of lesson plan components*. Document presented at a meeting of the Negro Leagues Baseball Museum and Kansas State University Partnership at Manhattan.

Barragree, C. (2006b, November). *Expert feedback chart*. Unpublished document, Kansas State University at Manhattan.

Barragree, C. (2006a, Fall). *Museum and public school partnership cycle of success*. Unpublished document, Kansas State University at Manhattan.

Barragree, C. (2006b, Fall). *The six stage process for museum and public school partnerships creating motivational standards-based curriculum materials in high school social studies*. Unpublished document, Kansas State University at Manhattan.

Barragree, C. (2006a). *Frame of reference checklist*. Unpublished document, Kansas State University at Manhattan.

Barragree, C. (2006b). *Planning curriculum components checklist*. Unpublished document, Kansas State University at Manhattan.

Ben-Peretz, M. (1990). *The teacher curriculum encounter freeing teachers from the tyranny of texts*. New York: Princeton University Press.

Bevan, B. (2003). Urban network: Museums embracing communities. In J. Spitz & M. Thom (Eds.), *Windows onto worlds*. (pp. 11-14). Chicago: The Field Museum.

Bomia, L., Beluzo, L., Demeester, D., Elander, K., Johnson, M., & Sheldon, B. (1997). *The impact of teaching strategies on intrinsic motivation*. (ERIC Document Reproduction Service No. ED418 925)

BrainPOP. (n.d.). Retrieved December 3, 2006, from http://www.brainpop.com/

California Department of Education. (2001). *Education technology planning: A guide for school districts*. Commission of Technology in Learning. Sacramento, CA: Author.

Center for Documentation of Cultural and Natural Heritage, Egypt. (2005). *Eternal Egypt*. Retrieved December 3, 2006, from http://www.eternalegypt.org/EternalEgyptWebsiteWeb/HomeServlet

Center for Museum Education. (1981). *Museum school partnerships: Plans & programs sourcebook #4*. Washington, DC: George Washington University.

Chandler, E., & Molt, L. (2005). *Unit planning for U.S. history*. Document presented at a meeting of the Negro Leagues Baseball Museum and Kansas State University Partnership at Manhattan.

Charles, R. (2005, Spring-Summer). Big ideas and understandings as the foundation for elementary and middle school mathematics. *Journal of Mathematics Education Leadership, 7,* 3.

Corbin, S. (1997, Fall). Comparisons with other academic subjects and selected influences on high school students' attitudes toward social studies [Electronic version]. *Journal of Social Studies Research, 21(2),* 1-6.

Corporation for Public Broadcasting. (n.d.). *American civics and history: A request for proposals.* Washington, DC: Author.

Council for Disability Rights. (n.d.). *A parent's guide to special education: Glossary of special education terms.* Retrieved August 23, 2006, from http://www .disabilityrights.org/glossary.htm

Daley, R. (2003, May). *No geographer left behind: A policy guide to geography education and the No Child Left Behind Act.* Washington DC: Education National Implementation Project.

Doswell, R. (2005, August). *Negro Leagues baseball: Important books and film.* Document presented at a meeting of the Negro Leagues Baseball Museum and Kansas State University Partnership at Manhattan.

EETT. (n.d.). *Definitions and terminology of educational technology and technology education.* New York State Education Department. Retrieved August 24, 2006, from http://www.emsc.nysed.gov/technology/nclb/definition.htm

Ellis, A., Fouts, J., & Glenn, A. (1991). *Teaching and learning secondary social studies.* New York: HarperCollins.

eSchool News. (2006). Retrieved August 15, 2006, from http://www.eschoolnews .com/

Getty Museum, The (n.d.). Retrieved December 3, 2006, from http://www.getty .edu/

Government of Western Australia. (n.d.). *Curriculum council.* Retrieved April 15, 2005, from http://www.curriculum.wa.edu.au/pages/framework/framework00 .htm

Hicks, E. (1986, September). *Museums and schools as partners.* (ERIC Document Reproduction Service No. ED278380)

Hirzy, E. (Ed.). (1996). *True needs, true partners: Museums transforming schools* [Electronic version]. Washington DC: Institute of Museum and Library Services.

Honolulu Community College. (n.d.). *Lesson planning procedures.* Faculty Development Committee. Retrieved December 5, 2006, from the Faculty Development Committee Guidebook Web site: http://honolulu.hawaii.edu/intranet/ committees/FacDevCom/ guidebk/teachtip/lesspln1.htm

Infobits. (1995-2006). Retrieved August 15, 2006, from http://www.unc.edu/cit/ infobits/

Institute of Museum and Library Services. (2002). *True needs, true partners: Museums serving schools 2002 survey highlights.* Washington, DC: Author.

Institute of Museum and Library Services. (2004, August). *Charting the landscape, mapping new paths: Museums, libraries, and K-12 learning* [Electronic version]. Washington, DC: Author.

Institute of Museum and Library Services. (n.d.). Retrieved July 10, 2006, from http://www.imls.gov/index/shtm

International Council of Museums. (2006, August 19). *ICOM statutes*. Retrieved December 6, 2006, from http://icom.museum/statutes.html

International Council of Museums. (2006, September 1). *Virtual library museums pages*. Retrieved December 6, 2006, from http://vlmp.icom.museum/

International Society for Technology in Education (ISTE). (2000). *National educational technology standards for students: Connecting curriculum and technology*. Washington, DC: Author.

International Society for Technology in Education. (n.d.). *About ISTE*. Retrieved January 23, 2006, from http://www.iste.org/Template .cfm?Section=About_ISTE&Template=/TaggedPage/TaggedPageDisplay .cfm&TPLID=21&ContentID=840

International Society for Technology in Education. (n.d.). Retrieved April 3, 2005, from www.iste.org

International Society for Technology in Education. (n.d.). *Educational technology standards and performance indicators for all teachers*. Retrieved December 3, 2006, from http://cnets.iste.org/teachers/t_stands.html

International Society for Technology in Education. (n.d.). *Technology foundation standards for all students*. Retrieved April 1, 2005, from http://cnets.iste.org /students/s_stands.html

Iowa City Community School District. (2006). *Glossary of special terms*. Retrieved August 23, 2006, from http://www.iowa-city.k12.ia.us/Teacher/SpecEd/sped/ Glossary.htm

Iowa State University, Ames, National K-12 Foreign Language Resource Center. (2000-04). *New Visions in Action*. Retrieved August 18, 2006, from http:// www.nflrc.iastate.edu/nva/newsite/docarch/td/2000PR06.html

Irvine Unified School District. (2000). *Coordinator IV: Education services*. Retrieved March 2, 2005, from http://www.iusd.k12.ca.us/human_resources/ job_descriptions/coord4ci.htm

Kizlik, B. (2006, November 22). *Lesson planning, lesson plan format, and lesson plan ideas*. Retrieved December 6, 2006, from http://www.adprima .com/lesson.htm

Learning Circuits. (n.d.). *Glossary*. American Society for Training & Development. Retrieved August 23, 2006, from http://www.learningcircuits.org/ASTD /Templates/LC/LC_OneBox.aspx?NRMODE=Published& NRORIGINALURL=%2fglossary&NRNODEGUID= %7bA1A2C751-7E81-4620-A0A3-52F3A90148EB%7d& NRCACHEHINT=NoModifyGuest#C

Learning Federation. (2005). *Glossary*. Retrieved August 24, 2006, from http://belts .sourceforge.net/systemadmin/glossary.html

Linder, B. (1987). Museum-school partnerships—A resource for principals. *NASSP Bulletin, 71*(503), 122-4.

Martorella, P. (1991). *Teaching social studies in middle and secondary schools*. New York: McMillan.

Massachusetts Department of Education. (2006, December). *Massachusetts history & social sciences curriculum framework*. Retrieved December 5, 2006, from http:/ /www.doe.mass.edu/frameworks/hss/final.doc

Massachusetts Institute of Technology. (n.d.). *Style guide: Glossary*. Retrieved August 23, 2006, from http://web.mit.edu/campaign/styleguide/glossary.html

McCombs, B. (n.d.). *Understanding the keys to motivation to learn*. Mid-continent Research for Education and Learning. Retrieved January 19, 2006, from http://www.mcrel.org/PDFConversion/Noteworthy/Learners_Learning_Schooling/barbaram.asp

McGraw-Hill Higher Education. (2003, August 4). Learning styles. In *Student success*. Retrieved December 5, 2006, from http://novella.mhhe.com/sites/0079876543/student_view0/weekly_update.html

Michigan Department of Education. (1996). *Michigan curriculum framework*. State of Michigan. Retrieved December 6, 2006, from http://www.michigan.gov

Micro2000. (2004). *Glossary*. Retrieved August 23, 2006, from http://www.micro2000uk.co.uk/hardware_glossary.htm

Midlink Magazine. (2004, August). *Rubrics and evaluation resources*. Retrieved June 3, 2006, from the North Carolina State University Web site: http://www.ncsu.edu/midlink/ho.html

Missouri Department of Elementary and Secondary Education. (1996, January 18). *The Show-Me standards. Social studies*. Missouri State Board of Education. Retrieved May 6, 2005, from http://dese.mo.gov/standards/ss.html

Missouri Department of Elementary and Secondary Education. (2004). *Framework for curriculum development in social studies K-12*. Missouri State Board of Education. Retrieved May 6, 2005, from http://www.dese.mo.gov/divimprove/curriculum/GLE/SSGLE10.20.04WORD.doc

Missouri Department of Elementary and Secondary Education. (2004, October 20). *Social studies grade-level expectations*. Missouri: Missouri State Board of Education.

Museum News. (n.d.) Retrieved December 6, 2006, from http://www.museumnews.net/

National Council for the Social Studies. (1994). *Expectations of excellence: Curriculum standards for social studies*. Silver Spring, MD: Author.

National Council for the Social Studies. (2006). *About NCSS*. Retrieved March 29, 2005, from www.ncss.org/about

National Council for the Social Studies. (n.d.). *Curriculum standards for social studies: Executive summary*. Retrieved March 31, 2005, from http://www.socialstudies.org/standards/execsummary/

National Council for the Social Studies. (n.d.). *Key features of powerful teaching and learning*. Retrieved March 31, 2005, from http://www.socialstudies.org/positions/powerful/

National Education Goals Panel. (1993, November). *Promises to keep: Creating high standards for American students*. Report on the Review of Education Standards from the Goals 3 and 4 Technical Planning Group to the National Education Goals Panel. Washington DC: Author.

National Endowment for the Arts. (2006). *NEA jazz in the schools*. Retrieved December 5, 2006, from http://www.neajazzintheschools.org/home.php

National Research Council. (2004). *Engaging schools: Fostering high school students' motivation to learn*. Committee on Increasing High School Students Engagement and Motivation to Learn. Washington, DC: Author.

Negro Leagues Baseball Museum. (n.d.). Retrieved March 29, 2006, from www.nlbm.com

Negro Leagues Baseball Museum and Kansas State University. (2005a, Fall). *Negro Leagues baseball lesson plan topic graphic organizer.* Document presented at the National Rural Educators Association Conference, Kansas City, KS.

Negro Leagues Baseball Museum and Kansas State University. (2005b, Fall). *Lesson planning for the NLBM.* Document presented at the meeting of the Negro Leagues Baseball Museum and Kansas State University Partnership at Manhattan.

Negro Leagues Baseball Museum and Kansas State University. (2005). The NLB and the law. In *Teacher Resources, Lesson Plans.* Retrieved December 5, 2006, from http://www.coe.ksu.edu/nlbemuseum/resource/lplaw.html

Negro Leagues Baseball Museum and Kansas State University. (2006a, Spring). Blogging baseball. In *Teacher Resources, Lesson Plans.* Retrieved December 5, 2006, from http://www.coe.ksu.edu/nlbemuseum/resource/lpblogging.html.

Negro Leagues Baseball Museum and Kansas State University. (2006b, Spring). *Philosophy and FAQ sheet.* Retrieved December 5, 2006, from http://www.coe.ksu.edu/nlbemuseum/resource/lpfaqs.html

Negro Leagues Baseball Museum and Kansas State University. (2006). Educator's toolbox. In *Teacher's Toolkit.* Retrieved December 5, 2006, from http://www.coe.ksu.edu/nlbemuseum/resource/toolkit.html

North Central Regional Educational Laboratory (NCREL). (n.d.). A sense of calling. In *Preparing technology-competent teachers for urban and rural classrooms: A teacher education challenge.* Retrieved February 24, 2006, from http://www.ncrel.org/tech/challenge/appendi.htm

North Dakota Department of Public Instruction. (n.d.). *Needs assessment.* Retrieved December 26, 2006, from http://www.dpi.state.nd.us/grants/needs.pdf

Nunley, K. (1998-2006). *Layered curriculum.* Retrieved August 15, 2006, from http://help4teachers.com/index.htm

Oliver, A. (1977). *Curriculum improvement: A guide to problems, principles and process* (2nd ed.). New York: Harper and Row.

O'Reilly, Safari Books Online. (2006). *Glossary.* Retrieved August 24, 2006, from http://safari.oreilly.com/0735615233/gloss01

Public Broadcasting Service. (1995-2007). Retrieved May 12, 2005, from www.pbs.org

Ravitch, D. (2005, November 7). Every state left behind [Electronic version]. *New York Times.* Retrieved September 7, 2006 from the Brookings Institution Web site: http://www.brookings.edu/views/op-ed/ravitch/20051107.htm

Reitz, J. (2004). *ODLIS: Online dictionary for library and information science.* Retrieved August 21, 2006, from http://lu.com/odlis/index.cfm

Safer, N. (2000-06). Teaching methods and management: Teaching methods and strategies. In *Universal design for learning.* Retrieved December 2, 2006, from http://www.teachervision.fen.com/teaching-methods/curriculumplanning/3756.html?detoured=1

Saxe, D. (1998, February). *State history standards: An appraisal of history standards in 37 states and the District of Columbia.* Washington, DC: Thomas B. Fordham Foundation. (ERIC Document Reproduction Service No. ED421511)

Scherer, M. (2002, Summer). Do students care about learning? *Educational Leadership, 60*(1), 2-78.

School Wise Press. (2006). *Glossary of educational terms*. Retrieved August 24, 2006, from http://www.schoolwisepress.com/smart/dict/dict6.html

Schumm, J., Vaughn, S., & Leavell, A. (1994). Planning pyramid: A framework for planning for diverse student needs during content area instruction. *The Reading Teacher, 47*, 608-615.

Sebolt, A. (1981). Museums and learning. In S. N. Lehman & K. Igoe (Eds.), *Museum school partnerships: Plans and programs sourcebook #4* (pp. 13-16). Washington, DC: Center for Museum Education, George Washington University.

Sheppard, B. (Ed.). (1993). *Building museum & school partnerships*. Washington, DC: American Association of Museums.

Spitz, J., & Thom, M. (Eds.). (2003). *Urban network: Museums embracing communities* Chicago: The Field Museum.

State of South Dakota. (2003, December 31). *SD EForm-1574 V2*. Retrieved December 6, 2006, from https://www.state.sd.us/eforms/secure/eforms/E1574V2-ApprovalofInserviceEdProgramApplication.pdf

System for Adult Basic Education Support. (n.d.). *Glossary of useful terms*. Retrieved January 13, 2006, from http://www.sabes.org/assessment/glossary.htm

Teacher Vision. (2000-2006). Adapt lessons to reach all students. In *Teaching methods and management: Special education*. Retrieved December 3, 2006, from http://www.teachervision.fen.com/teaching-methods/special-education/3759.html?detoured=1

Teacher Vision. (2000-2006a). The art of teaching: Big ideas. In *Teaching methods and management: Special education*. Retrieved December 3, 2006, from http://www.teachervision.fen.com/teaching-methods/special-education/3764.html

TechTarget. (2000-2006). *Whatis?com*. Retrieved August 23, 2006, from http://whatis.techtarget.com/definitionsAlpha/0,289930,sid9_alpA,00.html

Tomlinson, C. (2000a). Differentiated instruction: Can it work? *The Educational Digest, 65*, 25-31.

Tushnet, N. (1993, October). *Guide to developing educational partnerships*. Educational Partnerships Program, Programs for the Improvement of Practice. Office of Educational Research and Improvement (OERI). Southwest Regional Laboratory for Educational Research and Development.

United States Department of Education. (2003). *Overview: Fact sheet on the major provisions of the conference report to H.R. 1, the No Child Left Behind Act*. Retrieved August 23, 2006, from http://www.ed.gov/nclb/overview/intro/factsheet.html

United States Department of Education. (2004). *Digest of education statistics 2004*. Retrieved February 23, 2006, from http://nces.ed.gov/programs/digest/d04/definitions.asp#p

University of Kansas, The. (2006a) *Rubistar*. Retrieved December 6, 2006, from http://rubistar.4teachers.org/index.php

University of Kansas, The. (2006b). *Technology glossary*. Retrieved August 23, 2006, from http://www.4teachers.org/techalong/glossary/

Vaughn, S., Bos, C., & Schumm, J. (2000). *Teaching exceptional, diverse, and at-risk students in the general education classroom* (2nd ed.). Boston: Allyn & Bacon.

APPENDIX A

Missouri Department of Elementary and Secondary Education: Social Studies Grade-Level Expectations

Handbook on Developing Curriculum Materials for Teachers:
Lessons From Museum Education Partnerships, pp. 223–245
Copyright © 2010 by Information Age Publishing

Principles of Constitutional Democracy

1. Knowledge of the principles expressed in documents shaping constitutional democracy in the United States

Concepts	US History (Required by RSMO 180.011)	Government (Required by RSMO 170.011)	Geography	World History	Economics
A. (1) Principles of constitutional democracy in the United States	Examine the changing roles of government in the context of the historical period being studied: • philosophy • limits • duties • checks and balances • **separation of powers** • **federalism** Analyze the roles and influence of political parties and interest groups Assess the changing roles of the following: • checks and balances • **separation of powers** • **federalism** Define and explain judicial review	Apply the following concepts to historical and contemporary issues: • checks and balances • separation of powers • federalism • representation • popular sovereignty • due process of law • judicial review Determine the civic responsibilities of individual citizens. Identify and give examples of **democracies** and **republics** Assess the changing roles of government • philosophy • limits • duties		Examine changes in **democracy** and **republics** over time Apply the following in the context of the historical period being studied: • democracy • republic • changing role of government • representation	

224

B.
(2) Understanding the relevance and connection of constitutional principles

Describe the historical foundations of the United States governmental system

Evaluate the roles and influence of political parties and interest groups

Examine the relevance and connection of constitutional principles in the following documents:

- Mayflower Compact
- Declaration of Independence
- Articles of Confederation
- U.S. Constitution
- Federalist Papers
- Amendments to Constitution, emphasizing Bill of Rights
- Key Supreme Court decisions (e.g., *Marbury v. Madison*, *McCulloch v. Maryland*, *Miranda v. Arizona*, *Plessy v. Ferguson*, *Brown v. Topeka Board of Education*)

Examine the relevance and explain the connection of constitutional principles in the following documents:

- Magna Carta
- Enlightenment writings of Hobbes, Locke, Rousseau, Montesquieu and the Social Contract Theory

225

United States History

Concepts	*2a. Knowledge of continuity and change in the history of Missouri, the United States and the world*				
	US History (Required by RSMO 180.011)	*Government* (Required by RSMO 170.011)	*Geography*	*World History*	*Economics*
A. (1) Understand the migrations of people from many regions to North America	Describe the migrations of people from many regions of the world and the interactions of cultures and religious traditions that have contributed to America's history				
B. (2) Political development in the United States	Analyze the evolution of American **democracy**, its ideas, institutions and political processes from colonial days to the present, including: • Civil War and Reconstruction • struggle for civil rights • expanding role of government	Analyze the evolution of American **democracy**, its ideas, institutions and political processes from colonial days to the present, including: • American Revolution • Constitution and amendments • Civil War and Reconstruction • struggle for civil rights • expanding role of government			

C.
(3) Economic development in the United States

Describe the historical development of the American economy, including:

- impact of geographic factors
- role of the frontier and agriculture
- impact of technological change and urbanization on land, resources, society, politics and culture
  changing relationships between government and the economy

Describe the historical development of the American economy, including:

- impact of geographic factors
- role of the frontier and agriculture
- impact of technological change and urbanization on land, resources, society, politics and culture changing relationships between government and the economy

D.
(4) Foreign and domestic policy development

Describe and evaluate the evolution of United States domestic and foreign policies, including:

- Manifest Destiny
- imperialism
- two world wars
- Cold War

Analyze and evaluate the evolution of United States domestic and foreign policies including:

- New Deal
- global
- interdependence

United States History (Continued)

2a. Knowledge of continuity and change in the history of Missouri, the United States and the world

Concepts	US History (Required by RSMO 180.011)	Government (Required by RSMO 170.011)	Geography	World History	Economics
E. (5) Understanding cultural change	Describe the changing character of American society and culture (i.e., arts and literature, education and philosophy, religion and values, and science and technology)				
F. (6) Missouri history as it relates to major developments of United States history	Analyze Missouri history as it relates to major developments of United States history, including: • exploration and settlement • mid 1800s (conflict and war) • urbanization, industrialization, postindustrial societies				

World History

2b. Knowledge of continuity and change in the history of the world (World History)

Concepts	US History (Required by RSMO 180.011)	Government (Required by RSMO 170.011)	Geography	World History	Economics
A. (1) Knowledge of contributions and interactions of major world civilizations				Describe the dominant characteristics, contributions of, and interactions among major civilizations of Asia, Europe, Africa, the Americas and the Middle East in ancient and medieval times	
B. (2) Influence of the Renaissance and Reformation				Interpret the Renaissance and Reformation to include new ways of thinking, including humanism, new developments in the arts and influences on later developments	

World History (Continued)

2b. Knowledge of continuity and change in the history of the world (World History)

Concepts	US History (Required by RSMO 180.011)	Government (Required by RSMO 170.011)	Geography	World History	Economics
C. (3) Causes and effects of European overseas expansion				Assess the impact of the First Global Age (c. 1450 – c. 1770), including the **Columbian Exchange**; the origins and consequences of European overseas expansion; the effect of European arms and economic power on other parts of the world; resulting transformations in the Americas, Africa, Asia and Europe and conflicts among European maritime and land powers	
D. (4) Impact of Scientific Revolution				Examine and analyze the Scientific Revolution in the context of what it was, its antecedents and its impact on Europe and the world	

Evaluate the Enlightenment, including its principle ideas, its antecedents, its challenge to absolutist monarchies and others and its effects on world history

Evaluate the Enlightenment, including its principle ideas, its antecedents, its challenge to absolutist monarchies and others and its effects on world history

Identify and explain the major revolutions of the 18th and 19th centuries, including: political revolutions (American and French) and the Industrial Revolution (causes, development, reactions and other consequences, such as social, political and economic globalization)

Describe the evolution of diverse economic theories and practices, including: manorialism, mercantilism, **laissez-faire** capitalism and socialism. Describe the social and political effects these have had on various societies

Describe the evolution of diverse economic theories and practices, including: manorialism, mercantilism, **laissez-faire** capitalism and socialism. Describe the social and political effects these have had on various societies

World History (Continued)

2b. Knowledge of continuity and change in the history of the world (World History)

Concepts	US History (Required by RSMO 180.011)	Government (Required by RSMO 170.011)	Geography	World History	Economics
G. (7) Causes, comparisons and results of major twentieth-century wars	Examine all of the wars of the twentieth century (i.e., World War I and II), including: causes, comparisons, consequences and peace efforts			Examine all of the wars of the twentieth century (i.e., World War I and II), including: causes, comparisons, consequences and peace efforts	
H. (8) Causes, reactions and consequences of European and Japanese imperialism				Evaluate European and Japanese imperialism of the late 19th and 20th century and the independence movements in Africa and Asia: causes, reactions, short- and long-term consequences	
I. (9) Causes and consequences of major demographic changes				Outline major demographic changes and migrations from prehistoric times to the present, including: their causes and consequences (e.g. rural to urban, less developed to more developed)	

232

Principles and Processes of Governance Systems

3. Knowledge of principles and processes of governance systems

Concepts	US History (Required by RSMO 180.011)	Government (Required by RSMO 170.011)	Geography	World History	Economics
A. (1) Principles and purposes of government	Explain the importance of the following principles of government: • limited government • **majority rule** and minority rights • constitution and civil rights • checks and balances • merits of the above principles	Describe the purposes and structure of laws and government (with emphasis on the federal and state governments) • Explain the importance of the following principles of government: • limited government • majority rule • and minority rights • constitution and civil rights • checks and balances • merits of the above principles			
B. (2) Similarities and differences of governmental systems		Compare and contrast governmental systems, current and historical, including those that are democratic, totalitarian, monarchic, oligarchic and theocratic, and describe their impact		Compare and contrast governmental systems, current and historical, including those that are democratic, totalitarian, monarchic, oligarchic and theocratic, and describe their impact	

233

Principles and Processes of Governance Systems (Continued)

3. Knowledge of principles and processes of governance systems

Concepts	*US History (Required by RSMO 180.011)*	*Government (Required by RSMO 170.011)*	*Geography*	*World History*	*Economics*
C. (3) Processes of governmental systems		Interpret the processes pertaining to: • selection of political leaders (with an emphasis on presidential and parliamentary systems) • functions and styles of leadership (including authoritarian, democratic and *laissez faire*) • governmental systems • how laws and rules are made, enforced, changed and interpreted		Interpret the processes pertaining to: • selection of political leaders (with an emphasis on presidential and parliamentary systems) • functions and styles of leadership (including authoritarian, democratic and *laissez faire*) • governmental systems • how laws and rules are made, enforced, changed and interpreted	

Economic Concepts and Principles

4. Knowledge of economic concepts (including productivity and the market system) and principles (including the laws of supply and demand)

Concepts	US History (Required by RSMO 180.011)	Government (Required by RSMO 170.011)	Geography	World History	Economics
A. (1) Compare and contrast economic systems					Compare and contrast economic systems: traditional, market, command and mixed
B. (2) Understanding economic concepts	Apply the following major economic concepts in the context of the historical period studied: • **scarcity** • **opportunity cost** • **factors of production (human resources, natural resources** and **capital resources)** • **supply** and **demand** (shortages and surpluses) • **gross domestic product (GDP)** • **savings** and **investment** • **business cycle** • **profit**		Factors of **production (human resources, natural resources, capital resources)**		Apply major economic concepts, such as: • **scarcity** • **opportunity cost** • **factors of production (human resources, natural resources,** and **capital resources)** • **supply** and **demand** (shortages and surpluses) • **gross domestic product (GDP)** • **savings** and **investment** • **business cycle** • **profit** • government regulation and deregulation • budgeting

Economic Concepts and Principles (Continued)

4. Knowledge of economic concepts (including productivity and the market system) and principles (including the laws of supply and demand)

Concepts	US History (Required by RSMO 180.011)	Government (Required by RSMO 170.011)	Geography	World History	Economics
	• government regulation and deregulation • budgeting • income • unemployment and full employment • **inflation** and deflation				• income • unemployment and full employment • **inflation** and deflation

| C. (3) Understanding the roles of people, business, and government in economic system of the United States | Analyze the roles people, business, and government play in economic systems, such as:

• **monetary policy** (why the Federal Reserve System influences interest rates and money supply)
• **fiscal policy** (government taxation and spending)
• how monopolies affect people's lives and how they are regulated
• how boycotts, strikes, and embargoes affect trade and people's options
• why businesses may choose to build in or move to other regions or countries | Analyze the roles that people, businesses and government play in economic systems, such as:

• **monetary policy** (why the Federal Reserve System influences interest rates and money supply)
• **fiscal policy** (government taxation and spending) | Explain the roles people, business, and government play in economic systems, such as:

• **monetary policy** (why and how the Federal Reserve System influences interest rates and money supply)
• **fiscal policy** (government taxation and spending)
• how monopolies affect people's lives and how they are regulated
• how boycotts, strikes and embargoes affect trade and people's options
• why businesses may choose to build in or move to other regions or countries |
| D. (4) Knowledge of economic consequences of decisions | Determine the economic consequences of personal and public decisions | | Evaluate the economic consequences of personal and public decisions (e.g., use of credit; deficit spending) |

237

Economic Concepts and Principles (Continued)

4. Knowledge of economic concepts (including productivity and the market system) and principles (including the laws of supply and demand)

Concepts	US History (Required by RSMO 180.011)	Government (Required by RSMO 170.011)	Geography	World History	Economics
E. (5) Understanding the functions and effects of economic institutions	Survey the functions and effects of major economic institutions of the United States economy, such as corporations, labor unions and financial institutions				Analyze the functions and effects of major economic institutions of the United States economy, such as corporations, labor unions and financial institutions
F. (6) Knowledge of economic institutions	Explain the United States role in the global economy and of the roles of trade, treaties, international organizations and **comparative advantage** in the global economy			Explain the roles of trade, treaties, international organizations and **comparative advantage** in the global economy	Explain the roles of trade, treaties, international organizations and **comparative advantage** in the global economy
G. (7) Understanding the roles of government in a market economy	Identify the roles of government in a **market economy** (defining and protecting property rights, maintaining competition, promoting goals such as full employment, stable prices, growth and justice)	Identify the roles of government in a **market economy** (defining and protecting property rights, maintaining competition, promoting goals such as full employment, stable prices, growth and justice)			Analyze the roles of government in a **market economy** (defining and protecting property rights, maintaining competition, promoting goals such as full employment, stable prices, growth and justice)

Elements of Geographical Study and Analysis

5. Knowledge of major elements of geographical study and analysis (such as location, place, movement, regions) and their relationship to changes in society and the environment

Concepts	US History (Required by RSMO 180.011)	Government (Required by RSMO 170.011)	Geography	World History	Economics
A. (1) Uses of geographic research			Use and evaluate geographic research sources (e.g., maps, satellite images, globes, charts, graphs and databases) to interpret Earth's physical and human systems		
			Identify and solve geographic problems		
			Construct maps		
B. (2) Knowledge to use geography to predict and solve problems	Apply knowledge of the geography of Missouri, the United States and world to make predictions and solve problems		Apply knowledge of the geography of Missouri, the United States and world to make predictions and solve problems		

239

Elements of Geographical Study and Analysis (Continued)

5. Knowledge of major elements of geographical study and analysis (such as location, place, movement, regions) and their relationship to changes in society and the environment

Concepts	US History (Required by RSMO 180.011)	Government (Required by RSMO 170.011)	Geography	World History	Economics
C. (3) Understanding the concept of location	Locate major cities of Missouri, the United States and world; states of the United States and many of the world's nations; the world's continents and oceans; and major topographic features of the United States and world		Locate major cities of Missouri, the United States and world; states of the United States and many of the world's nations; the world's continents and oceans; and major topographic features of the United States and world. Communicate **locations** of **places** by creating maps and by describing their **absolute locations** and **relative locations**		
D. (4) Understanding the concept of place	Describe **physical characteristics** and **human characteristics** that make specific **places** unique.		Describe **physical characteristics** and **human characteristics** that make specific **places** unique.	Describe **physical characteristics** and **human characteristics** that make specific **places** unique.	

E. (5) Understanding relationships within places			
Explain how and why **places** change.	Explain how and why **places** change3	Explain how and why **places** change.	Explain how technology has expanded people's capacity to modify the physical environment.
Explain how and why different people may perceive the same place in varied ways.	Explain how and why different people may perceive the same place in varied ways.	Explain how and why different people may perceive the same place in varied ways.	Identify how changes in the physical environment may reduce the capacity of the **environment** to support human activity.
Distinguish major patterns and issues with regard to population distribution, **demographics**, settlements, migrations, cultures and economic systems in the United States and world	Explain how physical processes shape the earth's surface.		Identify and evaluate policies and programs related to the use of resources.
	Describe the distribution and characteristics of **ecosystems**, the forces that have led to their formation, and how they vary in biodiversity and **productivity.**		
	Analyze major patterns and issues with regard to population distribution, **demographics**, settlements, migrations, cultures and economic systems in the United States and world.		

Elements of Geographical Study and Analysis (Continued)

5. Knowledge of major elements of geographical study and analysis (such as location, place, movement, regions) and their relationship to changes in society and the environment

Concepts	US History (Required by RSMO 180.011)	Government (Required by RSMO 170.011)	Geography	World History	Economics
			Explain how technology has expanded people's capacity to modify the physical environment		
			Identify how changes in the physical environment may reduce the capacity of the **environment** to support human activity.		
			Identify and evaluate policies and programs related to the use of resources.		
F. (6) Understanding the relationships between and among places			Explain the factors that account for patterns in trade and human migration.		Explain the factors that account for patterns in trade and human migration.
			Describe major effects of changes in patterns of the movement of people, products and ideas		Describe the major effects of changes in patterns of the movement of people, products and ideas.
			Identify issues pertaining to the movement of people, products and ideas, and evaluate ways to address those issues		Identify issues pertaining to the movement of people, products and ideas, and propose, and evaluate ways to address these issues

G. (7) Understanding relationships between and among regions			
	List and explain criteria that give **regions** their identities in different periods of United States history.	List and explain criteria that give **regions** their identities in different periods of United States and world history.	List and explain criteria that give **regions** their identities in different periods of world history.
	Explain how parts of a region relate to each other and to the region as a whole (e.g., states to nation).	Explain how parts of a region relate to each other and to the region as a whole (e.g., states to nation).	Explain how parts of a region relate to each other and to the region as a whole (e.g., states to nation).
	Explain how **regions** relate to one another (e.g., river-drainage regions)	Explain how **regions** relate to one another (e.g., river-drainage regions).	Explain how **regions** relate to one another (e.g., river-drainage regions).
	Explain how and why **regions** change	Explain how and why **regions** change	Explain how and why **regions** change.
H. (8) Using geography to interpret events of the past explain the present and plan for the future		Use geography to interpret the past, explain the present and plan for the future	

Relationships of Individual and Groups to Institutions and Traditions

6. Knowledge of relationships of the individual and groups to institutions and cultural traditions

Concepts	US History (Required by RSMO 180.011)	Government (Required by RSMO 170.011)	Geography	World History	Economics
A. (1) Ideas and beliefs of different cultures	Compare and contrast the major ideas and beliefs of different cultures.				
B. (2) Changing of roles of various groups	Summarize how the roles of class, ethnic, racial, gender and age groups have changed in society, including causes and effects.				
C. (3) Major social institutions	Describe the major social institutions (family, education, religion, economy and government) and how they fulfill human needs.				
D. (4) Consequences of individual or institutional failure	Identify the consequences that can occur when: • institutions fail to meet the needs of individuals and groups • individuals fail to carry out their personal responsibilities				
E. (5) Causes, effects and resolution of cultural conflict	Determine the causes, consequences and possible resolutions of cultural conflicts				

244

Tools of Social Science Inquiry

7. Knowledge of the use of tools of social science inquiry (such as surveys, statistics, maps and documents)

Concepts	US History (Required by RSMO 180.011)	Government (Required by RSMO 170.011)	Geography	World History	Economics
A. (1) Developing a research plan and identifying resources	Develop a research plan and identify appropriate resources for investigating social studies topics				
B. (2) Selecting and analyzing primary/secondary sources	Distinguish between and analyze **primary sources** and **secondary sources**				
C. (3) Understanding fact, opinion, bias and points of view in sources	Distinguish between fact and opinion and analyze sources to recognize bias and points of view				
D. (4) Interpreting various social-studies resources	Interpret maps, statistics, charts, diagrams, graphs, timelines, pictures, political cartoons, audiovisual materials, continua, written resources, art and artifacts				
E. (5) Knowledge to create various social-studies' graphics	Create maps, charts, diagrams, graphs, timelines and political cartoons to assist in analyzing and visualizing concepts in social studies				

245

APPENDIX B

The Show-Me Standards

Note: Approved as a final regulation by the Missouri State Board of Education, January 18, 1996.

SOCIAL STUDIES

In Social Studies, students in Missouri public schools will acquire a solid foundation which includes knowledge of:

1. Principles expressed in the documents shaping constitutional democracy in the United States.
2. Continuity and change in the history of Missouri, the United States and the world.
3. Principles and processes of governance systems.
4. Economic concepts (including productivity and the market system) and principles (including the laws of supply and demand).
5. The major elements of geographical study and analysis (such as location, place, movement, regions) and their relationships to changes in society and environment.

Handbook on Developing Curriculum Materials for Teachers:
Lessons From Museum Education Partnerships, pp. 247–248
Copyright © 2010 by Information Age Publishing

6.   Relationships of the individual and groups to institutions and cultural traditions.
7.   The use of tools of social science inquiry (such as surveys, statistics, maps, documents).

APPENDIX C

Glossary of Terms

Academic Standard: Specify "what students should know and be able to do." They indicate the knowledge and skills—the ways of thinking working, communicating, reasoning, and investigating, and the most important and enduring ideas, concepts, issues, dilemmas, and knowledge essential to the discipline—that should be taught and learned in school (National Education Goals Panel, 1993, p. 6).

Administrator: The user role that enables managing school details and creating and managing users and classes within the school (Learning Federation, 2005).

American Association of Museums (AAM): Founded in 1906, the American Association of Museums (AAM) is dedicated to promoting excellence within the museum community. Through advocacy, professional education, information exchange, accreditation, and guidance on current professional standards of performance, AAM assists museum staff, boards and volunteers across the country to better serve the public (AAM,1999).

Handbook on Developing Curriculum Materials for Teachers:
Lessons From Museum Education Partnerships, pp. 249–256
Copyright © 2010 by Information Age Publishing

At-Risk Student: Students may be labeled at risk if they are not succeeding in school based on information gathered from test scores, attendance, or discipline problems (School Wise Press, 2006).

Benchmark: A detailed description of a specific level of student performance expected of students at particular ages, grades, or development levels. Benchmarks are often represented by samples of student work. A set of benchmarks can be used as "checkpoints" to monitor progress toward meeting performance goals within and across grade levels. In ABE, SPLs (Student Performance Levels) are examples of benchmarks; targets for instruction (System for Adult Basic Education Support, n.d.).

Big Ideas: A statement of ideas that are central to the learning of a subject area, one that links numerous subject area understandings into a coherent whole (Charles, 2005).

Common Content Language: Two or more groups using the same terminology for a specified topic area(s).

Curriculum: A course of study. The whole set of experiences learners have under the guidance of schools (Oliver, 1977, p. 7).

Curriculum Area Standard/Curriculum Standard: Guidelines specifying what should be learned, taught, or acquired in the study of a particular discipline (ISTE, 2000, p. 363).

Curriculum Coordinator: Provides leadership and coordination in the ongoing development and improvement of the curriculum and instructional program of the district (Irvine Unified School District, 2000).

Curriculum Framework: A curriculum framework is a document outlining content strands and learning standards for a given subject area. Curriculum frameworks provide a structure from which lessons and curricula can be organized and presented to the student. The specific knowledge and skills taught in the classroom are based on student needs and objectives as identified by the teacher and students (SABES, n.d.).

Curriculum Materials: The "texts" used by teachers in their daily professional lives that offer teachers a wide array of curriculum experiences for students depending on their purposes and the demands of the classroom situation (Ben-Peretz, 1990, pp. xiii-xiv).

Curriculum Sifting: Prioritize the critical learning objective(s) of the lesson and determining what "Big Ideas" should be the focus of the learning activity (Elliott, personal communication, September 3, 2006).

Diverse Learner: Any learner who displays or establishes differences in the following ways: race, ethnicity, cultural background, linguistic background, age, religion, gender, sexual orientation, learning, emotional, or physical disability, giftedness, socioeconomic status, or at-risk status (Iowa State University, 2000-04).

Educational Technology: Using multimedia technologies or audiovisual aids as a tool to enhance the teaching and learning process (EETT, n.d.).

Educator: One trained in teaching; a teacher; a specialist in the theory and practice of teaching; a person whose occupation is to educate (SABES, n.d.).

Frame of Reference: A set of ideas, as of philosophical or religious doctrine, in terms of which other ideas are interpreted or assigned meaning (Answers.com, 2006).

Frequently Asked Questions (FAQ): The FAQ (pronounced FAK) or list of "frequently-asked questions" (and answers) has become a feature of the Internet (TechTarget, 2000-06).

Google Alert: An automated Web search service that can help people and businesses monitor the Internet for developments and activities that could concern them. Results are sent to subscribers daily by e-mail (TechTarget, 2000-06).

Graphic Organizers: Create a note-taking guide, study sheet, or assignment that captures the lesson objective(s) in a visual manner.

Guide: A concise manual or reference book providing specific information, directions, instructions and other information about a subject or place (Answers.com, 2006).

High School: A secondary school offering the final years of high school work necessary for graduation, usually includes Grades 10, 11, 12 or Grades 9, 10, 11, and 12 (U.S. Department of Education, 2004).

Hotlink/Link: The result of HTML markup signifying to a browser that data within a document will automatically connect with either nested data or an outside source. Used in the design of hypertext (Learning Circuits, n.d.).

IEP/Individual Education Plan: The document developed at a meeting which sets the standard by which subsequent special education services are usually determined appropriate (The Council for Disability Rights, n.d.).

Inservice: "A planned sequence of experiences, activities, and studies designed to develop or improve the competencies and skills of educational staff" (State of South Dakota, December 31, 2003).

Instructional Strategies: A sequence of steps that builds upon the teacher's initial presentation of subject matter, supporting and expanding propositions made at the outset of the lesson (Martorella, 1991, p. 113).

Institute of Museum and Library Services (IMLS): The primary federal agency for funding and distribution of information about library and museum services (IMLS, 2004, p. 26).

Interactive: An electronic environment that is designed to allow the audience to interact with it. Often referred to as "multimedia," these environments may take the form of a Web site or computer program (Massachusetts Institute of Technology, n.d.).

International Society for Technology Education (ISTE): ISTE is a nonprofit professional organization with a worldwide membership of leaders and potential leaders in educational technology (ISTE, n.d., *About ISTE*, ¶1).

Internet: The high-speed fiber-optic network of networks that uses interconnects computer networks around the world, enabling users to communicate (Reitz, 2004).

Learning: Growth (usually a gain) in any dimension where experience mediates knowledge, skill, attitude, or behavior (IMLS, 2004, p. 26).

Learning Objective: Spell out specifically and clearly what students are expected to learn as the outcome of some measure of instruction (Martorella, 1991, p. 89).

Learning Outcome: A specific learning objective identified within a jurisdiction's curriculum framework (Learning Federation, 2005).

Learning Style: How a person learns, cognitive patterns of perception, and multi-dimensional aspects that affect learning (McGraw-Hill Higher Education, 2003).

Lesson Plan: A plan for specific learning objective identified within a jurisdiction's curriculum framework (Learning Federation, 2005).

Lesson Tiering: Develop multiple learning activities for the same lesson plan, with various levels of complexity, autonomy and difficulty (Elliott, personal communication, September 3, 2006).

Lifelong Learning (learning over a lifetime): Learning in which a person engages throughout his of her life. Lifelong learning includes but is not limited to learning that occurs in schools and other formal educational programs (IMLS, 2004, p. 27).

Modifications: Changes in curriculum or instruction that substantially change the requirements of the class or substantially alter the content standards or benchmarks (Iowa City Community School District, 2006).

Multimedia (Multi-media): Presenting data in more than one medium, such as combining text, graphics, and sound (Micro2000, 2004).

Multiple Modality Presentation: Using visual and auditory methods to present the lesson information in order to reach students with different learning styles (Elliott, personal communication, September 3, 2006).

Museum: An institution which performs all, or most, of the following functions: collecting, preserving, exhibiting and interpreting the natural and cultural objects of our environment (AAM and the Federal Council on the Arts and Humanities, 1969, p. 1).

Museum Education: A lifelong process of developing knowledge, skills, and character that takes place in a museum (Hicks, 1986, ¶1).

Museum Personnel: Professional museum workers include all the personnel of museums or institutions qualifying as museums   having received specialized training, or possessing an equivalent practical experience, in any field relevant to the management and operations of a museum … either in a professional or advisory capacity, but not promoting or dealing with any commercial products and equipment required for museums and services (International Council of Museums, 2006, August 19).

National Council for the Social Studies (NCSS): Founded in 1921, National Council for the Social Studies has grown to be the largest association in the country devoted solely to social studies education. NCSS engages and supports educators in strengthening and advocating social studies (NCSS, 2006).

National Educational Technology Standards (NETS): National standards for educational uses of technology that facilitate school improvement in the United States (International Society for Technology in Education, *Educational technology standards and performance indicators for all teachers*, n.d.).

Needs Assessment: A systematic process designed to acquire an accurate, thorough picture of the strengths and weaknesses of a museum and public school partnership which assists in the collection of any additional information that supports the planning efforts of the partnership members. Process that collects and examines information about museum and public school partnership issues and then utilizes that data to determine priority goals, to develop a plan, and to allocate funds and resources (adapted from the North Dakota Department of Public Instruction, n.d.).

Negro Leagues Baseball (NLB): A business structure representing the highest level of professional baseball available to African American and Latino athletes during the late nineteenth century through the mid 20th century (Doswell, 2005).

Negro Leagues Baseball Museum (NLBM): A privately funded, nonprofit organization dedicated to preserving the rich history of African American Baseball (NLBM, n.d.).

NLBM-KSU Partnership: A collaboration between the Negro Leagues Baseball Museum and Kansas State University.

No Child Left Behind: H.R. 1, The No Child Left Behind Act is a reform of the Elementary and Secondary Education Act (ESEA), enacted in 1965. It redefines the federal role in kindergarten through 12th grade education to help improve the academic achievement of all American students. (U.S. Department of Education, 2003).

Partnership: A relationship between individuals or groups that is characterized by mutual cooperation and responsibility, as for the achievement of a specified goal (see collaboration). In this usage partnership describes a spectrum of relationships between two or more organizations ranging from relatively informal cooperation through formal, legal agreement (IMLS, 2004, p. 28).

Public School: A school or institution controlled and operated by publicly elected or appointed officials and deriving its primary support from public funds (U.S. Department of Education, 2004).

Readability Level: Information about the level a document is written in, determined by the average number of syllables per word and words per sentence in relation to various U.S. reading scales (O'Reilly, 2006).

Readiness Level: The degree to which a student or students are ready to learn particular skills. Readiness levels may vary greatly among students in the same classroom (Elliott, personal communication, September 3, 2006).

Resources for Diverse Learners (RFDL): Commonly defined as modifications included in lesson plans that allow educators to diversify their teaching methods for varying student readiness levels (Elliott, personal communication, September 3, 2006).

Rubric: Specific sets of criteria that clearly define for both student and teacher what a range of acceptable and unacceptable performance looks like. Criteria define descriptors of ability at each level of performance and assign values to each level. Levels referred to are proficiency levels which describe a continuum from excellent to unacceptable product (SABES, n.d.).

School District: An education agency at the local level that exists primarily to operate public schools or to contract for public school services. Synonyms are "local basic administrative unit" and "local education agency" (U.S. Department of Education, 2004).

Search Engine: Any of a number of giant databases on the Internet which store data on Web sites and their corresponding URLs (University of Kansas, 2006b).

Social Studies: A collection of courses taught in secondary schools, which includes history, geography, economics, anthropology, political science, sociology, and psychology (Ellis et al., 1991, p. 4).

Standards: The broadest of a family of terms referring to statements of expectations for student learning including content and performance expectations, and benchmarks (SABES, n.d.).

Standards-Based Curriculum: Teaching directed toward student mastery of defined standards. Now that nearly all states have adopted curriculum standards, teachers are expected to teach in such a way that students achieve the standards (Association for Supervision and Curriculum Development, 2006a).

State Standards: Statements of expectation in a set of collections of different subject areas that may be proposed by a state for review (National Education Goals Panel, 1993, p. 9).

Student Motivation: A student's willingness, need, desire and compulsion to participate in, and be successful in, the learning process (Bomia et al., 1997, p. 1).

Technology: New developed and emerging materials, equipment, and strategies that enhance curriculum, classroom instruction, field experiences, clinical practice, assessments, and evaluation (North Central Regional Educational Laboratory, n.d., A sense of calling section, ¶1).

Technology-infused: To be filed with technology or cause to be filled with technology.

Virtual Museum: A collection of images, objects, or interactive experiences internationally brought together and presented through a computer (usually via Internet/Web pathways) (IMLS, 2004, p. 28).

Web/World Wide Web: All the resources and users on the Internet (TechTarget, 2000-06).

Webpage: A digital page within a Web site.

Web site: A Web site is a related collection of World Wide Web (WWW) files that includes a beginning file called a home page (TechTarget, 2000-06).

APPENDIX D

Further Resources

This section lists resources that museum and public school educators could use to obtain more information about museum and public school partnerships wishing to create motivational standards-based curriculum materials in high school social studies. Print and digital resources are cited, as well as professional organizations and programs.

Curriculum and Educator Materials:

Colonial Willamsburg Foundation. (2006). http://www.history.org/teach/

Liberty Memorial Association. (2004). *Lessons of liberty: Honor and courage.* Kansas City, MO: Project Explore.

Liberty Memorial Museum. (n.d.). *The lessons of liberty: Frequently asked questions.* http://www.libertymemorialmuseum.org/display.aspx?pgID=949

Michigan Alliance for the Conservation of Cultural Heritage. (2005). http://www.macch.org/lessons.php

Michigan Historical Museum. (2004-2005). *History, arts and libraries.* http://www.michigan.gov/hal/0,1607,7-160-17451_18670_18793---,00.html

Mississippi Historical Society. (2000-2006). *Mississippi history now.* http://mshistory.k12.ms.us/index.html

Negro Leagues Baseball eMuseum. (2006). http://www.coe.ksu.edu/nlbemuseum/

Handbook on Developing Curriculum Materials for Teachers:
Lessons From Museum Education Partnerships, pp. 257–262
Copyright © 2010 by Information Age Publishing

State Historical Museum of Iowa. (2004). http://www.state.ia.us/iowahistory/ museum/exhibits/mammoth/learn.htm

Wisconsin Historical Society. (1996-2006). http://www.wisconsinhistory.org /teachers/lessons/

Curriculum Standards:

Boehm, R., & Rutherford, D. (2004, November-December). Implementation of national geography standards in the social studies: A ten-year retrospective. *The Social Studies, 95(6)*, 228-230.

Cross, R., Rebarber, T., & Torres, J. (Eds.). (2004). *Grading the systems: The guide to state standards, tests, and accountability policies*. Washington, DC: Thomas Fordham Foundation.

Danker, A. (2000). Linking technology with social studies learning standards. *The Social Studies, 91(6)*, 263-266.

Darling-Hammond, L. (2001). *The Right to learn: A blueprint for creating schools that work*. San Francisco: Jossey-Bass.

Glass, K. (2005). *Curriculum design for writing instruction: Creating standards-based lesson plans and rubrics*. Thousand Oaks, CA: Corwin Press.

McArthur, J. (2004). Involving preservice teachers in social studies content standards: Thoughts of a methods professor. *The Social Studies, 95(2)*, 79-82.

O'Hara, S., McMahon, M., & International Society for Technology in Education. (2003). *Multidisciplinary units for grades 6-8* (1st ed.). Eugene, OR: The Society.

Pratt, F., Laney, J., & Couper, D. (2002). A multipurpose guide to teaching the ten thematic strands of social studies through life span education. *The Social Studies, 93(4)*, 170-175.

Ross, E. (2001). *The social studies curriculum: Purposes, problems, and possibilities* (Rev. ed.). Albany: State University of New York Press.

Sleeter, C., & Stillman, J. (2005). Standardizing knowledge in a multicultural society. *Curriculum Inquiry, 35(1)*, 27-46.

Social Studies. (2003, September/October). Assessment traps in K-12 social studies. *The Social Studies, 94(5)*, 212-15.

Stern, S. (2003, September). *Effective state standards for U.S. history: A 2003 report card*. Washington DC: Thomas Fordham Foundation.

Thornton, S. (2001). Legitimacy in the social studies curriculum. *Education across a century: The centennial volume, one hundredth yearbook of the National Society for the Study of Education* (pp. 185-204). Chicago: University of Chicago Press.

Guides/Handbooks:

Diamond, J. (1999). *Practical evaluation guide: Tools for museums and other informal educational settings* (American Association for State and Local History Book Series). Walnut Creek, CA: Altamira Press.

Grinder, A., & McCoy, E. (1985). *The good guide: A sourcebook for interpreters, docents and tour guides*. Scottsdale, AZ: Ironwood.

High School Student Motivation:

Corbin, S. (1994). *Lessons from the classroom: Male and female high school students' attitudes toward and achievement in social studies*. New York: Research and Evaluation Consultant.

Deci, E., & Ryan, R. (1985). *Intrinsic motivation and self-determination in human behavior*. New York: Plenum.

Desrochers, C., & Desrochers, M. (2000). Creating lessons designed to motivate students [Electronic version]. *Contemporary Education, 71(2)*, 51-55.

Fernandez, C., Massey, G., & Dornbusch, S. (1976). High school students' perception of social studies. *The Social Studies, 67*, 51-57.

Fouts, J. (1987). High school social studies classrooms and attitudes: A cluster analysis approach. *Theory and Research in Social Education, 15(2)*, 105-114.

Fraser, B. (1981). Deterioration in high school students' attitudes toward social studies. *The Social Studies, 72*, 65-68.

Haladyna, T. (1982). Correlates of attitude toward the social studies. *Theory and Research, 10*, 1-26.

Haladyna, T., & Shaughnessy, J. (1982). *A manual for the inventory of affective aspects of schooling*. Monmouth, OR: Teaching Research.

Kelly, M. (n.d.). *The art and craft of motivating students*. Retrieved January 19, 2006, from http://712educators.about.com/cs/motivation/a/motivation_p.htm

Kohn, A. (1993). *Punished by rewards*. New York: Houghton Mifflin.

Lewis, A. (2004, March). Schools that engage children. *Phi Delta Kappan, 85(7)*, 483-484.

Pintrich, P. (1996). *Motivation in education: Theory, research, and applications*. Hillsdale, NJ: Prentice Hall.

Sherman, T., & Kurhan, B. (2005). Constructing learning: using technology to support teaching and understanding. Learning and Leading with Technology. *International Society for Technology in Education, 32*(5), 10-13.

Museum Education:

Alexander, E. (1988). The American museum chooses education. *Curator, 31(1)*, 61-81.

American Association of Museums. (1992b). *Excellence and equity*. Washington, DC: Author.

American Association of Museums. (1998). *Museums places of learning*. Washington, DC: American Association of Museums.

Beer, V. (1992). *Do museums have "curriculum"?* In S. K. Nichols (Ed.), *Patterns in practice: Selections from the Journal of Museum Education* (pp. 209-214). Washington, DC: Museum Education Roundtable.

Bloom, J., & Mintz, A. (1990). Museums and the future of education. *Journal of Museum Education, 15(3),* 12-15.

Curran, E. (n.d.). Discovering the history of museum education. *Journal of Museum Education, 20(2),* 5-6.

Floyd, M. (2004). Interdisciplinary instruction using museums. *Phi Delta Kappa Fastbacks, 524,* 7-48.

Gallant, C. (1992). *A study of educational processes in museums.* Unpublished doctoral dissertation, Ohio State University, Columbus.

Goodlad, J. (1984). *A place called school: Prospects for the future.* New York: McGraw-Hill.

Harrison, N. (1980). *Development and implementation of educational programs in selected history museums and suggested practices for future programming.* Unpublished doctoral dissertation, University of Oklahoma, Oklahoma City.

Journal of Museum Education, Museum Education Roundtable. (1994). *Patterns in practice: Selections from the journal of museum education.* Washington, DC: American Association of Museums.

Larrabee, E. (1968). *Museums and education.* Washington, DC: Smithsonian Institution Press.

Moffat, H., & Woollard, V. (Eds.). (2004). *Museum and gallery education: A manual of good practice.* Walnut Creek: CA, Altamira Press.

Nichols, S., Alexander, M., & Yellis, K. (Eds.). (1984). *Museum education anthology: Perspectives on informal learning, a decade of roundtable reports, 1973-1983.* Washington, DC: Museum Education Roundtable.

O'Connell, P. (1992). *Decentralizing interpretation: Developing museum education materials with and for schools.* In S. K. Nichols (Ed.), Patterns in practice: Selections from the *Journal of Museum Education* (pp. 251-261). Washington, DC: Museum Education Roundtable.

Ravitch, D. (2003). *The language police: How pressure groups restrict what students learn.* New York: Alfred A. Knopf.

Soren, B. (1991). Education: Curriculum-makers across museums. *Journal of Museum Management and Curatorship, 10(4),* 435-438.

Museum and School Partnerships:

Berry, N. (1998, March). A focus on art museum/school collaborations. *Art Education, 51*(2), 8-12.

Boyer, C. (2007). Using museum resources in the K-12 social studies curriculum. *Social Studies Development Center.* Retrieved October 13, 2009, from http://www.indiana.edu/~ssdc/musdig.htm

Gardner, H. (1991, October 9). Making Schools More Like Museums. *Education Week, 6*(6), 40.

Hamilton-Sperr, P. (1995). *Museums in the life of a city: Strategies for community partnerships.* Washington, DC: American Association of Museums.

Harrison, M., & Naef, B. (1985). Toward a partnership: Developing the museum-school relationship. *Journal of Museum Education, 10(4),* 9-12.

Hodgson, J. (1986). Teaching teachers: Museums team up with schools and universities. *Museum News*, *64*(5), 28-35.

Kelman, S. (1992). *Collaborative efforts between museums and schools: Collaborations within collaborations*. Unpublished master's thesis, Bank Street College, New York.

Linder, B. (1987). Museum-school partnerships-a resource for principals. *NASSP Bulletin*, *74*(503), 122-124.

Munley, M. (1991). New partnerships with schools. *Journal of Museum Education*, *16*(3), 14.

Sebolt, A. (1980). *Building collaborative programs: Museums and schools: A manual for the development of collaborative programs*. Sturbridge, MA: Old Sturbridge Village.

Vliet, D. (2000). *Museum school partnerships: Educational resources for the new millennium*. Austin, TX: The Texas Association of Museums. Museline.

Social Studies/History Curriculum

Johnson, C. & Rector, J. (1997). The internet ten: Using the internet to meet social studies curriculum standards. *Social Education*, *61*(3), 167-169.

Leming, J. (1997). Social studies research and the interests of children. *Theory and Research in Social Education*, *25*(4), 500-505.

McTeer, J. (1979). *Student interest in social studies content and methodology*. (ERIC Reproduction Service No. ED139712).

Rabb, T. (2004, October). No child left behind historical literacy. *The Education Digest*, *70(2)*, 18-21.

Shaughnessy, J., & Haladyna, T. (1985). Research on student attitude toward social studies. *Social Education*. *49*, 692-695.

Social Studies. (2003, September/October). Where does social studies fit in a high-stakes testing environment? *The Social Studies*, *94*(5), 207-211.

Stern, B. (2005, Spring/Summer). *Debunking the myth: The social studies and rigor*. *International Journal of Social Education*, *20*(1), 52-60.

Stotsky, S. (2004). *The stealth curriculum: Manipulating America's history teachers*. Washington, DC: Thomas B. Fordham Foundation.

Sumrall, W., & Schillinger, D. (2004). A student-directed model for designing a science/social studies curriculum. *Social Studies*, *95*(1), 5.

Zevin, J. (2000). *Social studies for the twenty-first century: Methods and materials for teaching in the middle and secondary schools* (2nd ed.). Mahwah, NJ: Erlbaum.

Resources for Diverse Learners (RFDLs):

Edyburn, D. (2000). Assistive technology and students with mild disabilities. *Focus on Exceptional Children*, *32*(9), 1-24.

Edyburn, D. (2002). *What every teacher should know about assistive technology*. Upper Saddle River, NJ: Addison Wesley.

Kierman, L., & Tomlinson, C. (1997). *Why differentiate instruction?* Alexandria, VA: Association for Supervision and Curriculum Development.

Nordlund, M. (2003). *Differentiated instruction: Meeting the educational needs of all students in your classroom*. Lanham, MD: Scarecrow Press.

Rose, D., & Meyer, A. (2002). *Teaching every student in the digital age: Universal design for learning*. Alexandria, VA: ASCD.

Rose, D., Meyer, A., & Hitchcock, C. (Ed.s) (2005). *The universally designed classroom: Accessible curriculum and digital technologies*. Cambridge, MA: Harvard Education Press.

Tomlinson, C. (1995). *How to differentiate instruction in mixed-ability classrooms*. Alexandria, VA: ASCD.

Tomlinson, C. (1999). *The differentiated classroom: Responding to the needs of all learners*. Alexandria, VA: ASCD.

Tomlinson, C., & McTighe, J. (2006). *Integrating differentiated instruction and understanding by design: Connecting content and kids*. Alexandria, VA: Association for Supervision and Curriculum Development.

General Information:

AAM
http://www.aam-us.org/

AASLH
http://www.aaslh.org/

Achieve, Inc.
www.achieve.org

Altamira Press
http://www.altamirapress.com/

Diversity Classroom Collection & Small Press Diversity Materials Collection
http://catnet.ksu.edu/subguides/education/diversity.html

IMLS
http://www.imls.gov

Learning Point Associates
http://www.learningpt.org/

Museum Computer Network
http://www.mcn.edu/

National Center for Education Statistics (NCES)
http://www.nces.ed.gov/

National Council for the Social Studies (NCSS)
http://www.ncss.org/about/

Pew Internet & American Life Project
http://www.pewinternet.org

Thomas B. Fordham Foundation
http://www.edexcellence.net/foundation/publication/index.cfm

The Tripod Project
www.tripodproject.com

SECTION III

Developing Accessible Museum Curriculum

A Handbook for
Museum Professionals and Educators

by

Ann Elliott
Auburn Washburn Unified School District

Tara Baillargeon
Kansas State University

Cari D. Barragree
Kansas State University

and

Gerald D. Bailey
Kansas State University

CONTENTS

INTRODUCTION

This handbook is written to support professionals who wish to increase the scope and reach of curriculum materials they develop. The handbook contains practical, research-based strategies and applications. When applied during the initial design phase of the curriculum development process, these techniques will enhance the **accessibility** of curriculum, and therefore enhance the delivery of content to learners and patrons with varied learning needs. These tools are also effective when used to retrofit already existing curricular materials, however, they may be more difficult and time consuming to implement once materials have already been developed. Therefore, the reader is encouraged to reflect upon the many diverse learners and patrons that may benefit from a wider range of options and make a strategic decision to incorporate supports for those diverse groups as the development process unfolds. This decision will ultimately benefit many potential learners and patrons.

WHO SHOULD USE THIS BOOK?

This book will benefit museum professionals, including curators, exhibit designers, and educators who are interested in expanding the principals of architectural accessibility to the world of the mind. Museum patrons who are not engaged with the museum's collection do not benefit from their museum experiences. The process of cognition varies greatly among patrons, both those with and those without disabilities. Physical differences such as mobility and sensory diversity have a profound impact on a patron's cognitive experience. Therefore, enhancing the accessibility of the mental process a museum visitor engages in has the potential to deliver a museum's content to a wider audience. The methods in this handbook utilize the principles of universal design; a set of design strategies that are already in use in the physical environment of many museums.

Educational professionals, including teachers, administrators, and curriculum developers will also benefit from this handbook. It goes without saying that the educational system is greatly concerned with the process of cognition. Curriculum design has typically been the task of school educators and the methods and tools presented in this handbook are based on educational research and practice. Teachers will find these techniques useful in the lesson planning process as well.

When museum professionals decide to enhance the cognitive experiences of their patrons, they take on an educational role. Obviously, the school professional's role is also educational. Therefore, for the purposes of clarity, the handbook will refer to both groups in the target audience as "educators." This term focuses the reader on the mental process of cognition; that of learning. The handbook deals with methods to enhance the learning process. These strategies will be effective whether employed in a school or museum setting, as well as within a partnership between museums and schools.

WHY SHOULD READERS USE THIS BOOK?

Educators have as their primary goal the transfer of knowledge from one party to another. The learning process is a complex series of cognitive activities and research has revealed much about how the human brain functions. This knowledge has improved teaching methods in general; however, several other factors impact the learning process in a myriad of ways including the characteristics of individual learner preferences along with their interests and abilities. These factors, in turn, also determine the effectiveness of these teaching materials. Therefore, educators must be concerned with the variety of learners they will encounter and are wise to plan accordingly.

The diversity represented by any group of potential learners can be an important part of the learning equation. Learners' capacities are not inherent; capacities are defined by the interplay between learners' abilities and the tools they use. Curriculum that is designed to reach only a portion of this group will have a diluted effect on the group as a whole. Museums and schools are both institutions concerned with reaching a wide variety of patrons. Museums depend on patrons and donors to maintain their very existence and schools have been given the charge of teaching every learner. Information regarding accessibility laws can be found in chapter 1 of the handbook, but suffice it to say that educators from both museums and schools should be planning learning activities, (whether in the gallery or the classroom), that reach as many diverse learners as possible.

Consider This Example

Teachers who have access to only a few tools and *methods* for teaching and assessing learners' progress naturally tend to define *goals* that are closely tied to *methods*. Consider this *goal*, set by Patrick's teacher, Mr. Hernandez, as part of a class research project: "Students will collect information from a variety of books as part of their research." In a traditional classroom, with only traditional fixed *media* available, Mr. Hernandez might logically conclude that Patrick couldn't work toward the same goal as his classmates because of his slow reading and tendency to be easily discouraged.

What if, in addition to books, the resources available to Mr. Hernandez's students included digital text with reading support, a variety of image-rich sources, videos, and *scaffolds* to help Patrick stay focused and organize his information? In this classroom, it would be clearer that the goal's true purpose-learning to collect and synthesize information-does not depend upon the use of printed text. Mr. Hernandez might restate the *goal* more generally: "Students will collect information from a variety of sources." This rewording separates the *goal* from the *methods* for attaining it, broadening the options for the entire class. Patrick, instead of having to lower his sights because of difficulty accessing a particular medium, could rely on scaffolds and *supports* to achieve the same *goal* as his peers. (Rose & Meyer, 2002, chap. 5)

When educators design additional supportive tools for learners to use, diverse groups of learners can reach the same learning goal, but can use different paths to achieve it. In schools, this process is imperative as educators are challenged to "leave no child behind," and in museums the potential diversity represented by prospective patrons is unlimited.

Consider the teaching and learning process as a highway. Typically, educators have designed instruction "right down the middle," a phrase that is familiar to many in the field. The phrase refers to the process of planning and delivering learning activities designed for the "typical" learner and essentially leaving behind those learners whose skill levels or interest fall on either side of that one highway. Now consider the alternative; educators who consider the needs of a wider range of learners can incorporate curricular elements for those groups in the initial design process, much like architects design accessibility features in new buildings. When this is done, the learning highway contains many lanes or paths that can be used by diverse learners. Additionally, this highway can include multiple ways of entering and exiting the highway, so that diverse learners can access the learning in multiple ways, and demonstrate their learning in multiple ways. This multiple lane highway accommodates both a greater volume of traffic, and a greater diversity of travelers.

1. Instruction often resembles the construction of a one-way highway for learners. The learning journey begins with the selection of the content to be learned (A). The journey continues down the highway as learners engage with that content (B). The end of the learning journey is reached when learners demonstrate mastery of the content, often by producing a product (C).

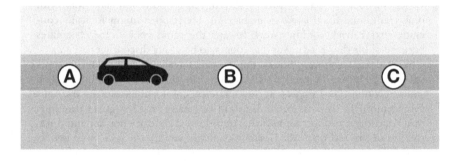

Figure 1–4.   The construction of a multilane highway, with additional lanes for entering and exiting, represents the increased accessibility of curriculum that is designed for diverse learners.

2. By adding lanes to the highway learners have more options to engage with the content (B). Additional lanes should not be restricted, but available to any traveler.

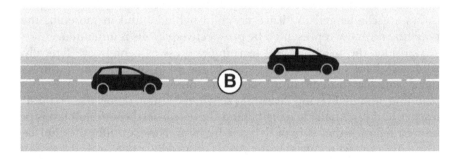

3. The more lanes there are, the more options travelers have (B). When travelers have the freedom to move from lane to lane they can make their learning journey in a flexible way—one that meets their needs from moment to moment.

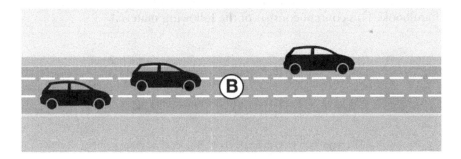

4. Adding additional lanes to the highway on which learners can enter the process, and exit the process truly increases accessibility (A). The entry lanes allow learners to have different sets of content objectives if necessary. The exit lanes allow learners to demonstrate their mastery of the content in multiple ways (C). This includes different types of end products.

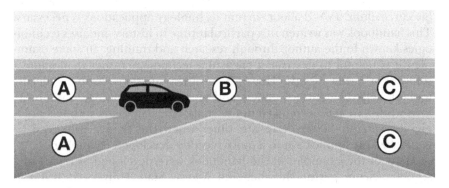

HOW SHOULD READERS USE THIS BOOK?

The handbook is organized into three major chapters with each chapter containing several specific sections. Each section can stand alone or the sections may be used in conjunction with each other. Therefore, readers have the flexibility to use the contents in a manner that best fits their immediate needs. This method of organization also allows the content to be presented in a very simple, pragmatic way. Readers are encouraged to skip around and refer to sections in any order. For this reason, the reader may notice some overlap in content. Many strategies can be applied in more than one section. In order to include as many practical tools as possible, some repetition is present. Definitions of words that appear in bold font can be found in the glossary.

Readers will notice icons and illustrations scattered throughout the handbook. This content consists of the following material.

1.   The mouse icon indicates helpful resources on the Internet.

2.   The book icon indicates helpful resources in print.

3.   The light bulb icon indicates the "Big Idea" or main point of a section.

4.   The cone icon indicates a warning or potential difficulty.

Figure 5.   Icons used in this section.

Given that technology will play a large role in the development of accessible curriculum, a word about current technology applications is necessary. This handbook was written in a particular time in history and uses technologies known to the author through research and training. In some examples, it is helpful to describe a particular technology rather than name a software or hardware title. However, in other situations, listing a specific tool will help the educator understand the application of that tool. Therefore, while care has been taken not to "date" the handbook with technologies present in 2007, there are times when the reader will need to generalize the application to a more recently developed technology.

Many of the examples in the handbook were developed as a part of a school/museum partnership between Kansas State University (KSU) in Manhattan, Kansas and the Negro Leagues Baseball Museum (NLBM) in Kansas City, Missouri. Curriculum materials created by the KSU/NLBM partnership are posted on the Internet. This internet site will be referred to as the NLB eMueum. The home page for the NLB eMuseum is shown in Figure 6, along with the URL address to access the materials on the Internet. Lesson plans were developed by educators from both environments and **scaffold** materials were included in the initial planning to enhance the cognitive accessibility of the materials for diverse learners. The reader will recognize social studies content delivered from the platform of the Negro Leagues Baseball history in these examples, and will identify the intended audience as learners 15 years of age and older. However, these examples will serve educators as models for the development of accessible curricular materials for multiple age groups. Additionally, the handbook contains examples that are not dependant upon a particular content area or age group.

Figure 6.   Negro Leagues Baseball eMuseum home page and URL address.

The handbook includes:

Chapter 1

Statutory foundations for accessibility

Research foundations

1. Universal Design for Learning
2. Differentiated Instruction

Chapter 2

Presentation

Process

Product

Chapter 3

Self-Assessment

Priorities

Appendixes

Examples

Glossary

Bibliography

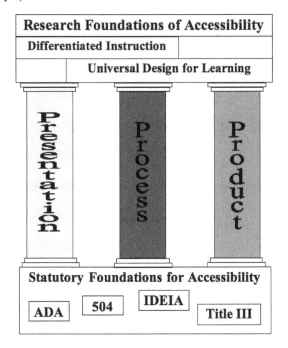

Figure 7.   Model for the design of accessible curriculum.

CHAPTER 1

THE IMPORTANCE
OF ACCESSIBILITY

As educators strive to deliver a rigorous curriculum to every learner, they use methods and strategies that increase the reach of the content, so that learners with diverse needs are provided meaningful access. These methods are applications of several sets of principals; universal design and differentiated instruction. This handbook explores each concept as it relates to curriculum and discusses the application of each to the design of accessible curriculum that may be developed for museums. The handbook contains a brief introduction to universal design and differentiated instruction, techniques for using each, and examples from curricular materials that have been developed for museums.

MUSEUM EDUCATION

Museums have included education as a primary goal for a long time. Educational values were included the charters of some of America's earliest museums. More recently, the Tax Reform Act of 1969 encouraged the adoption of educational goals by providing a tax benefit to non-profit organizations, such as museums (Kess, 1970).

Today, the American Association of Museum's (2005) accreditation program standards emphasize that museums assert their public service role and, "place education at the center of that role" (¶ 1). Museums report that the number of students, teachers, and schools they serve has contin-

Handbook on Developing Curriculum Materials for Teachers:
Lessons From Museum Education Partnerships, pp. 275–284
Copyright © 2010 by Information Age Publishing

ued to grow. Museums of all types and sizes offer educational programs and work with schools. Many employ museum educators whose job it is to deliver the museum's collection to patrons via the learning process. Although traditionally, the focus on these educational efforts may have been tied to a visit to the museum by school children, increasingly, the role of the museum educator has expanded to include adult learning, virtual learning and partnerships with educators in elementary, secondary and post-secondary schools. The increased availability of the Internet has allowed museums to reach patrons who may never physically visit the gallery, but will benefit from interacting with the collection on line. Many museum Web sites incorporate educational materials that include field trip guides, interactive exhibits, resource libraries, and lesson plans.

SECTION ONE: STATUTORY FOUNDATIONS FOR ACCESSIBILITY

- Legislation that mandates accessibility
- Section 504
- Americans with Disabilities Act
- Title III
- Individuals with Disabilities Education Improvement Act

Legislation That Mandates Accessibility

The Civil Rights Movement of the 1960s gave rise to the Disability Rights Movement. While minorities and women were protected by civil rights legislation passed by the United States Congress during the 1960s, the rights of people with disabilities were not protected by federal legislation until much later. However, several social factors contributed to the increased awareness of the need for accessibility. First, there was an increase in the number of elderly citizens as a result of increased life span and better health care. The average lifespan was 47 years in the early twentieth century, but increased to an average of 76 years by the later part of the century (Center for Universal Design [CUD], 2006a, ¶ 3). Additionally, after World War II, there was an increase in the number of disabled veterans living in the United States (CUD, 2006a, ¶ 4).

Section 504
These changes in the population presented new challenges to businesses and governmental agencies because many physical facilities were unusable to people with physical limitations. The lack of accessibility to

people with disabilities was not addressed until Section 504 of the Rehabilitation Act was enacted in 1973. This law prohibited discrimination on the basis of a disability towards otherwise qualified people by recipients of federal financial assistance.

Americans With Disabilities Act

The federal laws were strengthened with the passage of the Americans with Disabilities Act (ADA) in 1990 (United States Department of Justice, 2005) which prohibited discrimination on the basis of disability in businesses, places of employment, services, programs, public transportation, public accommodation and telecommunications.

Title III

Title III of the ADA went further to prohibit discrimination on the basis of disability by public accommodations and required places of public accommodation and commercial facilities to be designed, constructed, and altered in compliance with the accessibility standards established by the ADA. The ADA has raised public awareness to physical barriers that impede access and has represented a uniform nationwide mandate that ensures accessibility regardless of local attitudes.

Individuals With Disabilities Education Improvement Act

The Individuals with Disabilities Education Improvement Act (IDEIA) was reauthorized in 2004. This law was formerly the Education for All Handicapped Children Act, passed in 1975, and required that all children with disabilities receive a free, appropriate public education in the least restrictive environment. Public schools have obligations to students with disabilities under IDEIA, and as local government agencies, schools are also bound by the stipulations of Section 504 and the ADA.

These important pieces of federal legislation have impacted the disability community in terms of accessibility and will continue to play an important role. In 1997, the United States Census Bureau reported that one in five Americans had some form of disability and that this trend would continue to grow as the population aged (McNeil, 1997). People with disabilities represent a significant segment of society; visiting businesses, governmental agencies and schools.

SECTION TWO: RESEARCH FOUNDATIONS FOR ACCESSIBILITY

- Universal Design
  - Universal design in the physical environment
  - Universal design in museums

> o   Universal design in the cognitive environment
- Differentiated Instruction
- Universal design for learning and differentiated instruction

Universal Design

As architects began to implement these new standards, they discovered that specially designed elements for people with disabilities were expensive and aesthetically distracting. The realization emerged that design elements could be incorporated that would meet accessibility standards, be commonly provided and thus be less expensive, unlabeled, attractive, and even marketable, which could benefit all users. The idea of **universal design** was born (CUD, 2006a).

Universal Design in the Physical Environment

Robert Mace (1997), of the Center for Universal Design defines universal design as "the design of products and environments to be usable by all people to the greatest extent possible, without the need for adaptation or specialized design" (¶ 1). The intent of universal design is to "simplify life for everyone by making products, communications, and the built environment more usable by as many people as possible at little or no extra cost" (CUD, 2006a, ¶ 2).

The Center for Universal Design (1997) outlines the seven principles of universal design:

1. Equitable use.
2. Flexible use.
3. Simple and intuitive use.
4. Perceptible information.
5. Tolerance for error.
6. Low physical effort.
7. Size and space for approach and use.

Universal design features are usually standard practices that are placed differently, selected carefully, or omitted (CUD, 2006b). This is an important concept to our later discussion because the "mundane" nature of UD shapes our use of UD in the learning environment.

 What makes UD so effective and efficient is not the addition of innovative features, but rather the innovative use of elements that are readily available.

Figure 1.1.

Two classic examples of UD are curb cuts in sidewalks and electric door openers. Although originally designed to provide access to people with disabilities, these design elements are frequently used by those without disabilities. A person riding a bicycle can avoid a curb by crossing the street at a curb cut or a patron may choose the electric door opener on a building, even though that person may be physically able to manually open the door. These design elements represent universal design at its best by employing simple technologies that enhance accessibility for everyone.

Universal Design in Museums

In order to reach a wide spectrum of patrons with diverse needs, museum designers use the techniques of universal design to increase the accessibility of their exhibits (Adaptive Environments, 2003; Majewski, n.d.; Tokar, 2003). Leaders in exhibit development at the Boston Museum of Science (2001b) and the Smithsonian contend that UD provides intellectual access to patrons through the use of multisensory presentations and that "exhibitions must teach to different learning styles, respond to issues of cultural and gender equity, and offer multiple levels of information" (Majewski, n.d., ¶ 1). These concepts will also translate to our discussion of curriculum design.

 The Smithsonian Guidelines for Accessible Exhibition Design (Majewski, n.d.) serves as a resource for exhibition designers, curators, registrars, conservators, collections managers, designers, editors, developers, and educators. The guidelines present specific instructions regarding exhibit content, presentation, and physical access, and emphasize that care be given to ensure that display cases are easily accessed from either a sitting or standing position. Directions are included to ensure that labels and exhibit explanations are provided through more than one sensory channel, and advise the use of audio and visual materials to provide equal access to individuals with sensory impairments.

Figure 1.2.

Science museums and children's museums typically are concerned with bringing content to visitors in multisensory ways and the principals of universal design are useful to accomplish this goal (Association of Science Technology Centers, 2004; Boston Museum of Science, 2001b). Through the expanded use of technology, interactive and computer-enhanced presentations deliver material to the visitors that appeal to them visually, auditory and tactilely. By delivering museum content through several sensory channels, the cognitive experiences of visitors are enhanced, regardless of whether or not they have a disability. The effective use of multisensory representation as a method to increase learning has been reported in many research articles (Berninger, Abbott, Abbot, Graham, & Richards, 2002; Howard, Ellis, & Rasmussen, 2004; Jatala & Seevers, 2006; Prestia, 2004).

In summary, the practice of universal design includes several valuable concepts that extend beyond physical access, into the realm of thinking and understanding.

1. Universal design relies upon the strategic and innovative use of typical design elements to increase access.

2. Multisensory presentation results in multi-layered access.

3. Products that are universally designed are useful for people with and without disabilities. When made available to everyone, everyone can potentially benefit from their use.

4. Universal design is most effective when included in the initial design phase, rather than as a retrofit.

Universal Design in the Cognitive Environment

The theory of universal design has been expanded to the classroom as **universal design for learning (UDL)**. The Center of Applied Special Technology (CAST) in Wakefield Massachusetts and founded in 1984 developed UDL as a means to expand learning opportunities for people with disabilities. CAST promotes multiple means of representation, expression and **engagement** (2006) as critical elements of UDL and uses technology to accomplish this. The theoretical underpinnings of UDL are described by Rose and Meyer (1998, 2002). These researchers use Positron Emission Topography (PET) scan images that allow researchers to generate maps that detail specific brain areas that are activated as an individual performs particular mental tasks. According to Meyer and Rose (1998), the patterns of activity suggest the presence of three cortical systems, each functionally and anatomically distinct. These systems are the recognition system, the strategic system and the affective system.

In order to design supportive curriculum that enhances learning, curriculum developers must understand these networks in the brain and achieve a solid match between the network they are attempting to support and the curriculum they design. This match provides curricular flexibility (in the manner in which learners approach content, work with the content and acquire new learning) to provide appropriate support and challenge for a typically diverse spectrum of learners.

Another leader in the field, Dr. Dave Edyburn has written and presented extensively in the area of universal design for learning, particularly regarding the provision of strategically developed supplemental materials to facilitate thinking about a concept or subject in order to improve the learner's understanding. Dr. Edyburn also uses technology to create supplemental materials and remove barriers, allowing learners to interact with content despite developmental, cognitive or physical limitations (Edyburn, 2003a, 2005).

These techniques are currently used primarily by special education teachers, with students with disabilities, via an individualized plan as mandated by the Individuals with Disabilities Education and Improvement Act (IDEIA, 2004). However, as students with disabilities are educated in the general education classroom, resources that increase accessibility are coming with them. In turn, general educators are finding that many students benefit and are taking notice. With the passage of the **No Child Left Behind Act** in 2002, educators are now legally accountable for teaching a rigorous curriculum to all students (United States Department of Education, 2003). With this change has come a realization that more attention and effort are required to make curriculum accessible. Through the process of seeking curriculum materials with a wider scope, educators are only recently beginning to use universally designed materials in their mandate to teach every learner and leave no child behind.

In summary, Universal Design for Learning provides curricular flexibility (in activities, in the ways that information is presented, in the ways that students respond or demonstrate knowledge, and in the ways in which students are engaged) to provide appropriate support and challenge for a typically diverse spectrum of learners. The goal of UDL is accomplished when the consideration of usability is prioritized during the *initial* design phase; with careful planning that expands the flexibility of the curriculum material. Early consideration is exemplified when scaffold materials that support portions of the cognitive task are created alongside the traditional materials in order to expand access and opportunities for engagement (Edyburn, 2003a).

Differentiated Instruction

Differentiated instruction is a philosophy about teaching and learning that provides a method of expanding curricular scope in order to "anticipate and respond to students' learning differences" (Tomlinson, 1999, p. 9). Differentiated instruction promotes the concept that instruction should use the individual strengths and preferences of learners to maximize learning. Like universal design for learning, the emphasis of differentiated instruction is to plan for diversity and design instructional materials and methods that utilize the individual nature of the learner to create momentum towards the learning objective (Tomlinson, 1999).

These materials are varied in the degree of abstractness, complexity, open-endedness, problem clarity, and structure they represent (Kierman & Tomlinson, 1997, p. 6).

The principles of differentiated instruction include a series of decisions, made by educators regarding the manipulation of:

1. The content to be learned/input.
2. The process by which information is presented and by which the learner engages with that information/sense-making
3. The product or manner in which the learner uses the information/ output (Peirce & Adams, 2004, p. 59).

These three components could be modified according to the learner's:

1. Readiness level.
2. Learning style.
3. Interest (Orkwis, 1999; Tomlinson, 1999; Tomlinson & McTighe, 2006).

Decision making is crucial to this process and is based upon learner diversity. Planning for differentiation includes a two-step decision-making process. Step one includes a decision regarding which part of a lesson is to be differentiated. This is done by predicting potential barriers that might impede the learning process within the group and then planning which aspect of the lesson can be adjusted to compensate for those barriers. Step two utilizes a finer level of sorting; resulting in the decision about the manner in which the differentiation is to be implemented.

VanSciver (2005) shared this example of differentiation, among elementary students learning how to multiply. One group of students may be able to memorize their multiplication tables and understand the connection between addition and multiplication through conversation with the teacher. A different set of students may need to see how that process works through the use of manipulatives such as groups of checkers that they can physically move around to replicate the process of multiplication.

Tomlinson (2006) writes that educators who subscribe to the philosophy of differentiated instruction hold some common beliefs.

> Students who are the same age differ in their readiness to learn, their interests, their styles of learning, their experiences, and their life circumstances, and, the differences in students are significant enough to make a major impact on what students need to learn, the pace at which they need to learn it, and the support they need from teachers and others to learn it well. (p. 6)

The use of flexible groups is one method for delivering a differentiated learning activity. When grouping is flexible, groups change with the content and the learning activities accommodate a variety of teacher objectives (Peirce & Adams, 2004). This approach capitalizes on the high expectations that educators have for high-performing groups of learners and provides opportunities for educators to scaffold supports for those who struggle. The emphasis in this method is on the word *flexible*. This is the element that distinguishes this use of groups from previously used methods of ability grouping and tracking procedures.

Educators who subscribe to the philosophy of differentiated instruction reframe their thinking about a learner's academic functioning skills as "**readiness**" (Tomlinson, 1999). Readiness is assessed by determining a learner's current knowledge, understanding, and skill as it relates to what is being studied. It varies from learner to learner and within an individual learner; either according to content area, daily attitude, state of health, etc. This flexible way to look at skill sets facilitates more flexible planning because readiness cannot be captured in a static score on an intelligence test (Tomlinson, 1999; Van Garderen & Whittaker, 2006).

One method of differentiating is to use **tiered lessons**. In this type of lesson planning, the educator decides which part of the learning activity will be differentiated (content, process or product) and by what method it will be tiered (readiness, interest of learning style). Learners may be assigned different learning objectives and activities. However, the activities in which they engage reflect a consistent learning path towards those objectives.

The use of a planning pyramid (Schumm, Vaughn, & Harris, 1997) can be a helpful tool for educators when they design tiered lessons. The three-tiered pyramid represents a model for increasing the depth and breadth of planning in a particular content area. Different groups of learners will be held accountable for different content, process or product. For the purposes of explanation, this example of the pyramid will be described as an activity for which the decision has been made to differentiate the content by readiness level. The middle section of the pyramid is the largest and usually includes the learning objectives for lessons that are typically planned for learners whose readiness level can be predicted. This level may contain multiple learning objectives, but does not represent any adjustment. It can be compared to a lesson blueprint and would typically be representative of most traditional lesson plans. Differentiation occurs when the teacher expands this blueprint in both directions. The bottom level of the pyramid characterizes the most basic level of knowledge that is acceptable mastery for this content. In this example in which the decision has been made to differentiate the content of the lesson by readiness level, this tier may be appropriate for learners with cognitive limitations. These learning objectives are less complex and represent a grasp of the main points of the activity. In contrast, the top level of the pyramid describes the learning objectives that are above and beyond the predictable norm. It should be noted that the planning pyramid is not always limited to three levels. Educators may find it necessary to plan instruction on several levels depending on the diversity among their learners.

Universal Design for Learning and Differentiated Instruction

Although differentiated instruction and universal design have not been discussed previously in an integrated manner, they can be viewed as supportive theories with multiple converging concepts (Van Garderen & Whittaker, 2006). Each theory promotes modifications in the manner in which information is taken in by the learner, varied means of interacting with the information, and alternatives for demonstrating that the information has been received by the learner. The theories use similar methodologies to accomplish this flexibility but the most critical characteristic the theories share is the fundamental acknowledgement that all learners are different and bring differences to the experience. Those differences can be used to further the experience itself and are best accommodated during the planning process not after the fact.

The information in Figure 1.3 illustrates the allied nature of these two theories.

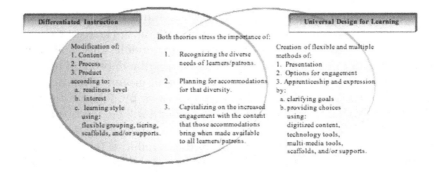

Figure 1.3.   Comparison of Differentiated Instruction and Universal Design for Learning.

 In differentiated instruction and in universal design for learning, the unique interests, skills and background knowledge a learner brings to the experience are critical elements in the planning process.

Figure 1.4.

CHAPTER 2

DESIGNING FOR ACCESSIBILITY

INTRODUCTION

This chapter will describe specific techniques that will increase the accessibility of learning materials. Essentially, the learning process becomes more accessible as the learner is given more options. These options can be delivered at various stages in the process of learning. In order to examine these alternatives, it is helpful to describe the process of learning as consisting of three basic steps:

1. The learner *recognizes* the content through some means of *presentation*.
2. The learner *engages* with the content to connect it to prior knowledge, commits it to memory and makes new connections to it; in other words, processes it.
3. The learner *expresses* the newly learned content to demonstrate mastery, usually through a *product*.

To design curriculum that is more accessible, educators can modify and design supports for any of these steps. Designing options in each of these areas allows learners to use the options that maximize their experience.

 What makes UD so effective and efficient is not the addition of innovative features, but rather the innovative use of elements that are readily available.

Figure 2.1.

Handbook on Developing Curriculum Materials for Teachers:
Lessons From Museum Education Partnerships, pp. 285–354
Copyright © 2010 by Information Age Publishing

This chapter will describe methods for designing supports for each of these stages. The chapter is organized according to these stages and educators may find it helpful to approach stages in a linear fashion.

Figure 2.2.

Conversely, because each section can stand alone as a complete set of strategies, educators may explore sections in the order that corresponds with their current needs. Readers may find one section more pertinent to their present experiences and therefore may wish to concentrate on only those sections that hold promise to a situation at hand.

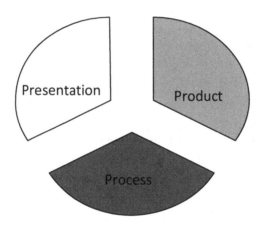

Figure 2.3.

SECTION ONE—PRESENTATION

Multiple means of representation give learners various ways of acquiring information and knowledge. (Center for Applied Special Technology, [CAST], 2006)

- Speech
  - o Advantages of speech
  - o Disadvantages of speech
  - o Increasing the flexibility of speech

- Images
  - Advantages of images
  - Disadvantages of images
  - Increasing the flexibility of images
- Text
  - Advantages of text
  - Disadvantages of text
  - Increasing the flexibility of text
- Combining speech, images and text

In order to learn any new content, the learner must be able to recognize the material. This recognition usually occurs in a teaching environment through the use of traditional media such as speech, text and images. The decision as to which media an educator chooses is often influenced by availability and the personal preference of that educator. Seldom are the inherent communicative strengths and weakness of these media considered in relation to their instructional purpose. Furthermore, educators seldom consider learner characteristics in this decision process. By doing so, educators can take advantage of learner preferences and strengths as well as support learner weaknesses.

Traditional instructional media and materials are rather inflexible, thus not well suited for differentiation, and educators who wish to provide alternatives are required to search out and/or create supplemental materials. However, computer-assisted media offer a wider range of presentation methods and make multiple means possible. Also, by planning for multiple means of presentation at the onset of the curriculum development process, several media versions of the content can be developed early on (Rose & Meyer, 2002).

Content that is presented in multiple media expands its accessibility to individual learners. Traditional media (speech, text and images), all offer both advantages and disadvantages as means of presentation. Used alone, the learner is subject to the limitations of each. However, used together the learner has choice. This choice translates into increased methods for acquiring the content, and represents a powerful method of differentiating content by readiness level, learning style and/or interest.

 Many learners will benefit from combinations of presentation methods and others will choose the media that best fits their learning style, preference, or that compensates for their limitations.

Figure 2.4.

SPEECH

Consider the use of speech, live or recorded, as a means to deliver content. While many learners find listening to content a satisfying experience, others may have difficulty gaining meaning from listening. An examination of the advantage and disadvantages of speech will indicate options to enhance the accessibility of content delivered through speech.

Advantages of Speech

The intonation, pace, volume and pitch of the human voice allow educators to express meaning beyond what words can convey. Live speech holds an additional advantage; that of nonverbal expression and gesture that enhances the communicative power of the words. Many learners who find text difficult for one reason or another will benefit from hearing content.

Disadvantages of Speech

Speech is time and memory dependant. The physical mechanism of hearing sound and the neurological process of making meaning from that sound is limited by the presence of the stimulation. As sound waves are produced, they must be detected and processed in order and within a set timeframe before the next set of sounds is produced. The listener must remember meaning as it is decoded and string multiple meaning strands together in order to understand sentences, then concepts. This means that the delivery and the listener must be matched in speed, volume, pitch, clarity and cognitive level.

Consider the alignment of these factors that are necessary for learning to occur and the loss of access if just one element is mismatched. A simple example is the volume with which a lecture is delivered. Individuals vary greatly in their ability to detect sound at various volumes. This variability may be the result of developmental, neurological or age factors. If the speaker does not produce enough volume, listeners may have difficulty hearing and therefore, will be unable to access the content. Likewise, the level of sophistication in vocabulary choice between the speaker and the listener may not match. If unknown words are used, the cognitive process of making meaning from sound will be hampered, thus impacting the learner's cognition. Typically, this match is achieved through a series of assumptions, any of which can be the wrong assumption. The result is a mismatch between speaker and learner (Rose & Meyer, 2002).

Increasing the Flexibility of Speech

Educators would be well served to plan ahead and to build in flexible means of using speech. The more flexible the presentation, the more matches possible. The following list represents techniques for building in flexibility, and thereby increasing accessibility:

1. Use digital speech that can be manipulated for rate, pitch and volume.
2. Use digital translators that can present material in different languages.
3. Use recordings that offer the listener the option to replay content.
4. Pair speech with text, images and touch.
5. Add vocabulary supports.
6. Add cognitive supports and scaffolds to provide frameworks on which the listener can recognize prior knowledge and build meaning for new learning.

PUTTING THESE TECHNIQUES TO WORK

Text to speech readers translate digital text to spoken language. Text must be available in digital form in order for it to be recognized. In general, if text on the computer can be highlighted on the screen, it is digital text. Much information on the Internet is presented in **Portable Document Format (PDF)** that must be read with the Adobe Acrobat computer software. This text is not digital, but rather is an image of text, much like a scanned picture of a printed page. In order to use this type of text it must be converted to digital media. There are software tools available to accomplish this conversion.

Digital speech is available from a variety of sources on the Internet. Several software companies offer free downloads. Explore the following sites to experiment with various tools or conduct an Internet keyword search for "speech to text" or "text readers."

 PDF Text Reader 1.1 from CTdeveloping at *www.ctdeveloping.com*. This free download allows you to open a PDF file in the reader window. This process converts the text to a digital image that can be edited, manipulated and/or moved to another word processing application or to a text reader. The free download is subject to personal use only. An educator and professional version are available for purchase.

Figure 2.5.

NaturalReader at *www.naturalreaders.com* allows a computer to convert text to audio files such as MP3 or WAV (to be played on a CD player or iPod) from text files, MS Word files, MS Internet Explorer webpages, Adobe PDF files and email. The user can adjust speed, voice, quality, volume, zoom size, font and background color. The reader is available in male and female voices in 5 languages. The website offers a free download, or the opportunity to purchase a package for as little as $39.99.

Figure 2.6.

ReadPlease at *www.readplease.com* opens a window on the desktop into which text is copied and pasted. Users can customize font and background color, use the low vision color option, and adjust voice choice and speed. The control buttons are easy to use so this tool works well when readers need to start and stop frequently (as in listening to test questions and choosing an answer or in listening to the reader read a printed worksheet). The reader also reads email **emotiocons** such as ☺ or ☻. The reader includes seven languages and highlights text as it is read. It requires digital text so PDF files are not readable. The free download is a 30 day trial.

Figure 2.7.

Examples of Materials With Modified Speech Components

This set of examples supplements a high school social studies lesson plan on the Buffalo Soldiers written for the NLB eMuseum. The original lesson plan contained a lecture to be given by the teacher, followed by several comprehension activities. The lecture was converted to an article by typing it into a word processing program. The original 877 word lecture was written at a twelfth grade reading level (Chandler, 2006a). Readability statistics were provided using Microsoft Word (see Figure 2.8 next page). The article was then rewritten to a lower reading level. This allowed multimedia presentation by producing digital text that could be read by a computer or a person. Additional punctuation was added to facilitate the smooth presentation by a text reading software program. The learner could access the information prior to the lecture, thereby activating prior knowledge and building a framework on which to anchor new learning. The reading difficulty level of the modified version and the summarized modified version are shown in Figures 2.11 and 2.13. (See also Figure 2.9 next page.)

Brief History of Buffalo Soldiers and Baseball
Excerpt for Original Lecture (877 words, 12.0 Grade Reading Level)

The History of the 9th and 10th Cavalry in the 24th and 25th Infantry Division and how these units came to be: "In 1866, Congress passed the legislation establishing two all-black cavalry and four all-black infantry regiments, each consisting of about 1,000 men. — The Cavalry units commanded by white officers were moved out west of the Mississippi River, mostly to fight renegade Indians. Because of their skills and reputation, the black soldiers consistently received some of the most dangerous and difficult assignments the Army had to offer.

"According to legend, the Cheyenne and Comanche tribes called the troops Buffalo Soldiers because their fighting spirit reminded them of the Buffalo."

These Buffalo soldiers would be involved in many fights and receive much credit for their valor in action against the Indian tribes of the west and fight in the Philippines and Cuba for Teddy Roosevelt in the Spanish-American War. They would see action and be stationed throughout Colorado, Utah, New Mexico, Texas, Oklahoma, Arizona, Hawaii, Philippines and Cuba. The 25th Infantry Regiment was stationed away from the action for a time in Washington State.

Using the readability statistics feature of Microsoft Word, the digital text can be analyzed for reading difficulty. The feature provides word count, sentence length and grade level. It should be noted that the highest difficulty level represented by the Flesch-Kincaid Grade scale is 12.0 or twelfth grade. Passages that are written at a higher difficulty level will also be displayed at a 12.0 readability level. Figure 8 displays a screen shot of the readability level for the original lecture used in the Buffalo Soldier lesson plan.

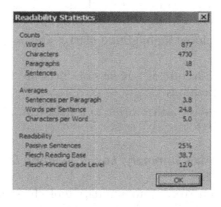

Figure 2.8.   Original lecture and the readability statistics for the original lecture on the history of the Buffalo Soldiers.

Warning: Text readers do not breathe, therefore the software will not pause between words. To add some inflection and natural pauses, type in commas and extra periods. This is especially important after headings.

Figure 2.9.

Example #1: Digital Text, Lower Reading Level, and Vocabulary Supports

In this example, the lecture was converted to a digital text version by typing it into a word processing program. The lecture was rewritten at the eighth grade reading level. Additionally, added vocabulary supports have been inserted in the text. These are displayed in underlined font. The vocabulary words are displayed in bold and the definitions in italic font. These cues alert the learner that this text is meant to support certain vocabulary words in the article. Additional commas have been inserted between the vocabulary words to act as a signal to the text reader software. Text to speech software will read these cues with a slight pause before and after the words, thus slightly setting them apart. Readability statistics have been provided using Microsoft Word. Notice that the number of words in the text has been reduced to 405 words and that the length of both the paragraphs and the sentences is considerably reduced.

The article could be used in any of the following ways to support diverse learners:

1. Read prior to the lecture to provide background information.
2. Used during the lecture to provide a visual map for the learner while the lecture is being delivered using speech.
3. Used with a colored highlighting marker as a note taking tool during the lecture.
4. Read after the lecture as a review or "firm up" activity to provide additional repetitions.
5. Used as a pre-visit article prior to a field trip. (See Figures 2.10a and 2.11b.)

Example #2: Executive Summary, Lower Reading Level, and Vocabulary Supports

Using the Microsoft Word AutoSummary tool, the same lecture article was also reduced to a shorter version. The software application creates an abstract of the article by sifting the content. The user can choose how much sifting the tool applies. One powerful, interactive feature of this software application is that it also includes a slider on the screen that can be manipulated by the learner as the document is displayed. This allows for exceptional accessibility because the learner can choose the depth and breadth of the content at the moment It is being presented. Educators can also create print copies in various versions to increase the options learners may choose from.

This example uses 50% of the material, and by doing so the software application boils down the critical elements for learners who may not

---

Brief History of Buffalo Soldiers and Baseball
Full Article, Alternate Reading Level (621 words - 8.0 GE)

Black soldiers.
In 1866, Congress, *the United States government*, passed the law creating **military regiments**, *or units*, made up of only Black soldiers. There were two units that fought on horseback. These units were called the cavalry units. There were another four that fought on foot. They were called infantry regiments. Each of these fighting units had about 1,000 Black men in them.

The **cavalry units**, *or those who used horses*, were led by White officers. The army sent them west to fight the Indians. They were good fighters. Because of this, they were given the most difficult **assignments**, *or jobs*. The Indians called these troops Buffalo Soldiers because their fighting spirit reminded them of buffalo. These Buffalo Soldiers won many fights against the Indians. They were famous for their bravery.

Soldiers and baseball.
When these soldiers were not fighting there was time to play. Baseball was the choice during the summer months. Black soldiers played against White soldiers. Sometimes Black soldiers played against the White people who lived near their forts.

Many people came to watch the games at Fort Douglas, in **Utah**, *a state in the western United States*. This team was called the Colored Monarchs. Players became famous. James Flowers was one of the many Black soldiers that played baseball during their time in the military.

Buffalo Soldiers played baseball at Fort Ethan Allen in **Vermont**, *a state in the northeastern United States*. The games were played on Sunday. That is, until a minister from the town complained. He said the games created a bad environment for the town's young people. The Fort's **commander**, *or leader*, argued that this was not the case but the Army stopped the baseball games between soldiers and people who lived in town. This decision forced the Buffalo Soldier to play games only against other soldiers.

On October 5, 1909, 900 men of the U.S. Army's 25th Infantry Regiment were transferred to Fort Lawton in **Washington State**, *in the north western most part of the United States*. They were famous for their baseball team. They won the US Army championship and were rated the best **amateur**, team in the county, *meaning they were not paid to play*. In the Army, Black soldiers played against White soldiers. Some

---

Figure 2.10a.   Lecture rewritten at a lower readability level.

good boxers. Sometimes fights broke out between Black and White players over a bad call by the **umpires,** *or person whose job it is to make sure the game is played by the rules*. Sometimes boxing matches were arranged between units.

Conclusion: It is clear that Buffalo Soldiers made a big impact in the U.S. Army. They also gained favor in the world of baseball. Baseball was changing from a pastime into a major athletic event (Chandler, 2006a).

Example #1: Modified Text

Readability Statistics ? X

Counts
Words   405
Characters   2020
Paragraphs   9
Sentences   40

Averages
Sentences per Paragraph   5.0
Words per Sentence   9.8
Characters per Word   4.8

Readability
Passive Sentences   22%
Flesch Reading Ease   55.4
Flesch-Kincaid Grade Level   7.9

OK

Figure 2.10b.

have the cognitive ability to benefit from the full detail. Notice that the number of words in the text has been reduced to 205 words and that the length of both the paragraphs and the sentences is considerably reduced. The vocabulary supports follow the same concept as above; however, in this example the word and cue are highlighted in gray.

A Brief History of Buffalo Soldiers and Baseball
Executive Summary (50%)
Alternate Reading Level (209 words – 8.4 GE)

Black soldiers.
In 1866, Congress, the United States government, passed the law creating military regiments, or units, made up of only Black soldiers. There were two cavalry units, because they used horses. The army sent them west to fight the Indians. The Indians called these troops Buffalo Soldiers because their fighting spirit reminded them of buffalo. These Buffalo soldiers won many fights against the Indians.

When these soldiers were not fighting there was time to play. Black soldiers played against White soldiers. Sometimes Black soldiers played against the White people who lived near their forts.

One team was called the Colored Monarchs. Players became famous. Buffalo Soldiers played baseball at Fort Ethan Allen in Vermont, a northeastern state. The games were played on Sunday but a local minister complained. He said the games were a bad influence on the young people. The Fort's commander, or leader, argued that this was not the case. The Army stopped the baseball games between soldiers and people who lived in town anyway. This decision forced the Buffalo Soldier to play games only against other soldiers.

Example #2 Auto Summary
of Modified Text

Readability Statistics	⊠
Counts	
Words	205
Characters	1076
Paragraphs	7
Sentences	19
Averages	
Sentences per Paragraph	3.8
Words per Sentence	10.0
Characters per Word	5.1
Readability	
Passive Sentences	15%
Flesch Reading Ease	51.9
Flesch-Kincaid Grade Level	8.4
	OK

Figure 2.11. Executive summary and readability statistics of simplified articles.

Microsoft Word contains a handy tool called AutoSummary. It can be found under the Tools menu. This feature condenses digital text into summaries or highlights key points. The feature also contains a toggle bar that allows the user to choose how much material is included. Once text is highlighted, the tool allows the user to display the entire document with highlights, just a summary of the highlighted text as a separate document, or a summary shown at the top of the original document.

Figure 2.12.

Example #3: Vocabulary Supports

In this excerpt from the lecture/article, vocabulary supports have been added using Microsoft Word. Using the markup menu, the educator can insert a written comment or a recorded sound comment. The comments can be made visible or invisible by selecting the view markup option. This technique allows some learners to read unimpeded, while others who need the additional supports can see and/or hear them. By clicking on the speaker icon in the third comment, the learner can hear a recorded comment.

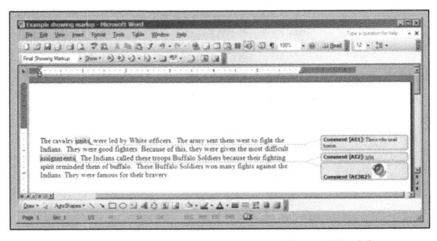

Figure 2.13.   Screen shot of a lecture presented as a Microsoft Word document Vocabulary supports are inserted as written comments and as sound recordings.

Example #4: Using ReadPlease

When copied and pasted into the ReadPlease window, the text appears as illustrated in Figure 2.16. Learners have the ability to change the voice, the speed of the voice, and the font size using tools on the window. Words are highlighted in yellow as they are read. ReadPlease does not read parenthesis, so they could be used to set apart vocabulary supports when this software is being used. Other text to speech readers read the parenthesis symbols, which may confuse learners. In that event, other methods described above would be more helpful.

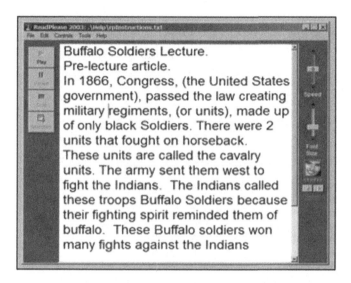

Figure 2.14.   Screen shot of a lecture presented as digital text, then pasted into the ReadPlease text reader software application.

Example #5: Supported Note-Taking Tool

A supported note-taking tool, created by an educator, can accompany the lecture on the Buffalo Soldiers. This handout supplies the learner with a scaffold in that it provides cues and supports to assist in organizing the material. It uses the task of physically recording information to encode what is being presented. Although a simple accommodation, this type of tool can make lecture format lessons more accessible to learners with **cognitive processing delays**, attention difficulties, memory limitations, cognitive disabilities, handwriting limitations, and deficits in organization and **executive functioning**. This type of tool is helpful as a post-visit supplement. (See Figure 2.15 next page.)

Example #6: Graphic Organizer

Graphic Organizers allow learners to build knowledge in a visual way. This supports the auditory processing that occurs while listening and reduces some of the **cognitive load** to sort material as it is initially encountered. There are many graphic organizers that vary from simple to complex. Educators will choose a design that supports the sophistication

---

A Brief History of Buffalo Soldiers and Baseball

Listen to the lecture and fill in the blanks.

History

1.   When did Congress pass laws that started black fighting groups? (year)_____.
2.   There were (how many) _____ cavalry units and (how many) _____ infantry groups?
3.   All together there were about (how many) _____ black soldiers in these groups.
4.   The officers in the cavalry units were (black/white)_____.
5.   They were sent to fight (Indians/the Spanish)_____ in the west.
6.   They (lost/won) _____ most of their fights.
7.   They were called Buffalo Soldiers by the (white officers/Indians) _____ because they were so brave.

Soldiers and baseball

8.   Black soldiers played baseball against (white soldiers/Indians)_____.
9.   Sometimes they played against (people they fought against/people who lived near the forts)_____.
10. The team's name from Fort Douglas, Utah was (The Cubs/The Colored Monarchs) _____.
11. One of the famous players was James (Smith/Flowers) _____.
12. In (what state?) _____, games were played on Sunday.
13. The games were stopped because the local minister thought they were (too competitive/a bad influence) _____.
14. After that, soldiers could only play baseball against (other soldiers/Indians) _____.
15. In 1909, the best amateur baseball team was the Army's 25th Infantry Regiment from Fort (Carson/Lawton) _____ in Washington State.
16. On this baseball team, black soldiers played against (white soldiers/townspeople) _____, and sometimes fights broke out.
17. The Buffalo Soldiers (won/lost)_____most of their games.
18. The Buffalo Soldiers influenced (the U.S. Army/the Spanish) _____ and the game of _____.

Figure 2.15.   Supported note-taking tool for a lecture on Negro Leagues history.

level of the framework they wish to provide for learners. This example represents a simplistic organizer. It could be used:

1. As a note taking tool during the lecture.
2. If completed by the educator prior to the lesson, as a pre-teaching tool.
3. As a "firm up" review activity.

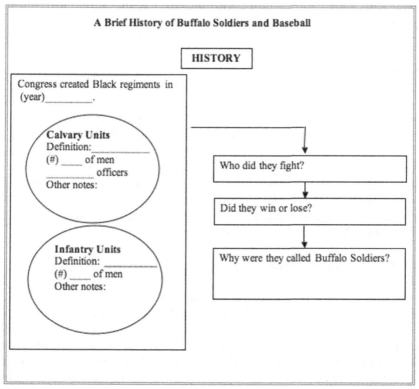

A Brief History of Buffalo Soldiers and Baseball

HISTORY

Congress created Black regiments in (year)_____.

Calvary Units
Definition:_____
(#)_____ of men
_____ officers
Other notes:

Infantry Units
Definition: _____
(#)_____ of men
Other notes:

Who did they fight?

Did they win or lose?

Why were they called Buffalo Soldiers?

Figure 2.16.   Graphic organizer for a lecture on Negro Leagues history.

IMAGES

Still images have long been staples in the presentation of content. Pictures, diagrams, charts and graphs all serve to convey meaning in highly engaging ways. However, the role of still images diminishes in the learning environment as learners grow from childhood to young adults. Picture books are prevalent means of transmitting knowledge for young learners, but the size and quantity of images are sacrificed for printed text in educational curriculum designed for older learners. Although this phenomenon is true in educational materials, it is not the case in curriculum designed for more aesthetic purposes. Coffee table books of photography, recipe books filled with colorful pictures and other artistic images are plentiful in environments other than the classroom. Still images are regularly used in museum galleries and materials.

Media has produced the moving images of video, movies and computer graphics. These mediums offer a wider range of sensory material by combining sound and pictures, and thus are gaining importance in the learning environment.

Advantages of Images

One advantage of still images is that they communicate all content at the same time. When the learner looks at a picture, there is no pre-set sequence that dictates order or pace as meaning is delivered. Additionally, no decoding is necessary because images convey information literally; therefore, images are not as dependant upon a cognitive match with the learner. Images also have the ability to convey emotion and feeling more directly than text. They can be used to simplify complex information such as a diagram or graph. Images also increase the likelihood that material will be remembered longer.

Disadvantages of Images

Images can be difficult for some learners to interpret because they rely on practice and training. An example of this limitation is that learners must be educated on how to read a bar graph or a scatter gram in order to understand the information it represents. Images may be highly culturally dependant, and thus prone to misinterpretation by members of other cultures. Finally, images may not be able to convey information that is highly abstract or conceptual, but rather are better suited to surface level knowledge (Rose & Meyer, 2002).

Increasing the Flexibility of Images

The limitations and uses of images should be considered when designing learning materials. Educators who plan and choose images as integral methods of content delivery will enhance the richness of their curriculum. The following list represents techniques for building in flexibility and thereby increasing accessibility:

1. Design multiple images that convey information in different ways to provide learners with options that match their interpretative skill level.

2. Provide multiple images that convey the same content to deepen the meaning through repetition and multiple representations.

3. Use still images alongside and inside text to reinforce portions of the content.

4. Use moving images such as movies and video to demonstrate fluid concepts, convey abstract and emotional content.

5. Combine images with speech to transmit information through multiple sensory channels.

 American Memory from the United States Library of Congress at *http://memory.loc.gov/ammem/index.htm.* This site houses photographs and songs in a searchable format. There are collections on topics from Washington to Houdini.

Figure 2.17.

PUTTING THESE TECHNIQUES TO WORK

Example #7: Text Alone vs. Text With an Image

Consider the difference between a text paragraph describing an object and the additional information that is added when an image is included. Here is a simple example.

Text Alone
The Desktop is the screen background on the monitor on which windows, icons, and dialog boxes appear. A window will open on top of this background, somewhere on the desktop. The taskbar is a narrow strip of information at the bottom of the screen that contains icons representing any open applications or documents. The start menu will open from the bottom left corner of the screen and expand upwards to display application icons on a menu.

Figure 2.18.   Example of text alone.

Text With an Image
The Desktop is the screen background on the monitor and appears as blue on the diagram below. A window will open on top of this background. The window that is open below displays the contents of My Computer. The taskbar is visible at the bottom of the screen and contains icons representing software applications that are open at the moment. The start menu can be found in the bottom left and contains a menu of programs the user may open for use.

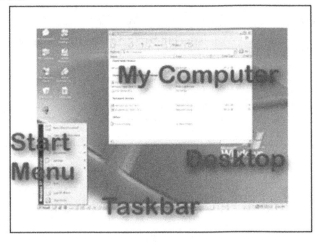

Figure 2.19.   Example of text with an image.

Text With a Movie Clip

Consider the following example of an interview with Negro Leagues player Harold Gould as he discusses the impact of segregation on players on the road. Although the reader can detect some of the emotion and nuances of his speech patterns by reading the text, the lesson becomes much richer with the addition of a short movie clip of the interview. This adds facial expression, intonation, speed and gestures to the presentation (see Figure 2.20 next page).

Example #8: Graphic Organizers and Concept Maps

Graphic organizers or concept maps are a very powerful support tool for diverse learners. A graphic organizer is a visual representations of information used for constructing meaning in reading, writing, and/or speaking. A graphic organizer can be developed quickly along with the initial

**Harold Gould talks about the impact of segregation
and the hardships of life on the road.**

In an interview at the Negro Leagues Baseball Museum, Harold recounts:

No, no, no hotel. You stop someplace, and Goose was great for that. He would say, "Well, two of you can go over Miss Mouldry's." and "Olla Brown's can put one of ya up." And there are shacks all around town, one house or another. And couldn't even use the bathrooms there. Couldn't wash up. You were dirty as a pig. I mean dirty. I mean dirty. Stinkin'. And that's the way it was. And most of the ball parks, the white ball parks in the South; you could not change no clothes in there. You can't change no, you just can't go in there. Don't go in there. One place down south we needed gas. Gas was very cheap then. We stopped and the boys wanted to relieve themselves, started going to the bathroom.

"You guys can't go in there."

"What do you mean don't go in there?"

"You can't go in there."

"Well, stop the gas. We ain't buying no more gas from ya."

"Well, wait a minute, just one of you go at a time."

We kept on pumping the gas, but only one could go at a time. But he didn't want to lose that sale cause it were gonna pump maybe twenty thirty gallons. That's how they were down there.

But most places down there, like in Atlanta, where ya think we played with Atlanta Crackers Ballpark you couldn't use the bathroom, couldn't go in the shower, couldn't change in there. Had to go out in people's houses to change our clothes. This was all over. All over the South. I mean all over. And then the stands would have White Ladies, Colored Women, you hear me? White Ladies, colored women. Then they'd have white men, colored men.

*Harold Gould talks about the impact
of segregation and the hardships
of life on the road*

Movie clip using Real Player software.

Figure 2.20.   Screen shot of movie clip of Negro Leagues player Harold Gould. Oral histories of Negro Leagues players can be found on the NLB eMuseum site, linked to the Negro Leagues Baseball Museum cite at: http://www.nlbm.com.

presentation material. Using the versatility of the computer, graphic organizers be customized for individual learners or groups of learners. Also,
multiple versions of the same graphic organizer can be created.

1. A graphic organizer can be used in any of the following ways: filled
    in can provide a cognitive framework to organize information for
    the educator, and the learner. This type of organizer can be used:

    (a) Before the learning experience as an introductory exercise
         to develop background knowledge.
    (b) During the learning experience as a modified note taking
         tool.
    (c) After the learning experience as a review or study guide.

2. An organizer with information partially filled in can provide cogni-
    tive prompts and structure for learners to organize new material.
    This type of organizer can be provided in different versions, with
    varying amounts of information provided. These can be used:

    (d) During the learning experience as a note taking tool.
    (e) After the learning experience as an assessment activity.
    (f) After the learning experience as a review or study guide.

SmartDraw from *http://smartdraw.com/*. This software contains many
templates for mind maps, organizational charts, task charts, flyers,
calendars, timelines, floor plans, etc. Templates and auto fill features allow
quick design of graphic organizers that can be saved as Microsoft Word,
Excel or PowerPoint, or Adobe PDF files. The website offers a free seven
day trial that seems fully functional, but places a watermark on the finished
product.

Figure 2.21.

Inspiration from *http://www.inspiration.com/freetrial/index.cfm*. This
software contains pictures, text and spoken words to be used in the creation
of graphic organizers. There are three versions available: Inspiration is
designed for learners ages 11 and older, Kidspiration for learners ages five
to ten years and InspireData is designed for learners ages nine and up to
interpret data by drawing conclusions and solving problems. The company
offers a free trial download

Figure 2.22.

Figures 2.23, 2.24, and 2.25 are three versions of the same graphic organizer. Using SmartDraw, the foundational graphic organizer was developed, saved into Microsoft Word, and then copied and modified twice as two separate files. In each of these versions, data was removed to leave only prompts. These three versions can be used in any of the ways described above. When paired with written text or speech, they become even more powerful. Learners with diverse reading, vision, and cognitive skills will benefit from seeing information in a visual format from having part of the cognitive framework presented for them and from different levels of prompting provided as they fill in new information. These

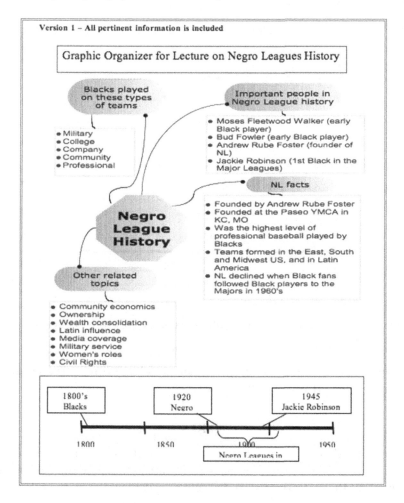

Figure 2.23.   Completed graphic organizer for the Brief History of the Negro Leagues.

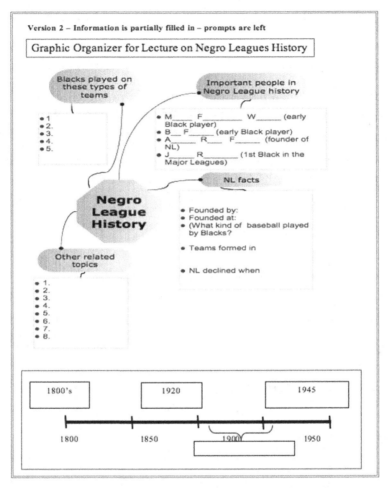

Figure 2.24.   Partially completed graphic organizer for the Brief History of the Negro Leagues.

graphic organizers support a curriculum developed on Negro Leagues History for the NLB eMuseum (Doswell, 2006a).

TEXT

There is no doubt that printed text is a central method for presenting content. Text is often used exclusively in instructional settings with the assumption that material that is printed is available to be learned. Educators may relegate other mediums to supplemental status because text is such a powerful medium.

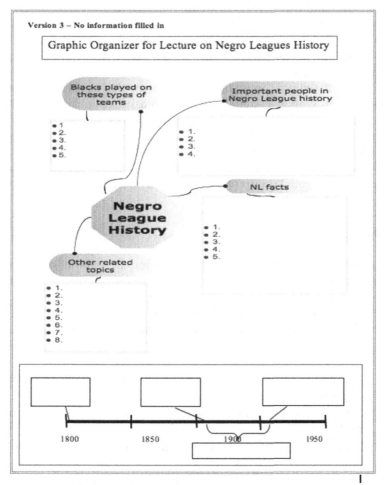

Figure 2.25.   Blank graphic organizer for the Brief History of the Negro Leagues.

Advantages of Text

Text provides a static representation of content with the ability to be present despite the limitations of time and place. This characteristic of being ever-present allows text to overcome the transient nature of speech. Text reduces the memory demands of speech by providing a lasting record.

Disadvantages of Text

One of the significant limitations of text is that it lacks the inherent expressiveness of speech. The reader is left to supply the emotive qualities on their own and this process is highly sensitive to individual differences that may produce content that is very different than was intended by the writer (Rose & Meyer, 2002). Another limitation of printed presentation material is that meaning can only be derived from reading the text. Learners vary greatly in their ability to decode and comprehend text. Thus, content delivery must be matched with the learners' skill level. Although tools such as readability scales can assist educators as they produce textual content, the print becomes a "one size fits all" delivery system and thus does not likely match a widely diverse group of learners. Obviously, the ability to gain knowledge from text is dependent upon the reader having the sensory ability to see the print. Again, this factor excludes the potential group of users who may have limited sight.

Increasing the Flexibility of Text

Because text is such a powerful tool to impart knowledge, strategic attention to the cognitive match between material and learner is critical. In order to plan for diversity among learners, educators should design curriculum materials that provide flexible text. The following list represents techniques for building in flexibility and thereby increasing accessibility:

1. Use digital text that can be manipulated by the reader in terms of size and contrast.
2. Combine speech and text together to double the sensory channels used by the learner.
3. Combine images with the text to deliver content that is not print-dependant.
4. Use icons to create picture-enhanced reading materials.
5. Write multiple versions of textual content, at varying readability levels.
6. Provide the same content using video and/or still photographs.
7. Use the Microsoft Word Auto Summary tool to highlight key points, and to create executive summaries.

It is evident that several of the methods listed above simply alter the method in which text is presented and others actually change the content of the material. This technique is described by Dr. Dave Edyburn as **cognitive rescaling** (Edyburn, 2004a). Edyburn advocates the use of technology tools to modify the difficulty of the cognitive processes needed to process content. Several of his strategies for cognitive rescaling include the use of the Auto Summary tool in Microsoft Word and the use of icons to insert pictures into reading materials. These strategies are exemplified next.

PUTTING THESE TECHNIQUES TO WORK

Some of the techniques discussed in this section also appear in the section above that deals with speech. Because the option of using text to speech readers to translate digital text to spoken language is such a powerful support, it is helpful to explore that technique here as well.

 Combining text and speech to provide multisensory inputs is a powerful support for many learners. Digital text facilitates this option.

Figure 2.26.

Text must be available in digital form in order for it to be recognized. In general, if text on the computer can be highlighted on the screen, it is digital text. Much information on the Internet is presented in **Portable Document Format (PDF)** that must be read with the Adobe Acrobat computer software. This text is not digital, but rather is an image of text much like a scanned picture of a printed page. In order to use this type of text it must be converted to digital media. There are also software tools available to accomplish this.

Digital speech is available from a variety of sources on the Internet. Several software companies offer free downloads. Explore the following sites to experiment with various tool or conduct an Internet keyword search for "speech to text" or "text readers."

 PDF Text Reader 1.1 from CTdeveloping at *www.ctdeveloping.com*. This free download allows one to open a PDF file in the reader window. This process converts the text to a digital image that can be edited, manipulated and/or moved to another word processing application or to a text reader. The free download is subject to personal use only. An educator and professional version are available for purchase.

Figure 2.27.

NaturalReader at *www.naruralreaders.com* allows a computer to convert text to audio files such as MP3 or WAV (to be played on a CD player or iPod) from text files, MS Word files, MS Internet Explorer webpages, Adobe PDF files and email. The user can adjust speed, voice, quality, volume, zoom size, font and background color. The reader is available in male and female voices in five languages. The website offers a free download or the opportunity to purchase a package for as little as $39.99.

Figure 2.28.

 ReadPlease at *www.readplease.com* opens a window on the desktop into which text is copied and pasted. Users can customize font and background color, use the low vision color option, and adjust voice choice and speed. The control buttons are easy to use so this tool works well when readers need to start and stop frequently (as in listening to test questions and choosing an answer or in listening to the reader read a printed worksheet). The reader also reads email **emotiocons** such as ☺ or ☻. The reader includes seven languages and highlights text as it is read. It required digital text so PDF files are not readable. The free download is a 30-day trial.

Figure 2.29.

Example #9: Modifying Font

A simple support such as providing print materials in large and/or bold font can prove very useful to many diverse learners. There are several individual reasons a learner may choose a larger/bolder print. Obviously, learners with different vision capabilities such as poor acuity, eye strain, color blindness or partial vision may benefit, but others may find larger/bolder font helpful when in low light environments or when fatigue is a factor. The mere fact that larger font limits the amount of information per page can be a helpful "chunking" technique, that of breaking information into smaller, more manageable sections. Chunking assists learners who may experience limited attention or vitality, differences in cognitive functioning and in motivation.

The following excerpt is from curriculum written for the NLB eMuseum (Doswell, 2006a). Changing the font size and style allows the educator and the learner to encounter the text differently.

> **Version 1 - Original text**
> African-Americans began to engage the game of baseball in the mid to late 1800s. They played on military teams, college teams, and company teams. They eventually found their way to professional teams with white players. Moses Fleetwood Walker and Bud Fowler

Figure 2.30.   Original text from a lecture on Negro Leagues History.

> **Version 2 - Larger font, stretched out**
> African-Americans began to engage the game of baseball in the mid to late 1800s. They played on military teams, college teams, and company teams. They eventually found their way to professional teams with white players. Moses Fleetwood Walker and Bud Fowler were among the first to participate. However, racism and "Jim Crow" laws would force them from these teams by 1900. Thus, black players formed their own units, "barnstorming" around the country to play anyone who would challenge them.

Figure 2.31.   Modified text from a lecture on Negro Leagues History. Text is enlarged and spread out.

Some learners experience black text on a white background as problematic. By making the text digital and placing it in a text box, the size and style can be modified and background and font colors can be changed by individual learners to meet their needs (see Figure 2.32 next page). Accessibility would be enhanced even more if these techniques were employed in a digital interactive environment such as on a computer screen. Learners could choose the text size, style and colors that best met their needs. This would represent universal design for learning at its best.

Version 3 – Digital text in a text box

African-Americans began to engage the game of baseball in the mid to late 1800s. They played on military teams, college teams, and company teams. They eventually found their way to professional teams with white players. Moses Fleetwood Walker and Bud Fowler were among the first to participate. However, racism and "Jim Crow" laws would force them from these teams by 1900. Thus, black players formed their own units, "barnstorming" around the country to play anyone who would challenge them.

African-Americans began to engage the game of baseball in the mid to late 1800s. They played on military teams, college teams, and company teams. They eventually found their way to professional teams with white players. Moses Fleetwood Walker and Bud Fowler were among the first to participate. However, racism and "Jim Crow" laws would force them from these teams by 1900. Thus, black players formed their own units, "barnstorming" around the country to play anyone who would challenge them.

Figure 2.32.   Example of modified text using different font and background colors for a lecture on Negro Leagues History.

Example #10: Digital Highlighting

This paragraph was taken from a lesson plan on women and the Negro Leagues for the NLB eMuseum (Chandler, 2006b). It was designed to be an article read before the lesson. Using Microsoft Word Auto Summary tool, the most important 50% of the content has been highlighted (Edyburn, 2004a). This tool allows either the educator or the learner to manipulate the amount of content to be marked by highlighting, thus providing a great deal of flexibility.

Pre-Reading Article
Grade level 8.2

This lesson is about how women were involved with Negro Leagues Baseball. There are three ways they were involved:
1.   As coaches and managers.
2.   As players.
3.   As wives of players.

Part One: Coaches and managers
   In 1935, Abe Manley started a Negro Leagues Baseball team named the Newark Eagles. His wife Effa Manley, was the manager of the team. She was a tough manager and she said the team was successful because the players were good. Effa Manley's father was Black, and her mother was White. Her skin was light, and even though she could have pretended to be White, she chose to be Black. She was pretty and smart. She fought for the rights of Blacks. She met her husband, Abe, at the 1932 World Series. He was a rich man who was involved in illegal business activities.
   Effa managed the team, called plays and decided who played what position. She went on the road with them and was respected by the players. When the White professional baseball Leagues began signing Black players, Effa's teams were next. She lost three of her players to the major Leagues. She was the only woman to manage a professional baseball team in the history of baseball.

Figure 2.33.   Modified text using the highlighting tool on Microsoft Word.

Example #11: Executive Summaries

   Microsoft Word Auto Summary also allows educators to cut out a percentage of highlighted text and create a summary. This example consists of the 50% highlighted material from the same article, only presented in a shorten version.

Pre-Reading Article
Grade level 8.2

This lesson is about how women were involved with Negro Leagues Baseball:
1. As coaches and managers.
2. As players.
3. As wives of players.

Part One: Coaches and managers
   In 1935, Abe Manley started a Negro Leagues Baseball team named the Newark Eagles. His wife Effa Manley was the manager of the team. Effa Manley's father was Black and her mother was White. Effa managed the team, called plays and decided who played what position. When the White professional baseball Leagues began signing Black players, Effa's teams were next. Effa ran the team for 3 years and was the first woman to own a Negro Leagues team.

Figure 2.34.   Modified text using the executive summary tool on Microsoft Word.

Combining Speech, Images and Text

When educators provide information in multiple formats, potential barriers are removed. As curriculum is developed, early in the planning stage, educators with a mind toward expanded access will create additional versions of the content to be presented. This process may be time consuming and expensive with traditional materials such as print, taped material and/or books. However, the increased use of digital technologies to store and present information has expanded the scope of options open to educators. Digital files have the capacity to combine and transform text, speech and images to create a more diversified set of options. The following list contains several examples of digital methods for combining media presentation:

1. Talking books.
2. American Sign Language (ASL) tracks.
3. Descriptive videos.
4. Text reading software.

PUTTING THESE TECHNIQUES TO WORK

Another cognitive rescaling strategy is the presentation of text that has been enhanced by **icons** (Edyburn, 2004a). The addition of small pictures or icon to a selection of text offers learners another mechanism to discern meaning. These are especially helpful for learners whose reading skills are limited. There are several software packages available to assist educators by automating the process.

 BoardMaker is a graphics database containing over 3,000 symbols in bitmapped clip art form. The program allows one to quickly find and paste pictures into a display, resize, store, retrieve and paste scanned or custom drawn pictures. The picture icons in the database are from the Picture Exchange Communication (PECS) system, a common form of icon-based communication for people who are nonverbal. A single user copy costs $299. Available at *http://www.mayer-johnson.com*.

Figure 2.35.

PCS Sign Language Animations are used to reinforce learning of sign language. Over 500 animated signs, pulling from both American Sign Language (ASL) and Signed Exact English (SEE), supplement the core PCS Sign Language Library (Volume I). These animations are designed to reinforce the sign, they are not recommended to serve as a comprehensive teaching program. A single use license costs $79. Available at *http://www.mayerjohnson.com.*

Figure 2.36.

 Media Magic 2 and Media Weaver 3.5 These two software packages contain multimedia word processors (Media Magic 2 for learners age 4 to 9, and Media Weaver for learners age 8 and up). They contain a rebus bar and word predictors, vocabulary words, pictures and recorded speech, text to speech and paint functions. Single user license costs $49. Found at *www.sunburst.com.*

Figure 2.37.

 Picture It allows educators to type in text, then with a click of the mouse add pictures and icons to enhance the readability. The software contains over 600 literacy support pictures with both black and white and color versions, clip art and the capability to import pictures. A single user license costs $295 from *www.slatersoftware.com.*

Figure 2.38.

 Writing With Symbols is a word/picture processing program allows you to type words with the option of having picture symbols appear with each word. It allows learners who do not recognize text to write with pictures and it allows text users to have a pictorial spell checker. A single use license costs $199. *Available from www.mayerjohnson.com.*

Figure 2.39.

Example #12: Icon-Enhanced Text

This is a sample of text supported with pictures. This example was made with Picture It and was available at http://www.slatersoftware.com as a free sample. It is part of a short biographical essay on George Washington Carver.

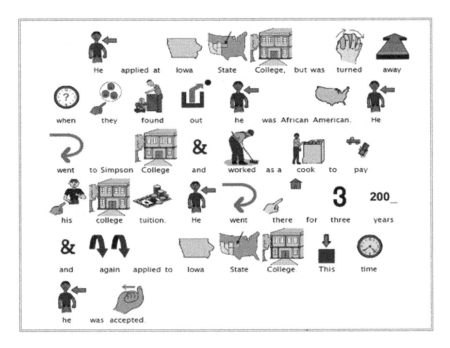

Figure 2.40.   Modified text using icons to enhance vocabulary.

Example #13: Combining Text, Images and Video

Appendix A consists of a full lesson plan from the Negro Leagues. It contains examples of text, images, and video. Note taking tools have been developed to highlight important information and activate background knowledge and graphic organizers accompany the lesson plan to be used in any or all of the ways described above.

 Teaching Every Student in the Digital Age: Universal Design for Learning
by David Rose and Anne Meyer. (2002) ASCD. Available in digital form at
http://www.cast.org/teachingeverystudent/ideas/tes/

Figure 2.41.

In their book *Teaching Every Student in the Digital Age: Universal Design for Learning* David Rose and Anne Meyer outline specific strategies to support presentation. In chapter 5, the authors include:

1. Providing multiple examples.

   Educators often use examples of specific content to help learners acquire concepts. The larger the number of examples and the better those examples embody the concept, the more effective they are. Using digital media to provide multiple examples in a variety of sensory channels also enhances effectiveness by reaching learners who may have difficulty with a particular method of sensory input. Rose and Meyer suggest using collections of text, image, sound and video examples that can be digitally stored and expanded from year to year. Digital media offers the additional advantage of interactivity. Learners can manipulate digital examples to discover patterns and properties that represent the concept.

2. Highlight critical features.

   Educators assist learners in the identification of key features and patterns in the examples they provide. Learners must recognize the essential attributes of an example or set of examples to recognize the concept those examples represent. The use of labels on an image example provides this focus. Likewise, educators use intonation, pace and volume, gestures and facial expressions to highlight key points in examples that use speech. Text features such as italics, underlining, and font styles can mark critical elements in print examples. Digital tools applied to digital media examples can expand the capacity of educators to focus learners' attention on key features. These may include the ability to zoom in to a specific part of an image, color highlighting, animation, and the process of overlaying text and images onto video. Some tools allow educators to provide a continuum of supports that can be accessed by individual learners to meet their needs at the moment. An example of this type of support is a scrolling application that enlarges font through the use of a computer mouse or changes the color and intensity of a highlighting mark on the screen.

3. Provide multiple media and formats.

   It is clear that a single means of presentation does not reach every potential learner. Using text and print images (the traditional methods) excludes the learner who may have a different capacity for visual input. Presenting examples using speech alone does not reach the learner with **auditory or language processing differences**. Presentation using multiple methods of delivery increases learning in two important ways. First, learners can choose methods that most effectively match their needs; if one modality is not a viable input channel for a particular learner, another channel may be used. Second, multiple representations provide more repetitions of the content, thereby providing repeated practice opportunities. Research has shown that using multiple modalities not only increases access for learners with diverse needs, it improves learning generally for all learners (Siegil, 1995).

4. Support background knowledge.

    The process of learning is one of incorporating new knowledge into previous knowledge. Obviously, learners differ considerably in the background knowledge they bring to the learning environment. Educators support this process by helping learners tie their background knowledge to new concepts and by providing missing related information. These goals are accomplished when educators require the learner to reflect upon their own experiences in relation to the new content they are presenting. Learning key vocabulary prior to encountering words in the midst of the presentation, providing vocabulary supports during the presentation, and the use of graphic organizers are also effective methods to connect background knowledge. Digital media are helpful supports in this area because they are flexible and because they can be linked to other information such as those on the internet. Learners can access supports as they need them.

SECTION TWO—PROCESS

Multiple means of engagement, to tap into learners' interests, offer appropriate challenges, and increase motivation (Center for Applied Special Technology [CAST], 2006).

-   Scaffolds
    o Study guides
    o Cognitive prostheses
    o Instructional unit resource guides
    o Webquests
    o Manipulatives
    o Virtual reality and simulations
    o Tiered learning activities

Students with diverse learning needs often have some skills sets that are more developed than others. As we discussed previously, learners have preferred learning channels and benefit when new concepts are presented in using that learning channel. Likewise learners differ in their ability and preferences as they manipulate and learn information. This set of learning activities relate to the process of learning or engaging with the material. Most learners can engage with content, even that which is fairly complicated and abstract, if they are provided with support. We will focus on three methods for providing support during the engagement process:

1. Scaffolds
2. Cognitive prosthesis
3. Tiered learning activities

Scaffolds

Rose and Meyer (2002) discuss scaffolds as a means for learners to practice a new skill in context and advocate the use of scaffolds to support some parts of the new skill while the learner practices other, specific parts. Rose and Meyer use the example of a set of training wheels on a beginner's bicycle. The training wheels support part of the balance required for the new skill, but allow the beginning rider to practice using the pedal, handle bars, etc. In the world of curriculum design, similar tools can support the learning process. Like training wheels, curricular scaffolds are only useful to a learner who needs them. Using them beyond that point inhibits the learning experience.

 WARNING! The use of scaffolds and supports for learners who do not need them leads to shallow and unchallenging learning experiences. When given the choice to use supports, most learners will make a choice to use them only if they are needed. However, in situations where learners may not be able to make the best choice for themselves, educators will need to support good decisions.

Figure 2.42.

Study Guides

The use of study guides is a common **curricular scaffold**. A study guide can help the learner organize and prioritize reading material, provide a visual image of complex concepts, or represent a cognitive framework on which new information can be attached to previously known information. Educators often design study guides that consist of questions to be answered during reading. Reflective questions, as well as those that require the reader to find certain pieces of data will help focus the reader, activate background knowledge and provide a framework on which to organize new information.

PUTTING THESE TECHNIQUES TO WORK

The amount of cues or supports any learner may require may vary according to their readiness level, the degree of interest they have in the subject, and their particular learning style.

> CAST's eTrekker Project has created a software tool to assist learners in the process of gathering information on the internet. It contains scaffolds for the organization of information in all three areas (presentation, process and product) and is flexible to allow educators to customize the tools for individuals or groups of diverse learners. Learn more about it at *http://udl.cast.org.*

Figure 2.43.

Example #14: Research Tool

Educators frequently use the Internet as a way for learners to access information. Study guides are particularly helpful when learners are conducting research. Anyone who has spent any time "surfing the Web" will soon find out that doing meaningful research using the Internet can be time consuming and confusing. One can get easily lost in the tangle of linked pages, become drawn off the topic, and encounter sources that may be of questionable value to the task at hand.

Version 1—Structured and Specific

Consider the following excerpt from a high school social studies lesson plan on the Negro Leagues written for the NLB eMuseum (Barragree, 2006a). The learning activity for this lesson is to research material from an assigned period in history and then use that information to create a magazine page.

> Group students into groups of four, then student groups choose one time period to research together... Each student in each group then selects one issue or event to "cover" from the time period selected. As students are researching their selected issue or event, they fill in headlines, headings, names, photographs, etc. on their page layout. Ensure students understand

this is a very important step before they begin creating their magazine. (Barragree, 2006a)

This lesson activity is designed to use two, 60 minute class periods. The instructions are very open-ended and provide a lot of room for individual choices, judgment and critical thinking skills. While some learners will welcome this limitless approach, others will find it threatening and overwhelming. In response to this need, a scaffold was created in the form of a research tool to guide learners through the research process. This tool limits choice, but focuses learners on the process of retrieving crucial information from several Web sites and provides a hard copy record of that information so that when the learners return to their cooperative learning group, they can make a valuable contribution. The tool was created by Lori Mott (2006).

RESEARCH TOOL for TIMEWARP – 1900 vs. Now
http://www.time.com/time/time100/timewarp/timewarp.html

Check each item off as you complete it.

1. _____ On the Home Page, locate the tab that says United States (at the top of the page). Click it and read the information about how the United States has changed during the years 1900-1998. Pick one item that you think your group would like to include in your magazine and write it below.

2. _____ In 1900 _____ .
   _____ In 1998 _____ .

3. _____ On the left side of the page, find the box that says *TIME* 100 Polls. Click on the third item – Event of the Century. There are 20 events listed. Choose two important ones that you would like to share with your team. Record them below.

4. _____ Event _____ Year _____ .

5. _____ Back on the left side of the page, find the *TIME* 100 Polls, and click on the second item – Person of the Century. There are 20 people listed. Choose one important one you want to find out more about and share with your team. Record their name below.

6. _____ Name _____ .

7. _____ Go to *www.askjeeves.com*.

8. _____ Type in the name of the important person you chose –followed by the word "biography". For example, in the search box, you would type Adolph Hitler biography. Click the SEARCH button.

9. _____ You will find a page of potential websites with information about your important person. They will include pictures and text. There may be a picture of your person at the top. If there is, you will need to print it out, or copy it here. To copy, put your pointer on the picture, and hold down the right button on your mouse. The menu will appear, and move the pointer to COPY. Once COPY is highlighted, click once with the left mouse button. This will copy the picture.

10. _____ (If you printed out your picture, skip this step.) To paste your picture, put your pointer over the X below, and click the right button on your mouse again. The menu will appear and you will choose PASTE. Click the left mouse button again. This will paste the picture onto this worksheet.

Figure 2.44a.   Structured research tool.

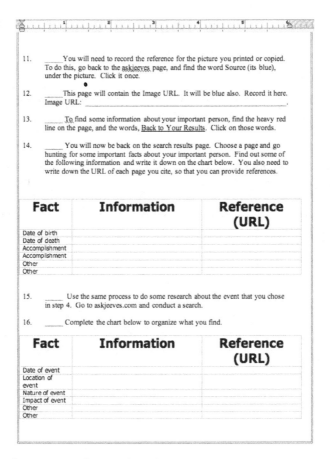

Figure 2.44b.   Structured research tool.

Version 2—Open-Ended

This version of a research tool is much less structured. It provides initial instructions to ensure that learners start their research in a reliable source, but then allows more individual freedom and choice on the part of the learner. This example is taken from another Negro Leagues lesson plan for the NLB eMuseum, in which learners are asked to find examples of oral tradition, folklore and/or opinion in order to create a magazine page (Barragree, 2006b). The instructions have been edited to include only that information that pertains to the scaffold process.

3. Although the lesson plan suggests that students research and find three examples of African American and/or Negro Leagues oral

tradition/folklore, some students may not be able to accomplish this in the time allowed or without considerable adult support. Consider asking them to find one example.

4. When assigning groups, assign one student to find an example from the slave interviews. Direct them to http://memory.loc.gov/ammem/snhtml/snvoices00.html and have them pick a narrative from the list.

5. Assign another student to find an example from the Negro Baseball Leagues history. Direct them to *http://www.charliethejuggling-clown.com/baseball.htm* to read about the Indianapolis Clowns, one of the NLB clown teams.

6. Provide the note-taking card (see Figure 2.46) for students to keep track of their research. This information will be used when they join their group to report on what they found. It will allow them to offer meaningful input to the group's decision.

I researched a story about: _____

One (or some) of the important people were : _____

The thing about it that stuck with me the most was: _____

I found some fact/folklore/opinion in this story. It was: _____

I think it would make a good storyboard because: _____

Figure 2.45.   Open-ended research tool

Example #15: Reading/Note-Taking Tool or Concept Maps

Note-taking tools and concept maps were discussed earlier as a way for diverse learners to record new information while it is being presented. This process can be further enhanced when the information recorded on the note taking tool is reorganized, augmented or sifted by the learner and placed in a graphic organizer. These cognitive steps deepen the learner's engagement with the material, thus encoding and creating new meaning from the content.

This chart represents a very simple note taking tool for use during research, but it could also be used for a lecture or video situation. It was developed to accompany a Negro Leagues lesson plan for the NLB eMuseum (Baillargeon, 2006). Learners sift information to sort out the "Big Ideas" listed across the top of the chart and focus on three organizations that have been formed to meet the needs of African Americans. By providing this structure, learners determine pertinent from non-pertinent information.

Aftermath For Freedom Seekers - BIG Idea Comparison Chart				
Name of Black Institution	**Mission**	**Location**	**Activities**	**History**
				(when and why it was formed)
National Association for the Advancement of Colored People (NAACP)	Ensure political, educational, social and economic equality of rights of minority groups. To eliminate racial hatred and racial discrimination.	National office- Baltimore Maryland, 7 Regions serving 5 countries	demonstrations court cases lobbying	Formed in 1909 to fight for civil rights.
National Urban League	Empowering African Americans to enter the economic and social mainstream. To make "The American Dream" possible for African Americans.	New York	voter registration drives boycotts, training program, lobbying, volunteerism, government programs	1910-A merger of other groups-to bring educational and employment opportunities to blacks
Negro Baseball Leagues	Provide professional opportunities for black baseball players	Formed in Kansas City, MO	leagues, barnstorming, tours, promoted economic development in communities,	1920-Leagues formed to give black players opportunities to play despite segregation and racism in professional leagues.

Figure 2.46. Note-taking tool to capture "big ideas."

By providing learners with an additional tool such as a Venn Diagram, learners can compare and contrast the information from the Big Idea Chart.

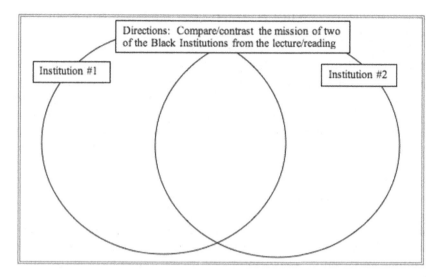

Figure 2.47.   Venn Diagram as a note-taking tool.

Cognitive Prostheses

A **prosthesis** is a device designed to replace a missing part of the body or to make a part of the body work better (United States National Library of Medicine, 2006). Cognition refers to the process of thinking. Therefore, a **cognitive prosthesis** is defined as a device that replaces or improves the function of a thinking process. Originally designed for patients suffering from brain injury, cognitive prosthesis are often developed by computer scientists and rehabilitation professionals who work with patients with brain injuries. Although the application of assistive technology in this sense is primarily for rehabilitation purposes, the result is a compensatory strategy which can be used to maximize an individual's strengths and abilities in order to compensate for acquired deficits (Cole & Matthews, 1999). Mundane examples of cognitive prostheses include alarmed wristwatches, speed dialing, calculators and **Personal Digital Assistants (PDAs).** These tools enhance cognitive processes by supporting portions of the cognitive load of specific tasks.

We all use cognitive prostheses every day. Consider the timer on the kitchen oven. This device keeps track of passing time, which is a function that many people have the ability to do with their minds. However, chefs may choose to use the timer to perform this function in order to devote their thoughts to the coordination of the meal, to converse while cooking, or any number of other mental activities. The same is true of the alarm clock. While some people may be able to awaken themselves by "programming" a mental process that interrupts sleep, most of us require an additional support to accomplish this task.

This application can be extended to the learning environment. Tools such as cognitive prostheses are powerful ways to increase access in the cognitive environment and hold great potential for curriculum developers who subscribe to the principals of universal design for learning. Some typical, well known examples of cognitive prostheses in this domain include spell checkers, copy/paste functions, readability statistics, handheld translators, and electronic dictionaries. This handbook explores the expansion of this concept to include auto summary features, Internet search engines, and speech to text readers.

One controversial cognitive prosthesis from the world of education is the use of a calculator. Educators have debated the relevance of mathematical equations solved with a calculator, arguing that the device performs computation instead of the student. Yet, it is common to see graphing and scientific calculators being used in upper level mathematics classes in many educational settings. The question here is not the value of calculators, but rather the purpose for their use. Just because a chef is mentally able to keep track of passing time does not mean that he/she may not benefit from the use of an oven timer. This is an important fact to keep in mind as educators discuss the value of these tools in the learning process.

David Edyburn (2000, 2003a, 2004b, 2005) has written extensively on the use of assistive technology to assist students with diverse learning needs. He contends that technological applications can and should be used as cognitive prostheses and trains educators in their use. While assistive technology has traditionally been seen **as augmentative communication devices**, or modified computer keyboards, and used with individuals who experience physical disabilities, Edyburn suggests that software such as text-to-speech, and Internet search engines can also benefit learners who experience cognitive disabilities such as memory difficulties, reading disabilities, and cognitive limitations. He contends that learners, especially those in the upper grades experience so much failure as a result of their limited access to the curriculum, that there is an appropriate time to augment their performance, even compensate for their limitations with technological solutions.

The purpose of this handbook is to expand the access to curriculum materials for any and all learners with diverse needs. The decision to use or not use any of the techniques and strategies included in the handbook lies with the educator. Therefore, the use of cognitive prostheses is included in order that educators can make informed decisions regarding their potential use.

Important considerations when designing cognitive prostheses
When making decisions about the use of cognitive prostheses, educators could benefit from reflecting on the following issues:
1.   What is the purpose/goal of the activity?
2.   What added benefit would the cognitive prosthesis provide?
3.   Would the use of a cognitive prosthesis limit the learner's experience?
4.   What is the setting in which the cognitive prosthesis will be used?
(What is helpful and appropriate in a museum setting will differ from a classroom setting.)

Figure 2.48.

This set of general design methodologies will make materials more accessible to individuals with cognitive challenges. They can be applied to computer screens or print materials:

1.   Use of clear, uncluttered layout.
2.   Use of graphics and animation that contribute to, rather than distract from learning.
3.   Use of consistent commands, features and directions from screen to screen or page to page.
4.   Combined use of pictures and audio prompts for navigation.
5.   Use of linear designs of software operation.
6.   Inclusion of options to manipulate appropriate sequencing and pacing.
7.   Inclusion of opportunities for repetition and positive practice.
8.   Use of "error minimization" features, such as removing buttons from the screen at times when use is inappropriate.
9.   Use of frequent audio feedback, both for error correction and positive reinforcers.
10. Use of customization options that allow professionals to adapt the materials to the unique needs of a variety of learners.

PUTTING THESE TECHNIQUES TO WORK

There are many software packages and Internet sites available on the Internet that will assist learners with cognitive learning tasks. The first group consists of tools learners can use to complete learning activities. The software assists learners by supporting portions of the cognitive load. Carol Ann Tomlinson writes extensively in the area of differentiated instruction. One of her most useful tools is The Equalizer, shown Figure

ReadPlease at *www.readplease.com* opens a window on the desktop into which text is copied and pasted. Users can customize font and background color, use the low vision color option, and adjust voice choice and speed. The control buttons are easy to use so this tool works well when readers need to start and stop frequently (as in listening to test questions and choosing an answer or in listening to the reader read a printed worksheet). The reader also reads email **emotiocons** such as ☺ or ☻. The reader includes seven languages and highlights text as it is read. It requires digital text so PDF files are not readable. The free download is a 30 day trial.

Figure 2.49.

2.50 (Tomlinson, 1999). Each of the "sliders" adjusts the learning activity in a particular domain. By reflecting on the relative cognitive load inherent in the activity, educators can strategically adjust the activity to reach diverse learners.

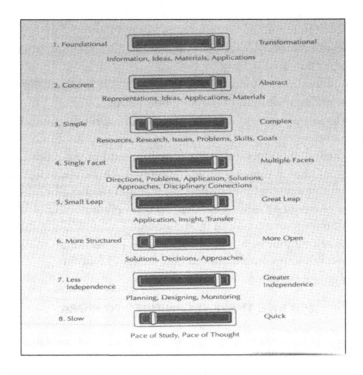

Figure 2.50.   Tomlinson's representation of The Equalizer, a tool to guide decision making as an educator differentiates instruction.

Cognitive prosthesis can be easily developed as curriculum is designed. Consider the ease with which the graphic organizer in example #8 is duplicated using a word processing software application. Different levels of support are created as portions of the content are supplied for the learner. Features such as word banks also provide support for the cognitive load of a learning activity.

Example #16: Picture/Word Bank

This cognitive prothesis was designed to accompany a lesson plan that was written for the NLB eMuseum (Mott, 2006b). The learning activity was the design of a T-shirt depicting the negative aspects of segregation. In order to provide cognitive support, examples and images were included to initiate the cognitive process so that the learner could participate in the activity.

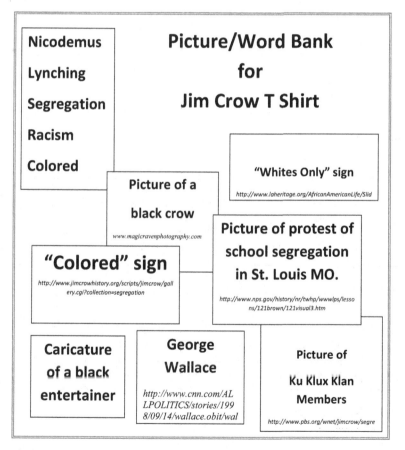

Figure 2.51.   Word and picture bank.

ReadMark, at *http://www.geocities.com/threehillssoftware/readmark.html* provides a description and link to download a 30-day trial version. This product creates a movable marker on the screen that can be moved by using the mouse or arrow keys on top of a document, a web page, or any other image; and can be used as a place holder for reading on a computer screen.

Figure 2.52.

Inspiration software at *www.inspiration.com* allows learners to create dynamic, interactive graphic organizers, and supports the writing process. The company offers a free download.

Figure 2.53.

Ask Jeeves is an easy to use search engine that will accept queries in the form of a question. Search results are simple to follow and stay in a separate window. This feature makes the site less confusing to use than some other search engines. Find it at *www.askjeeves.com*.

Figure 2.54.

4Kids.org is a team of educators, writers, artists, technology specialists and students that produces a weekly newspaper article and maintains the www.4Kids.org website. Their vision is to pursue more effective ways of creating learning environments for all children through advancing technologies such as the Internet. Find it at *www.4Kids.org*. The site contains a listing of links to knowledge-based sites that are learner-friendly.

Figure 2.55.

How Stuff Works. This science site allows learners to explore how all the things we use every day really work. At *www.howstuffworks.com* you can investigate an internal combustion engine or the human body.

Figure 2.56.

World Fact Book is provided by the Central Intelligence Agency at
www.odci.gov/cia/publications/factbook. This social studies site contains
information on continents, countries, oceans, land formations, and much
more. It includes peoples from around the world, governments and climates.

Figure 2.57.

The **Students for the Exploration and Development of Space (SEDS)**
at www.seds.org is an astronomy site that includes a Web telescope which
allows students to see comets, black holes and far-off galaxies. There are
also excellent images and sounds, such as the latest Pathfinder photos of
the "Red Planet."

Figure 2.58.

Kathy Schrock's Guide for Educators is a categorized list of sites useful
for enhancing curriculum. Find it at http://school.discovery.com/schrockguide.

Figure 2.59.

Trackstar is a site that allows educators to create maps or "tracks" of
websites. The site clusters selected web sites together and creates a lesson
plan for learners to follow, educator directions can be embedded inside.
Find it at http://trackstar.4teachers.org.

Figure 2.60.

Instructional Unit Resource Guides

Edyburn advocates a lesson planning process that incorporates
resources from the Internet, a tiering system for lesson content. He trains
educators to develop these lessons using a template called Instructional
Unit Resource Guides.

Example #17: Instructional Unit Resource Guide

A complete example is included as Appendix B. The example was
developed by Barb Melvin, Occupational Therapist and Carolyn Dale,
High School Language Arts Teacher during a workshop conducted by
Edyburn in March, 2006.

WebQuests

This inquiry-oriented activity involves interacting with resources on the Internet. They can be appropriate for almost any age learner or content. According to Dodge (2001), there are six parts to a successful WebQuest. They are:

1. Introduction—This is where the learner is oriented to what is coming. This section should raise the learner's interest by making the topic relevant, visually interesting, important, urgent, and/or fun.

2. Task—A description of what the learner will have done at the end of the exercise. This can be a product or a verbal act. It is important that the learner is allowed input into what the task will be and that options are provided.

3. Process—Here, the educator makes suggestions regarding the steps of discovery, including strategies for dividing the task and descriptions of the roles to be played or perspectives to be taken by each learner. An educator may also provide learning advice, which relates to helping learners with interpersonal skills. This is also where an answer sheet or a guided notes template may be included.

4. Resources—These can be pre-selected Web pages the educator has located to help the learner accomplish the task at hand. An educator may choose to create the Web pages or to utilize ones already present on the Internet. Other resources, such as books, interviews, and video can be used as well.

5. Evaluation—In this section, the educator not only evaluates the learner's progress but the effectiveness of the WebQuest as well. An evaluation rubric is most commonly used for this purpose. Learners should be made aware of the assessment process from the very beginning and a copy of the rubric should be included in the Web-Quest.

6. Conclusion—The conclusion provides an opportunity to:

    (a)   Summarize the experience.
    (b)   Encourage reflection about the process.
    (c)   Extend and generalize what was learned.
    (d)   Give the learner a sense of closure.
    (e)   Open a path into the next lesson (p. 3).

WebQuest is a website hosted by Bernie Dodge. It contains articles about webquests, a database of webquests that have been submitted by educators, and a site that will provide educators with the structure to create their own webquest. Find it at *http://webquest.org*.

Figure 2.61.

Example #18: WebQuest

Appendix C contains an example of a WebQuest developed for learners ages 13 and up on the subject of civil rights leaders.

Manipulatives

The use of hands-on learning activities is a powerful way to increase access. Learners who prefer kinesthetic input channels will benefit greatly from the opportunity to use touch and physical movement to encode information. The use of manipulative objects moves the cognitive process from an abstract to more concrete domains. Models and physical exemplars are often included in museum curriculum materials and serve an important function as they bring concepts to real life.

When physical objects are not available, educators can create hands on activities with ideas and concepts. This process of creating a "cognitive manipulative" replicates the hands-on advantage of moving information from one physical location to another, but is accomplished with concepts instead of objects (S. Robinson, personal communication, March, 2000). This technique can be applied to almost any print resource and is a powerful way to make a learning activity a group activity. A rudimentary application of this strategy is the sorting of facts into groupings according to an assigned attribute. Consider this example that uses content from Example #11.

Example #19: Cognitive Manipulative Sorting Activity

Use this worksheet that was developed as a scaffold to a lecture on the social and political organizations that emerged during and after the civil rights era.

Aftermath For Freedom Seekers - BIG Idea Comparison Chart

Name of Black Institution	Mission	Location	Activities	History
				(when and why it was formed)
National Association for the Advancement of Colored People (NAACP)	Ensure political, educational, social and economic equality of rights of minority groups. To eliminate racial hatred and racial discrimination.	National office- Baltimore Maryland, 7 Regions serving 5 countries	demonstrations court cases lobbying	Formed in 1909 to fight for civil rights.
National Urban League	Empowering African Americans to enter the economic and social mainstream. To make "The American Dream" possible for African Americans.	New York	voter registration drives boycotts, training program, lobbying, volunteerism, government programs	1910-A merger of other groups-to bring educational and employment opportunities to blacks
Negro Baseball Leagues	Provide professional opportunities for black baseball players.	Formed in Kansas City, MO	leagues, barnstorming, tours, promoted economic development in communities.	1920-Leagues formed to give black players opportunities to play despite segregation and racism in professional leagues.

Figure 2.62.   A cognitive manipulative chart.

Remove the content from the chart and use it as the sorting tool.

Name of Black Institution	Mission	Location	Activities	History
				(when and why it was formed)
National Association for the Advancement of Colored People (NAACP)				
National Urban League				
Negro Baseball Leagues				

Figure 2.63.   Blank template for the cognitive manipulative.

Place the details on separate cards or slips of paper. Cut them apart and shuffle them.

training programs	National office-	demonstrations	lobbying
court cases	Baltimore Maryland,	barnstorming tours	voter registration drives
government programs	7 Regions serving	empowering African	provide professional
Kansas City, MO	5 countries	Americans to enter the	opportunities for black
eliminate racial hatred	leagues	economic and social	baseball players.
and racial discrimination.	1909 to fight for	mainstream.	represented the highest
1920-formed to	civil rights	volunteerism	level of baseball for
give black players	1910-a merger of other	promoted economic	African Americans
opportunities to play	groups-to bring	development in	boycotts
despite segregation and	educational and	communities	ensure political,
racism in professional	employment opportunities	to make the "The Americ	educational, social and
leagues.	to blacks	Dream " possible for	economic equality of
New York	lobbying	African Americans.	rights of minority groups.

Figure 2.64.   Details for the cognitive manipulative.

Use the cards as a cooperative learning activity in either of the following ways:

1. Place all the cards in the center of a table, have each learner draw a card, read it to the group then place it on the chart where it belongs.

2. Assign each learner as a representative of one of the activity organizations. Deal out all the cards. Player 1 draws one card from the player on his/her left. If the card belongs on the chart for the organization he/she represents, the player places the card on the correct place on the chart, if not, the player holds onto the card. Play continues in this way until all the detail cards are placed correctly on the chart.

Almost any text material or print resource can be turned into a cognitive manipulative just by cutting it apart. Cognitive manipulatives make great cooperative learning activities. Most interactive museum exhibits are elaborate cognitive manipulatives.

Figure 2.65.

Virtual Reality and Simulations

When physical models are unavailable or impractical, virtual versions can fulfill a similar function. There are many Web sites and software applications that offer this option. Content can be explored in lab-like settings without the need for renewable supplies and resources and without the safety and supervision concerns frequently associated with laboratory activities. The increasing affordability of LCD projectors make these applications a viable alternative to live demonstrations for large groups because an educator can project the image from one computer onto a screen.

Example #20: Situational Simulation

The Internet contains many examples of simulation activities designed by educators. These allow learners to go beyond role play and actually get physically and emotionally involved in the learning.

Paths of Resistance deals with Jim Crow laws. It can be found at *http://www.jimcrowhistory.org/resources/simulations.htm*.

Figure 2.66.

Example #21: Online Games

Many museums host Web pages of online learning activities.

Exploratorium in San Francisco. Find it at *http://www.exploratorium.edu/explore/online.html*.

Figure 2.67.

Tiered Learning Activities

One of the techniques for differentiation that provides increased access to the learning process is the use of a planning pyramid (Schumm, Vaughn, & Harris, 1997). This tool allows educators to sift curriculum content for diverse groups or individuals. Planning tiered learning embodies the spirit of universal design because it emphasizes strategic decision making during the initial design phase. Educators must determine what aspect of the learning activity is to be manipulated (content, process or product) and how it will be modified (readiness, interest or learning style). Learners may be assigned different learning objectives and be assigned different learning activities. However, the activities in which they engaged reflect a consistent learning path towards those objectives.

PUTTING THESE TECHNIQUES TO WORK

For the purposes of explanation, this example of a three tiered pyramid will be described as an activity for which the decision has been made to differentiate the content by readiness level. The middle section of the pyramid is the largest and usually includes the learning objectives for lessons that are typically planned for learners whose readiness level can be predicted. This level may contain multiple learning objectives, but does not represent any adjustment. It can be compared to a lesson blueprint and would typically be representative of most traditional lesson plans. Differentiation occurs when the teacher expands this blueprint in both directions. The bottom level of the pyramid characterizes the most basic level of knowledge that is acceptable mastery for this content. In this example in which the decision has been made to differentiate the content of the lesson by readiness level, this tier may be appropriate for learners with cognitive limitations. These learning objectives are less complex and represent a grasp of the main points of the activity. In contrast, the top level of the pyramid describes the learning objectives that are above and beyond the predictable norm. It should be noted that the planning pyramid is not always limited to three levels. Educators may find it necessary to plan instruction on several levels, depending on the diversity among their learners.

Example #22: Tiered Learning Activity

This is an example of a history learning activity designed for learners ages 13 and up. It represents differentiation in the process level by readiness. This lesson plan was created by John Marron (n.d.), and is included here in its entirety.

Tiered Lesson Plan: Causes of the Civil War

Standard

This lesson will cover national standard of US history era five/standard thirteen/level four/number two: "Understands events that fueled the political and sectional conflicts over slavery and ultimately polarized the North and the South (e.g., the Missouri Compromise, the Wilmot Proviso, the Kansas-Nebraska Act)" (www.mcrel.org)

Background

Prior to giving this assignment the students will receive lectures and readings explaining the rising conflicts prior to and throughout the 1850's. They will receive material through lectures and readings on the following historical figures and events: Nat Turner, Elijah Lovejoy, William Lloyd Garrison, Henry Clay, John Calhoun, Stephan Douglas, Fredrick Douglass, Harriet Beecher Stowe's Uncle Toms Cabin, John Brown and Harper's Ferry, Dred Scott Case, Abraham Lincoln, Lincoln/Douglas debates, Kansas-Nebraska Act, and the Presidential Nominating Conventions of 1860.

Tiered by process

This lesson will be tiered by process. Different groups of students will receive different assignments to exhibit their understanding of the ideas presented. The easier assignments will be longer in length to accommodate for the difference in the difficulty of assignments.

Tiered by readiness

This lesson will be tiered by readiness. The students who are able to think, synthesize and evaluate the facts given them, will be given an evaluation assignment. The students who are able to analyze the facts will be given analytical problems. Finally, the students who learn only by memorization and comprehension will be given a basic assignment.

Guide in tiering

I will tier this lesson by groups of readiness, in ways that I think will be the most beneficial for the different students. I will take into account, their ability to evaluate history, analyze history, or comprehend history. I will group the students as I feel it will be the best way for them to learn. Although I will be dividing the assignments into three different groups of types of students, the students will NOT be working in groups to

Figure 2.68a.   Example of a tiered lesson on the Civil War.

answer these questions. The will work as individuals, and they will present individual ideas and views.

Make up of tiers

Tier I will be made up of students who I feel will benefit best from a simpler form of learning, such as defining and giving the significance of various key terms or people and answering basic questions. Some of the terms they will be expected to identify will be:

Slavery, Nat Turner, Elijah Lovejoy, William Lloyd Garrison, abolitionists, Henry Clay, John Calhoun, Stephan Douglas, popular sovereignty, Fredrick Douglass, Harriet Beecher Stowe's Uncle Toms Cabin, John Brown and Harper's Ferry, Dred Scott Case, Abraham Lincoln, republicans, democrats, Lincoln/Douglas debates, Kansas-Nebraska Act, and the Presidential Nominating Conventions of 1860, etc.

Tier II would be comprised of students that I felt capable of taking historical facts and analyzing them to show how these people/events led to the escalation of conflict that led to the civil war. I would give these students various questions that asked them to link certain events to the causes of the civil war. Some example questions that I may ask of these students are:

1) How did the publishing of Harriet Beecher Stowe's Uncle Toms Cabin help lead to civil war?

2) What did the Dred Scott Case decide? What did it mean for slaves and former slaves? Did the Supreme Court overstep its constitutional limits in their decision?

3) What were the differing points of view in the Lincoln/Douglas debates?

4) What key figure in this time period favored popular sovereignty? How did other key figures react to his ideas?

5) What were the views of the abolitionists? What were the differences in views held by Lovejoy, Garrison, and Douglass?

6) What role did John Brown and Harper's Ferry play in escalating the rift between North and South?

7) What caused the Democratic Presidential Appointing Convention in Charleston, SC to break up? What were the effects of this?

These students will be expected to answer these questions in a complete manner. Most answers should consist of at least one or two paragraphs, sometimes more. They will be expected to show full understanding of these terms, and how they led to an escalation of conflict between the North and the South.

Tier III students will be those students who I feel have a good grip on the ideas presented and can think critically and explain how these key terms/figures/events eventually led to the civil war. I would ask these students to present a 3-4 page essay on how the key points of the lecture and readings ended up causing the civil war. These students will be expected to provide their own ideas on why these situations occurred and what the effects of these events were. These students will be given more freedom to handle the material. Their own ideas will shape their responses and mold the essay.

Figure 2.68b.   Example of a tiered lesson on the Civil War.

Assessment

These students will be eligible to earn equal points on their respective assignments. For example, this assignment may be worth 50 points. The Tier I students would have 25 terms to identify at two points apiece. The Tier II students would have 10 questions at five points per question. The Tier III students' essays would be worth 50 points in itself. In this way, the students doing the harder work would only be expected to present one essay, and be able to receive the same credit as the students who must do 25 easier identifications.

On the test, I would assess their knowledge through basic multiple-choice questions to measure their understanding of key concepts and ideas. These questions would all have been covered in lectures or assigned readings. I would then give about 25 identifications (worth five points apiece) and 5 essays (worth 10 points apiece). The students would be responsible for completing a combination of these totaling to 30 points. In this manner, the students who learned by knowledge and comprehension would have the option of using the method by which they were assigned to show their knowledge of the key concepts. Those who were able to analyze and/or evaluate the history would have the option of writing essays to demonstrate their knowledge of the subject. This way no student would have an unfair advantage over others because of the differing assignments.

Figure 2.68c.   Example of a tiered lesson on the Civil War.

SECTION THREE—PRODUCT

Multiple means of expression, to provide learners' alternatives for demonstrating what they know. (Center for Applied Special Technology, [CAST], 2006)

- Product Options
  - Multiple products
  - Layered learning activities
  - RAFTS
  - Blogs
  - Podcasts
  - Self-assessments

To support expression, educators should provide multiple, flexible methods of expression and apprenticeship. Demonstrating new skills requires learners to put all the pieces of the process together and elicits feedback from a broader audience. These activities affect motivation and self-efficacy and are very important. By providing varied methods of demonstration, educators can provide meaningful experiences to diverse learners. When designing curriculum, educators may be unacquainted with the learners who will eventually use the materials. Therefore, multiple means of expression should be developed so there are options available to diverse learners.

Layering the curriculum is a specific tiering technique. It was developed by Kathie Nunley (2003) and uses new brain research to create a planning pyramid that differentiates the lesson product by interest. Layering allows learners a great deal of control as they choose their learning activity from a "menu." The "Big Ideas" of the lesson are divided into layers (usually 3 layers are used because this coincides with the typical grading pattern of A, B or C grades that are considered to be satisfactory performance). Layers are distinguished from one another by the complexity of the tasks according to Bloom's Taxonomy. Simple, basic concepts go into the "C" layer; more complex thinking skills go in the "B" layer; and the most complex, higher-level thinking skills are assigned to the "A" layer. Each layer contains several activity choices that represent different learning styles, readiness levels and accessibility paths.

 Dr. Kathie Nunley's Layered Curriculum website contains newsletters and training resources on her technique of layered curriculum. It also contains lesson plan samples using layering. Find it at *http://help4teachers.com/index.htm.*

Figure 2.69.

PUTTING THESE TECHNIQUES TO WORK

Differentiating the learning activities is an effective way to provide flexible products. A menu of possible products offered to learners allow them to differentiate their own learning. Here is a list of possible product options educators might use:

1. Make a model of ...
2. Draw a map showing ...
3. Write a journal form the point of view of ...
4. Make a **Venn Diagram** comparing and contrasting ...
5. Write a poem about ...
6. Do a written report on ...
7. Write a myth or legend explaining ...
8. Produce a video news report about ...

9. Role play ...
10. Create song lyrics and music to tell about...
11. Make a time line showing ...
12. Make a speech about ...
13. Write a diary entry dated ...
14. Design a game to teach about...
15. Interview, ... creating at least five interview questions.
16. Do a PowerPoint presentation on ...
17. Do an oral report using visuals about ...
18. Explain ... in paragraph form
19. Write a short story about ...
20. Make a word search about ...
21. Design a study guide for ...
22. Conduct an e-mail interview with ...
23. Make a mobile showing ...
24. Use a digital camera to ...
25. Make a scrapbook of ...
26. Create a mural showing ...
27. Make a chart to show ...
28. Arrange a display showing ...
29. Create a mosaic depicting ...
30. Write and direct a one-act play about ...
31. Evaluate the effect of ...
32. Do a concept map or web showing...
33. Develop a picture dictionary on the topic of ...
34. Create a brochure about ...
35. Create jeopardy questions about ...
36. Make a picture postcard showing ...
37. Write an editorial expressing your opinion about ...
38. Tape a radio report telling about ...
39. Make a **diorama** showing ...
40. Write an epilogue to ...
41. Write a letter describing ...
42. Draw a comic strip about ...
43. Construct an information cube with the following information on it ...
44. Construct puppets and put on a puppet show about ...

45. Develop a pro and con chart about …
46. Make a flow chart showing …
47. Search the Internet for information about …
48. Make a crossword puzzle about …
49. Make a collage of …
50. Design a symbol of …
51. Design a T-shirt showing …
52. Make an illustrated booklet of …
53. Generate a graph to show …
54. Debate with a fellow learner …
55. Do a slide show on the computer about …
56. Make a poster showing …
57. Design a bookmark about …
58. Write a **shape story** about …
59. Do a scale drawing of …
60. Do a sand painting for …
61. Lead a discussion on …
62. Read a book about …
63. Design a plan to …

Dr. Carol Ann Tomlinson's Equalizer is repeated on the next page because it is relevant when considering the type of product learners will be required to complete (1999). Each of the domains on The Equalizer represents differing levels of cognition and sophistication. Therefore, this tool is useful when developing alternative activities.

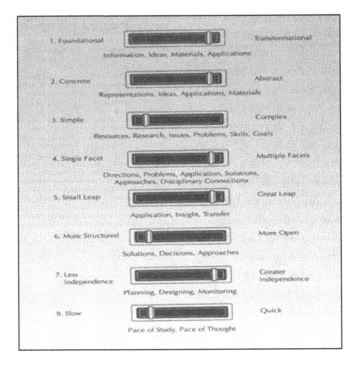

Figure 2.70. Tomlinson's representation of The Equalizer, a tool to guide decision making as an educator differentiates instruction.

Example #23: Multiple Product Options

This lesson consists of a lecture on the Buffalo Soldiers and a menu of product options. Consider all the possible ways learners could demonstrate their mastery of the content in this lesson plan taken from the NLB eMuseum curriculum (Chandler, 2006a).

Brief History of Buffalo Soldiers and Baseball
Full Article, Alternate Reading Level (621 words - 8.0 GE)

Black soldiers

In 1866, Congress passed the law creating military regiments, made up of only Black soldiers. There were two units that fought on horseback. These units were called the cavalry units. There were another four that fought on foot. They were called infantry regiments. Each of these fighting units had about 1,000 Black men in them.

The cavalry units, were led by White officers. The army sent them west to fight the Indians. They were good fighters. Because of this, they were given the most difficult assignments. The Indians called these troops Buffalo Soldiers because their fighting spirit reminded them of buffalo. These Buffalo Soldiers won many fights against the Indians. They were famous for their bravery.

Soldiers and baseball

When these soldiers were not fighting there was time to play. Baseball was the choice during the summer months. Black soldiers played against White soldiers. Sometimes Black soldiers played against the White people who lived near their forts.

Many people came to watch the games at Fort Douglas, in Utah. This team was called the Colored Monarchs. Players became famous. James Flowers was one of the many Black soldiers that played baseball during their time in the military.

Buffalo Soldiers played baseball at Fort Ethan Allen in Vermont. The games were played on Sunday. That is, until a minister from the town complained. He said the games created a bad environment for the town's young people. The Fort's commander argued that this was not the case but the Army stopped the baseball games between soldiers and people who lived in town. This decision forced the Buffalo Soldier to play games only against other soldiers.

On October 5, 1909, 900 men of the U.S. Army's 25th Infantry Regiment were transferred to Fort Lawton in Washington State. They were famous for their baseball team. They won the US Army championship and were rated the best amateur team in the county. In the Army, Black soldiers played against White soldiers. Some problems did happen. The Buffalo Soldiers won most of their games. They were also good boxers. Sometime fights broke out between Black and White players over a bad call by the umpires. Sometimes boxing matches were arranged between units.

Option 1: Activity for this lesson plan is to have students map out the geographic locations on a world map where the Buffalo Soldiers were stationed. Have them next, look at the climate of these areas and decide what kind of conditions these soldiers would have played baseball in. *http://www.drought.unl.edu/whatis/climographs.htm.*

Figure 2.71a.   Example of a learning activity with multiple products.

Option 1: Activity for this lesson plan is to have students map out the geographic locations on a world map where the Buffalo Soldiers were stationed. Have them next, look at the climate of these areas and decide what kind of conditions these soldiers would have played baseball in. *http://www.drought.unl.edu/whatis/climographs.htm.*

Option 2: Have students do a website search and find other information about black soldiers and attempt to find the names of soldiers that played baseball or were veterans that played during the years of the Buffalo Soldier.

Option 3: Activity: Students are to write a RAFT (see below) that explores the possible social issues raised by the Buffalo Soldiers' Sunday baseball games at Fort Ethan Allen. The use of the RAFT below allows for considerable differentiation in depth of material, synthesis of information, creativity, and autonomy and interest levels.

Buffalo Soldiers at Fort Ethan Allen

Picture of Buffalo Soldiers Out West

http://personalweb.smc vt.edu/thefort/ history/BuffaloSoldiers. htm

The Buffalo Soldiers brought character and life to Fort Ethan Allen. In their everyday recreation they played baseball and basketball. They often played baseball games against the civilian teams in the area until this was stopped by a complaint. A local minister, who was upset that these games were held on Sundays, wrote to the War Department and stated that they furnished an "Attraction for the young people to an environment which was not the best for them." The commander of the Tenth replied that no one was compelled to come to these games, but the military responded to the minister's pressure and the Sunday games were banished.

The commander was upset by this action; he remarked that there was more vice just outside the post in "disreputable dives" than took place in the form of Sunday baseball games. Unfortunately the policy did not change, so the men were forced to play against other military or professional teams.

Picture of George Osborne, a Buffalo soldier stationed at Fort Ethan Allen.

http://personalweb.smcvt.edu/thefo rt/ history/BuffaloSoldiers.htm

R – Role: Your role is that of the Fort Commander.

A – Audience: Your audience is US Army headquarters, your superior officer.

F – Form: A letter of appeal.

T – Topic: The benefits of Sunday baseball games and why they should not be banned.

Figure 2.71b.   Example of a learning activity with multiple products.

Option 4: Below is a Power Point presentation developed as an alternative activity. The original activity requires the learner to write an essay and this version applies technology to record the learner's thoughts. The structure and organization is presented to the learner, thus compensating for potential difficulties in cognition, writing ability or executive functioning. This support allows the learner to focus their energy on the content, not the presentation.

Buffalo Soldiers Power Point Activity

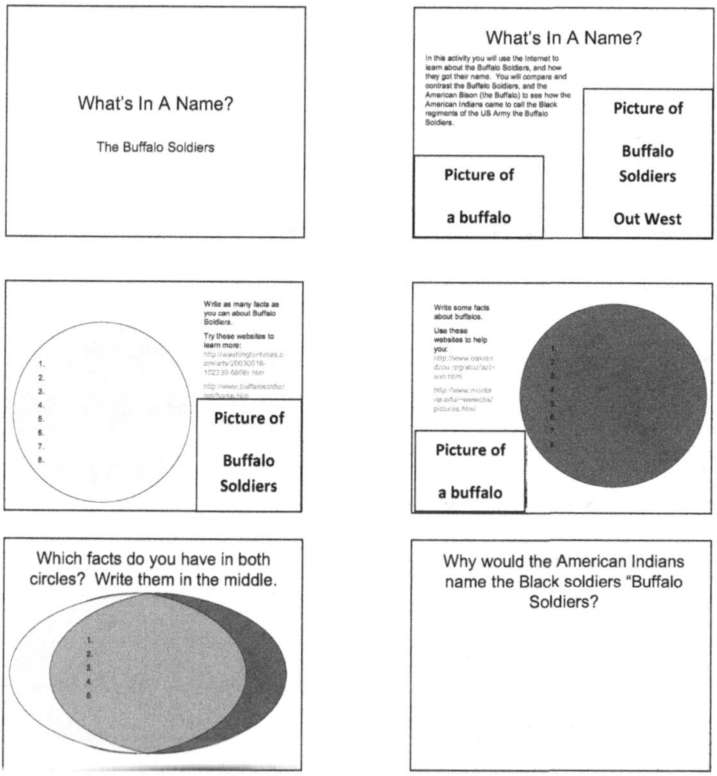

Figure 2.71c. Example of a learning activity with multiple products.

Example #24: Layered Learning Activities

This example was written for the NLB eMuseum (Barragree, 2006c) and contains multiple product options for learners to choose. Note that each level of learning activities (assignments) requires an oral defense. Learner must complete and defend all the activities in the C level to progress to the B level, etc. Higher level thinking skills are required in the A level than the other two. This aspect is what makes layered curriculum such an effective way to differentiate by interest and readiness level.

Negro Leagues Baseball

You must complete the required number of points in each section and defend each submission individually and orally before moving on to the next section. A maximum of two assignments per person will be accepted per day so manage your time accordingly.

C Level Assignments: A maximum of 40 points can be earned at this level.	Points Possible	Points Earned	Teacher's Signature
Write a one page paper on one of the following players: Fleetwood Walker, Satchel Paige, Josh Gibson, or "Cool Papa Bell".	5		
Listen to the taped selection of Black Diamond by McKissack and McKissack and write a one page summary of the information.	5		
Go to the following website and listen to interviews with NLB players and relatives, orally tell or write a one page paper on what NLB was like during this time.	5		
Draw five NLB player trading cards, include a drawing of the player, position played, and team(s) played for, team logo, and career starting and ending dates.	5		
Write a diary entry from a NLB player's perspective for four days, include a description of at least one game.	5		
Listen to music from Ella Fitzgerald or Duke Ellington. Tell or write the meaning of one of their songs.	5		
Read the article at: http://www.infoplease.com/spot/negroleagues1.html and create a timeline from the information.	5		
Watch one of the Negro Leagues videos and tell or write about the conditions NLB players endured and how they were treated by Whites and society as a whole.	5		
Recreate a typical NLB stadium using whatever materials you want.	5		
Draw signs (one point per sign) depicting "separate but equal" facilities and/or treatment.	5		
What are Jim Crow laws? Describe, draw, or write a summary.	5		
Define segregation, integration, discrimination, racism, and slavery (one point per word).	5		
Tell, draw, or write one paragraph answering this question. Does slavery still exists today, and if so, why?	5		
Reenact a situation in which you or someone you know was discriminated against, and explain why you think it was discrimination.	5		

Figure 2.72a.   Example of a layered learning activity.

	Points Possible	Points Earned	Teacher's Signature
Define Negro Renaissance and name three important contributors of the time.	5		
Write a poem or a song that reflects upon NLB.	5		
Draw a cartoon depicting any NLB team(s), player(s), or owner(s).	5		
Create an artist's sketch of a woman involved in the NLB, be sure to color and label the sketch for full credit.	5		
B Level Assignments: Choose one for 20 points	Points Possible	Points Earned	Teacher's Signature
Research NLB innovations, how did they contribute to the success of NLB? What, if any, other innovations could have helped save NLB? How would these have helped? What else could have been done to prolong NLB? Write a 3–4 page paper.	20		
Listen to Ted Williams' Hall of Fame induction speech. Write a 3–4 page paper detailing if you agree with his proposal to induct NLB players into the Hall of Fame, and support your position with historical information.	20		
What was the major turning point in NLB? Why? Write a 3–4 page paper and support your position with historical information.	20		
A Level Assignments: Choose one for 30 points	Points Possible	Points Earned	Teacher's Signature
Research Black women in NLB, choose one woman to write a six page historically based story about NLB from her perspective.	30		
Create an interactive timeline showing the history of NLB from its inception to its demise. Then post your timeline to a classroom website. See me for the directions on how to create an interactive timeline.	30		
Research court cases dealing with segregation and/or discrimination and/or integration. Write a summary of at least 3 cases. Choose one case, and write a trial transcript of what you think occurred in court include both the defending and prosecuting points of view.	30		

Figure 2.72b. Example of a layered learning activity.

Example# 25: RAFTs

 RAFTs are powerful learning activities because they offer a wide variety of options that can be differentiated by readiness level, interest level or learning style. Some options can use technology supports.

Figure 2.73.

RAFTs are writing prompts that can be differentiated by varying the concrete/abstract level, creativity level, concept depth level, and so forth. RAFTS offer a variety of product options as well. R = role, A = audience, F = format, T = topic. By offering learners different combinations of options, learners can choose options that fit their individual needs, thus increasing motivation.

This series of RAFTS was developed for the NLB eMuseum (Doswell, 2006a) on the topic of the First Colored World Series in 1924. The Kansas City Monarchs prevailed over Hilldale of Philadelphia. The RAFT chart contains 100 different writing combinations.

Role	Audience	Format	Topic
A newspaper reporter for the Kansas City Times	The citizens of Philadelphia	An invitation	The potential profit to be made from the Negro World Series
Ed Bolden	The coach of the Hilldale of Philadelphia	A letter or article	The thrill of the moment
A 12 year old Black boy from Philadelphia	The family of the character chosen in the Role column	A poem	The implications of this series on race relations
The mother of Jose Mendez	The patrons of the the local newspaper	A song	The caliber of Negro League Players
The mayor of Kansas City in 1924	The pitcher of the opposing team	An illustration	A play-by-play of a portion of one of the games

Figure 2.74.   Example of multiple RAFT options for a learning activity.

Example #26: Blogs

This example is from a lesson plan created for the NLB eMuseum (Barragree, 2006d). The lesson includes a description of blogs and a step-by-step set of instructions for creating a blog that was used as the learning activity for the lesson.

Description of a blog: A Web log (or blog) is a Web-based space for writing where all the writing and editing of information is managed through a Web browser and is immediately and publicly available on the Internet. A blog site is managed by an individual who compiles lists of links to personally interesting material, interspersed with information and editorial. Individuals use the public aspect of the blog to check where other people "are at" and to see what others are learning, but also to gauge their own progress compared to others. Blogs are able to integrate the personal aspect of a traditional learning journal that documents a learner's thoughts and ideas about a topic(s) with the publishing capabil-

---

Blog Activity

Learning activity: Students will use the blog to organize their thoughts and findings on oral traditions, folklore, negro Leagues baseball, NL players, and other cultures' oral traditions and folklore. The blogging experience is about not only putting thoughts on the web, but hearing back from and connecting with other students and like-minded people. Therefore students are able to observe others' learning through reading each other's learning journal blogs.

Creating a blog: eBlogger allows for lots of control. Go to the "Settings" page and you can modify things like time stamps, who can comment, etc. The best way to control access is to limit members of the blog. You can then add members by adding in their email addresses which makes it a private blog. You can even create a mirror blog for others to read and respond as well.

1..   Click on "Set up Blog Now."
2.   Enter some basic information-name, email address, etc.
3.   Choose a pre-made template for your blog or make your own if you like.
4.   Under "Settings" click on members and add member (student) email addresses. An invite email is sent to each member and they must accept in order to begin blogging. This allows you to see who has accessed the blog.
5.   Under "Settings" click on archive, select the frequency you want to archive the blog postings.
6.   Under "Settings" click on comments, under who can comment set it to only members of this blog. Now only members (students) you have allowed can comment on this page.
7.   After you make all the changes you want under "Settings", be sure to click on the republish button to update your changes.
8.   To begin blogging, click on "Posting" and blog

Figure 2.75.   Example of a learning activity using a blog.

ity of the Web. The blog is a way of documenting learning and collecting information for self-analysis and reflection.

e.Blogger allows users to set up blogs, free of charge. Find it at *www.blogger.com/start.*

Figure 2.76.

Example #27: Podcasts

Podcasting's initial appeal was to allow individuals to distribute their own "radio shows," but the system quickly became used in a wide variety of other ways, including distribution of <u>school lessons,</u> official and unofficial audio tours of museums, conference meeting alerts and updates, and by police departments to distribute public safety messages. The recent wide availability of MP3 players makes podcasts an up and coming media format. To create a podcast, learners would initially create a story, either in print or using a video camera. There are instructions posted on the Internet to convert a digital movie to a podcast and there are software packages available to record them directly.

Audacity is a free, easy-to-use audio editor and recorder for Windows, Mac OS X and Linux. Creates podcasts; record audio up to 24-bit 96kHz; convert tapes and records to MP3 or CD; edit OGG, MP3 and WAV files; cut, copy, splice, and mix sounds together, change the speed or pitch of a recording. Import sound files, edit them, and combine them with other files or new recordings. Export recordings in several common formats. Download it free from *http://www.topdrawerdownloads.com/download/104513.*

Figure 2.77.

Example #28: Self-Assessment

Having learners reflect upon their learning is a powerful tool. Like other supportive materials, self-assessment tools should offer flexible response formats. Consider this example from one of the NLB eMuseum lesson plans.

Version 1: Structured and tight
Answer the questions below to create a written assessment of the work that you did
during the project.

A. Content Knowledge
What new things did you learn while you worked on this project? List at least 3.
1. _____
2. _____
3. _____

B. Collaboration and Teamwork
Fill out the chart to list how you helped your team.

	What I did	How it helped
1.		
2.		
3.		

C. Technology Improvement
List at least one new thing you learned about using technology to get your ideas
across:_____

Figure 2.78.   Example of a structured self assessment tool.

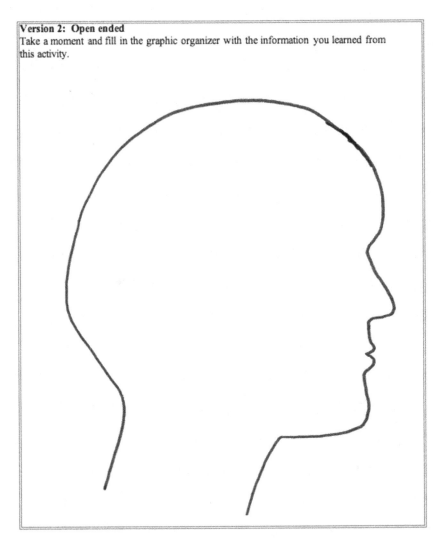

Version 2: Open ended
Take a moment and fill in the graphic organizer with the information you learned from this activity.

Figure 2.79.   Open ended self assessment tool.

CHAPTER 3

PLANNING FOR ACCESSIBILITY

INTRODUCTION

The 28 examples included in this handbook were created by a team of educators from museums and schools. Not all museums will have the luxury of this kind of team, however all museums can increase the accessibility of materials they create. Partnerships with school educators, especially special educators will prove very helpful in this process. Additionally, time and technology resources may be limited for some museums. Many of the techniques included in this handbook use simple tools that are probably on the desktop in the museum office. One computer that is connected to the Internet is all that is needed to download most of the software tools that were used in these examples.

SELF-ASSESSMENT

Educators from both museums and schools may find it helpful to critique curriculum materials using this rating scale. Items have been created using Carol Ann Tomlinson's Equalizer model (1999) and Robert Mace's principles of universal design (1997). Educators can examine curriculum for elements of accessibility in the areas of cognitive load, readiness, interest, motivation and learning style. It may also be helpful to have colleagues use the scale to rate materials created by each other in order to

Handbook on Developing Curriculum Materials for Teachers:
Lessons From Museum Education Partnerships, pp. 355–359
Copyright © 2010 by Information Age Publishing
355

ensure that intuitive assumptions have not been made during the design phase that would decrease the materials' accessibility.

Curriculum Material Accessibility Scale

The higher the score on these 20 questions, the higher the level of accessibility.

1. Information and ideas are ...	Foundational .... Transformational
	5 4 3 2 1
2. Representations and applications are ...	Concrete .... Abstract
	5 4 3 2 1
3. Problems, goals, research and issues are ...	Simple .... Complex
	5 4 3 2 1
4. Directions, solutions, approaches and applications are ...	Single Faceted .... Multifaceted
	5 4 3 2 1
5. Application, insight and transfer skills are ...	Small leaps .... Great Leaps
	5 4 3 2 1
6. Solutions, decisions and approaches are ...	More Structured .... More Open
	5 4 3 2 1
7. Planning, designing and monitoring are ...	More Dependent .... More Independent
	5 4 3 2 1
8. Pace of study and thought is ...	Slow .... Quick
	5 4 3 2 1
9. Presentation of content contains ...	At Least 3 Methods .... Only 1 Method
	5 4 3 2 1
10. Process of engagement is ...	Flexible .... Rigid
	5 4 3 2 1
11. Product offers ...	At Least 3 Options .... Only 1 Option
	5 4 3 2 1
12. Activity uses ...	At Least 2 Sensory Mode .... Only 1 Sensory Mode
	5 4 3 2 1
13. Required use of the materials is ...,	Simple and Intuitive .... Complex/Requires Instruction
	5 4 3 2 1
14. Information and ideas are ...	Easily Perceived .... Indistinct
	5 4 3 2 1
15. Tolerance for error is ...	High .... Low
	5 4 3 2 1
16. Physical effort required is ...	Low .... High
	5 4 3 2 1
17. Space for approach and/or use is ...	Large .... Small
	5 4 3 2 1
18. Format of text is ...	Digital .... Print
	5 4 3 2 1
19. Materials are ...	Interactive .... Static
	5 4 3 2 1
20. Variety of materials is ...	Large .... Small
	5 4 3 2 1

References:

Center for Applied Special Technology. (2006). *What is universal design for learning?* Retrieved February 5, 2006, from http://www.cast.org/research/udl/

Mace, R. (1997). *What is universal design?* Retrieved January 24, 2006, from http://www.design.ncsu.edu:8120/cud/newweb/about_ud/aboutud.htm

Tomlinson, C. (1999). *The differentiated classroom: Responding to the needs of all learners.* Alexandria, VA: Association for Supervision and Curriculum Development.

Figure 3.1.   Curriculum material accessibility scale.

PRIORITIES

Once educators become aware of the critical need to make their curriculum materials accessible, the biggest barrier to achieving this goal will be the availability of resources. Initially, educators would be well served to set small goals that will require minimal additional resources of:

1. Time
2. Staff
3. Equipment

This goal setting process should be guided by the educator's ability to prioritize. It is much easier to design accessible supportive materials for new curriculum than it is to retrofit existing curriculum. Start with a new project. As text is being prepared, create a digital version and store the material using a digital method. This will allow the manipulation of that text in a variety of ways. Seek out supportive images that supplement the content of that text. Explore digital photographs and movie clips. Finally, identify the "big ideas" of the material. What is it you want all learners to gain from the experience, despite their diverse skill levels, interests and physical attributes? Create one scaffold that captures these big ideas and store it digitally, along with the text and image files. This basic set of data will provide a foundational set of materials from which other scaffold materials can be created. It may be helpful to store this data set as separate files, but together in a folder for easy retrieval. Educators will be able to find materials quickly if the format of the digital file is also recorded. Using a chart like Figure 3.2 may be helpful.

SUMMARY

When professional educators working in schools or museums, seek to increase the scope of the curriculum they design they will benefit from these techniques. When applied during the initial design phase of the curriculum development process, these techniques will enhance the accessibility of curriculum and; therefore, enhance the delivery of content to learners and patrons with varied learning needs. These tools are also effective when used to retrofit already existing curricular materials; however, they may be more difficult and time consuming to implement after the fact. Therefore, the reader is encouraged to reflect upon the many diverse consumers that may benefit from a wider range of options and make a strategic decision to incorporate supports for those consumers as

Title of the content:		
TEXT		
File name:	Location:	Format:
IMAGES/SOUNDS		
File name:	Location:	Format:
BIG IDEAS: 1.	**2.**	
3.	**4.**	
File name:	Location:	Format:

Figure 3.2.   Curriculum material accessibility scale.

the development process unfolds. This decision will ultimately benefit many potential consumers.

Museum patrons who do not think about the museum's collection do not benefit from their museum experiences. The process of cognition varies greatly among patrons, both those with and those without disabilities. Physical differences such as mobility and sensory diversity have a profound impact on a patron's cognitive experience. Therefore, enhancing the accessibility of the mental process a museum visitor engages in has the potential to deliver a museum's content to a wider audience. The methods in this handbook utilize the principles of universal design; a set of design strategies that are already in use in the physical environment of many museums. The handbook seeks to expand these applications to the cognitive experiences that are delivered through curriculum materials.

It goes without saying that the educational system is greatly concerned with the process of cognition. Curriculum design has typically been the task of school educators and the methods and tools presented in this handbook are based on educational research and practice. Teachers will find these techniques useful in the lesson planning process as well.

The diversity represented by any group of potential learners can be an important part of the learning equation. Learners' capacities are not inherent; capacities are defined by the interplay between learners' abilities and the tools they use. When educators design additional supportive tools for learners to use, diverse groups of learners can reach the same learning goal, but can use different paths to achieve it. In schools, this process is imperative as educators are challenged to "Leave No Child Behind" and in museums the potential diversity represented by prospective patrons is unlimited.

Anyone who embraces the task of imparting knowledge must do so with an eye toward accessibility. This can be done by bringing rich learning experiences to all learners via materials that are truly accessible. When accomplished in the early planning stages, designing accessible materials is a creative, natural process.

REFERENCES

4Kids.org. (n.d.). Retrieved November 19, 2006 from www.4Kids.org

Adaptive Environments. (2003). *Universal design*. Retrieved January 31, 2006, from http://www.adaptiveenvironments.org/index.php?option =Content&Itemid=3

American Association of Museums. (2005). *Accreditation program standards*. Retrieved March 4, 2007, from http://www.aam-us.org/museumresources/ accred/upload/Characteristics%20of%20an%20Accreditable %20Museum%201-1-05.pdf

Association of Science Technology Centers. (2004). *Accessible practices*. Retrieved March 26, 2006, from http://www.astc.org/resource/access/index.htm

Amberton University. (n.d.) *Glossary of library terms*. Retrieved December 20, 2006 from http://www.amberton.edu/VL_terms.htm

Baillargeon, T. (2006). *Aftermath of freedom fighters lesson plan*. Retrieved December 15, 2006 from http://coe.k-state.edu/nlbemuseum/resource/lessonplans.html

Barragree, C. (2006a). *Publishing history lesson plan*. Retrieved December 15, 2006 from http://coe.k-state.edu/nlbemuseum/resource/lessonplans.html

Barragree, C. (2006b). *Folklore and oral history lesson plan*. Retrieved December 15, 2006 from http://coe.k-state.edu/nlbemuseum/resource/lessonplans.html

Barragree, C. (2006c). *Negro leagues baseball lesson plan*. Retrieved December 15, 2006 from http://coe.k-state.edu/nlbemuseum/resource/lessonplans.html

Barragree, C. (2006d). *Blogging baseball lesson plan*. Retrieved December 16, 2006 from http://coe.k-state.edu/nlbemuseum/resource/lessonplans.html

Berninger, V., Abbott, R., Abbot, S., Graham, S., & Richards, T. (2002). Connections between language by hand and language by eye. *Journal of Learning Disabilities, 35*(1), 30 56.

Boston Museum of Science. (2001b). *Star Wars: Where science meets imagination: Accessibility*. Retrieved February 11, 2006, from http://www.mos.org/doc/1870

Boston Museum of Science. (2001c). *Universal design (accessibility)*. Retrieved January 23, 2006, from http://www.mos.org/exhibitdevelopment/access/index.html

Center for Applied Special Technology. (2006). *What is universal design for learning?* Retrieved February 5, 2006, from http://www.cast.org/research/udl/

Center for Universal Design. (1997). *The principles of universal design version 2.0.* Raleigh: North Carolina State University. Retrieved July 16, 2006, from http://www.design.ncsu.edu:8120/cud/about_ud/docs/English.pdf

Center for Universal Design. (2006a). *About universal design.* Retrieved July 14, 2006, from http://www.design.ncsu.edu/cud/about_ud/about_ud.htm

Center for Universal Design. (2006b). *Universal design in housing.* Retrieved July 14, 2006, from http://www.design.ncsu.edu/cud/about_ud/docs/UD_Housing .pdf

CITES. (2006). *Glossary of acronyms and technical terms.* Retrieved December 20, 2006 from http://www.cites.uiuc.edu/glossary/index.html

Chandler, E. (2006a). *Buffalo soldiers lesson plan.* Unpublished manuscript.

Chandler, E. (2006b). *Women and negro baseball leagues lesson plan.* Retrieved December 15, 2006 from http://coe.k-state.edu/nlbemuseum/resource /lessonplans.html

Cole, E., & Matthews, M. (1999). Cognitive prosthetics and telerehabilitation: Approaches for the rehabilitation of mild brain injuries. *Proceedings of Basil Therapy Congress* (pp. 111-120). Basel, Switzerland.

DataCore Technology, Inc. (2006). *Glossary of terms.* Retrieved December 19, 2006 from http://www.data-core.com/glossary-of-terms.htm

Dodge, B. (2001). FOCUS: Five rules for writing great WebQuests. *Learning & Leading with Technology, 28*(8), 6-8.

Doswell, R. (2006a). *Colored world series lesson plan.* Retrieved December 15, 2006 from http://coe.k-state.edu/nlbemuseum/resource/lessonplans.html

Doswell, R. (2006b). *A brief history of the negro leagues.* Retrieved December 15, 2006 from http://coe.k-state.edu/nlbemuseum/resource/lessonplans.html

Duck, W. (n.d.) Retrieved November 26, 2006, from http://webquest.org/

Edyburn, D. (2003a). *Assistive technology for students with mild disabilities: From consideration to outcome measurement.* Paper presented at Closing The Gap, Minneapolis, MN.

Edyburn, D. (2004a). Cognitive rescaling strategies. *Closing the gap.* Retrieved November, 23, 2006, from http://www.paec.org/fdlrstech/SummerInstitute/ fdlrs2004/Edyburn/PDFs/Cognitiverescaling.pdf

Edyburn, D. (2004b). Rethinking assistive technology. *Special Education Technology Practice, 5*(4), 16-23.

Edyburn, D. (2005). *A primer in universal design (UD) in education.* Retrieved March 11, 2006, from http://www.uwm.edu/~edyburn/ud.html

Howard, G., Ellis, H., & Rasmussen, K. (2004). From the arcade to the classroom: Capitalizing on students' sensory rich media preferences in disciplined-based learning. *College Student Journal, 38*(3), 431-441.

IDEA (2004). *Selected sections of individuals with disabilities education act. H.R. 1350, SECTION 602: Definitions.* Retrieved July 9, 2006 from http://www.kansped .org/ksde/laws/idea04/602.doc

Katz, J., Stecker, N. A., & Henderson, D. (1992). Introduction to central auditory processing. In J. Katz, N. A. Stecker & D. Henderson (Eds.), *Central auditory processing: A tran disciplinary view* (pp. 3-8). St. Louis, MO: Mosby Year Book.

Kess, S. (1970). *Explanation of Tax Reform Act of 1969: P.L. 91-172*. Chicago: Chicago Review Press.

Kierman, L., & Tomlinson, C. (1997). *Why differentiate instruction?* Alexandria, Va.: Association for Supervision and Curriculum Development.

Library of Congress. (n.d.). *HR1350*. Retrieved March 26, 2006, from http://thomas.loc.gov/cgi-bin/query/F?c108:1:./temp/~c108ku8qRE:e16556

Mace, R. (1997). *What is universal design?* Retrieved January 24, 2006, from http://www.design.ncsu.edu:8120/cud/newweb/about_ud/aboutud.htm

Majewski, J. (n.d.). *Smithsonian guideline to accessible exhibition design*. Retrieved January 23, 2006, from http://www.si.edu/opa/accessibility/exdesign/start.htm http://web.mit.edu/campaign/styleguide/glossary.html

Marron. (n.d.). *Tiered lesson plan: Causes of the civil war*. Retrieved November 26, 2006 from http://www.bsu.edu/web/jfmarron/tlpcauses.html

McNeil, J. (1997). *Disabilities affect one fifth of all Americans*. Census Brief 97-5. Retrieved July 14, 2006, from http://www.census.gov/prod/3/97pubs/cenbr975.pdf

Melvin, B. & Dale, C. (2006). *Persuasive writing: Instructional unit resource guide*. Unpublished manuscript.

Mott, L. (2006a). *Research tool for time warp activity*. Retrieved December 15, 2006 from http://coe.k-state.edu/nlbemuseum/resource/lessonplans.html

Mott. L. (2006b). *The dirty laundry of segregation*. Unpublished manuscript.

National Multiple Sclerosis Society. (2004). *Glossary*. Retrieved March 26, 2006, from http://www.nationalmssociety.org/I%20-%20N.asp

Nebraska Department of Education. (n.d.). *Glossary*. Retrieved December 19, 2006 from http://www.nde.state.ne.us/READ/FRAMEWORK/glossary/general_u-z.html

Negro Leagues Baseball Museum. (n.d.). Retrieved March 29, 2006, from www.nlbm.com

North Central Regional Educational Laboratory. (2004). *Glossary of education terms and acronyms*. Retrieved February 17, 2006, from http://www.ncrel.org/sdrs/areas/misc/glossary.htm

Nunley, K. (2003). Layered curriculum brings teachers to tiers. *Education Digest* 69(1), 31-37. Retrieved November 30, 2006 from http://proquest.umi.com.er.lib.ksu.edu/pqdlink?Ver=1&Exp=11-29-2011&FMT=7&DID=424927581&RQT=309&clientId=48067

Orkwis, R. (1999). *What is curriculum access?* The ERIC Clearinghouse on Disabilities and Gifted Education. Retrieved March 26, 2006, from http://ericec.org/digests/e586.html

Peirce, R., & Adams, C. (2004). Tiered lessons: One way to differentiate mathematics instruction. *Gifted Child Today, 27*(2), 58-67.

Prestia, K. (2004). Incorporate sensory activities into the classroom. *Intervention in School and Clinic, 39*(3), 172-175.

Rehabtool. (2004). *What's assistive technology?* Retrieved December 19, 2006 from http://www.rehabtool.com/at.html#Speech%20and%20Augmentative%20Communication%20Aids

Rose, D., & Meyer, A. (1998). *Learning to read in the digital age*. Retrieved October 1, 2006, from http://www.cast.org/teachingeverystudent/ideas/tes/

Rose, D., & Meyer, A. (2002). *Teaching every student in the digital age: Universal design for learning.* Retrieved October 1, 2006, from http://www.cast.org/teachingeverystudent/ideas/tes/

Schumm, J. S., Vaughn, S., & Harris, J. (1997). Pyramid power for collaborative planning. *Teaching Exceptional Children, 29*(6), 62-66.

System for Adult Basic Education Support. (n.d.). *Glossary of useful terms.* Retrieved April 14, 2006, from http://www.sabes.org/assessment/glossary.htm

Tokar, S. (2003). *Universal design: An optimal approach to the development of hands-on exhibits in science museums.* Retrieved January 12, 2006, from http://www.stevetokar.com/images/pdf_files/Tokar_UD_thesis.pdf

Tomlinson, C. (1999). *The differentiated classroom: Responding to the needs of all learners.* Alexandria, VA: Association for Supervision and Curriculum Development.

Tomlinson, C. (2000). Reconcilable differences? Standards-based teaching and differentiation. *Educational Leadership, 58*(1), 6-11.

Tomlinson, C., & McTighe, J. (2006). *Integrating differentiated instruction and understanding by design: Connecting content and kids.* Alexandria, VA: Association for Supervision and Curriculum Development.

United States Department of Education. (2003). *Overview: Fact sheet on the major provisions of the conference report to H.R. 1, The No Child Left Behind Act.* Retrieved February 16, 2006, from http://www.ed.gov/nclb/landing.jhtml

United States Department of Justice. (2005). *ADA references and technical materials.* Retrieved February 12, 2006, from http://www.usdoj.gov/crt/ada/publicat.htm#Anchor-ADA-44867

United States National Library of Medicine. (2006). Medical encyclopedia. Retrieved November 19, 2006, from http://www.nlm.nih.gov/medlineplus/ency/article/002286.htm

Van Garderen, D., & Whittaker, C. (2006). Planning differentiated, multicultural instruction for secondary inclusive classrooms. *Teaching Exceptional Children, 38*(3), 12-20.

VanSciver, J. (2005). Motherhood, apple pie, and differentiated instruction. *Phi Delta Kappan, 86*(7), 534.

WordReference. (2005). *English dictionary.* Retrieved April 1, 2006, from http://www.wordreference.com/definition

BIBLIOGRAPHY

4Kids.org. (n.d.) Retrieved November 19, 2006 from www.4Kids.org

Adaptive Environments. (2003). *Universal design*. Retrieved January 31, 2006, from http://www.adaptiveenvironments.org/index.php?option= Content&Itemid=3

American Association of Museums. (2005). *Accreditation program standards*. Retrieved March 4, 2007, from http://www.aam-us.org/museumresources/ accred/upload/Characteristics%20of%20an%20Accreditable %20Museum%201-1-05.pdf

Association of Science Technology Centers. (2004). *Accessible practices*. Retrieved March 26, 2006, from http://www.astc.org/resource/access/index.htm

Amberton University. (n.d.) *Glossary of library terms*. Retrieved December 20, 2006, from http://www.amberton.edu/VL_terms.htm

Baillargeon, T. (2006). *Aftermath of freedom fighters lesson plan*. Retrieved December 15, 2006, from http://coe.k-state.edu/nlbemuseum/resource/lessonplans.html

Barragree, C. (2006a). *Publishing history lesson plan*. Retrieved December 15, 2006, from http://coe.k-state.edu/nlbemuseum/resource/lessonplans.html

Barragree, C. (2006b). *Folklore and oral history lesson plan*. Retrieved December 15, 2006, from http://coe.k-state.edu/nlbemuseum/resource/lessonplans.html

Barragree, C. (2006c). *Negro leagues baseball lesson plan*. Retrieved December 15, 2006, from http://coe.k-state.edu/nlbemuseum/resource/lessonplans.html

Barragree, C. (2006d). *Blogging baseball lesson plan*. Retrieved December 16, 2006, from http://coe.k-state.edu/nlbemuseum/resource/lessonplans.html

Berninger, V., Abbott, R., Abbot, S., Graham, S., & Richards, T. (2002). Connections between language by hand and language by eye. *Journal of Learning Disabilities, 35*(1), 39-50.

Boston Museum of Science. (2001a). *Star Wars: Where science meets imagination: Accessibility*. Retrieved February 11, 2006, from http://www.mos.org/doc/1870

Boston Museum of Science. (2001b). *Universal design (accessibility)*. Retrieved January 23, 2006, from http://www.mos.org/exhibitdevelopment/access/index.html

Center for Applied Special Technology. (2006). *What is universal design for learning?* Retrieved February 5, 2006, from http://www.cast.org/research/udl/

Center for Universal Design. (1997). *The principles of universal design version 2.0.* Raleigh: North Carolina State University. Retrieved July 16, 2006, from http://www.design.ncsu.edu:8120/cud/about_ud/docs/English.pdf

Center for Universal Design. (2006a). *About universal design.* Retrieved July 14, 2006, from http://www.design.ncsu.edu/cud/about_ud/about_ud.htm

Center for Universal Design. (2006b). *Universal design in housing.* Retrieved July 14, 2006, from http://www.design.ncsu.edu/cud/about_ud/docs/UD_Housing.pdf

CITES. (2006). *Glossary of acronyms and technical terms.* Retrieved December 20, 2006, from http://www.cites.uiuc.edu/glossary/index.html

Chandler, E. (2006a). *Buffalo soldiers lesson plan.* Unpublished manuscript.

Chandler, E. (2006b). *Women and negro baseball leagues lesson plan.* Retrieved December 15, 2006, from http://coe.k-state.edu/nlbemuseum/resource/lessonplans.html

Cole, E., & Matthews, M. (1999). Cognitive prosthetics and telerehabilitation: Approaches for the rehabilitation of mild brain injuries. *Proceedings of Basil Therapy Congress* (pp. 111-120). Basel, Switzerland.

CT Developing. (2006). *PDF text reader.* Retrieved October 15, 2006 from http://www.ctdeveloping.com/ctdeveloping/products/pdftextreader_info.asp

DataCore Technology, Inc. (2006). *Glossary of terms.* Retrieved December 19, 2006 from http://www.data-core.com/glossary-of-terms.htm

Deshler, D. D., Robinson, S., & Mellard, D. F. (2004). Instructional principles for optimizing outcomes for adolescents with learning disabilities. In M. K. Riley & T. A. Citro (Eds.), *Best practices for the inclusionary classroom: Leading researchers talk directly with teachers.* Weston, MA: Learning Disabilities Association Worldwide.

Discoveryschool. (2006). *Kathy Schrock's guide for educators.* Retrieved November 19, 2006, from http://school.discovery.com/schrockguide/

Dodge, B. (2001). FOCUS: Five rules for writing great WebQuests. *Learning & Leading with Technology, 28*(8), 6-8.

Doswell, R. (2006a). *Colored world series lesson plan.* Retrieved December 15, 2006, from http://coe.k-state.edu/nlbemuseum/resource/lessonplans.html

Doswell, R. (2006b). *A brief history of the negro leagues.* Retrieved December 15, 2006, from http://coe.k-state.edu/nlbemuseum/resource/lessonplans.html

Duck, W. (n.d.). *WebQuest.* Retrieved November 26, 2006, from http://webquest.org/

Edmunds, A. L. (1999) Cognitive credit cards: Acquiring learning strategies. *Teaching Exceptional Children, 31*(4), 68073. Retrieved November 30, 2006. from http://vnweb.hwwilsonweb.com.er.lib.ksu.edu/hww/shared/shared main .jhtml?_requestid=88555

Edyburn, D. (2000). Assistive technology and students with mild disabilities. *Focus on Exceptional Children, 32*(9), 1-24.

Edyburn, D. (2001a). Critical issues in special education technology research: What do we know? What do we need to know? In M. Mastropieri & T. Scruggs

(Eds.), *Advances in learning and behavioral disabilities* (Vol. 15, pp. 95-118). New York: JAI Press.

Edyburn, D. (2001b). Models, theories and frameworks: Contributions to understanding special education technology. *Special Education Technology Practice, 3*(2), 16-24.

Edyburn, D. (2003a). *Assistive technology for students with mild disabilities: From consideration to outcome measurement.* Paper presented at Closing the Gap, Minneapolis, MN.

Edyburn, D. (2003b). Learning from text. *Special Education Technology Practice, 5*(2), 16-27.

Edyburn, D. (2004a). Cognitive rescaling strategies. *Closing the Gap.* Retrieved November, 23, 2006, from http://www.paec.org/fdlrstech/SummerInstitute/fdlrs2004/Edyburn/PDFs/Cognitiverescaling.pdf

Edyburn, D. (2004b). Rethinking assistive technology. *Special Education Technology Practice, 5*(4), 16-23.

Edyburn, D. (2005). *A primer in universal design (UD) in education.* Retrieved March 11, 2006, from http://www.uwm.edu/~edyburn/ud.html

Edyburn, D. (2206). Cognitive prostheses for students with mild disabilities: Is this what assistive technology looks like? *Journal of Special Education Technology, 21*(4), 62-65.

Edburn, D. (2007). Re-examining the role of assistive technology in learning. *Closing the Gap, 25*(5), 1-5.

How Stuff Works. (2006). Retrieved November 19, 2006, from www.howstuffworks.com

Howard, G., Ellis, H., & Rasmussen, K. (2004). From the arcade to the classroom: Capitalizing on students' sensory rich media preferences in disciplined-based learning. *College Student Journal, 38*(3), 431-441.

IDEA. (2004). *Selected sections of individuals with disabilities education act H.R. 1350, SECTION 602: Definitions.* Retrieved July 9, 2006 from http://www.kansped.org/ksde/laws/idea04/602.doc

Inspiration. (n.d.). *Inspiration software.* Retrieved November 19, 2006, from http://www.inspiration.com

Jatala, S., & Seevers, R. (2006). Nature and use of curriculum in special education. *Academic Exchange Quarterly, 10*(1), 192-197.

Katz, J., Stecker, N. A., & Henderson, D. (Eds.). (1992). Introduction to central auditory processing. In *Central auditory processing: A tran disciplinary view* (pp. 3-8). St. Louis, MO: Mosby Year Book.

Kay, R. (2006). Evaluating strategies used to incorporate technology into preservice education: A review of the literature. *Journal of Research on Technology in Education, 38*(4). 383-408.

Kess, S. (1970). *Explanation of Tax Reform Act of 1969: P.L. 91-172.* Chicago: Chicago Review Press.

Kierman, L., & Tomlinson, C. (1997). *Why differentiate instruction?* Alexandria, VA: Association for Supervision and Curriculum Development.

Library of Congress. (n.d.). *HR1350.* Retrieved March 26, 2006, from http://thomas.loc.gov/cgi-bin/query/F?c108:1:./temp/~c108ku8qRE:e16556

Mace, R. (1997). *What is universal design?* Retrieved January 24, 2006, from http://www.design.ncsu.edu:8120/cud/newweb/about_ud/aboutud.htm

Majewski, J. (n.d.). *Smithsonian guideline to accessible exhibition design.* Retrieved January 23, 2006, from http://www.si.edu/opa/accessibility/exdesign/start.htm http://web.mit.edu/campaign/styleguide/glossary.html

Marron. (n.d.). *Tiered lesson plan: Causes of the civil war.* Retrieved November 26, 2006 from http://www.bsu.edu/web/jfmarron/tlpcauses.html

McNeil, J. (1997). *Disabilities affect one fifth of all Americans.* Census Brief 97-5. Retrieved July 14, 2006, from http://www.census.gov/prod/3/97pubs/cenbr975.pdf

Melvin, B., & Dale, C. (2006). *Persuasive writing: Instructional unit resource guide.* Unpublished manuscript.

Microsoft Corporation. (2003). *Microsoft Office.* Retrieved October 15, 2006, from http://www.microsoft.com/shared/core/1/webservice/navigation.asmx /DisplayDownlevelNavHtml?navPath=/global/SiteTemplates /5257839b-b661-44b7-9194-2bc147d897b0.xml&groupName=Office

Mott, L. (2006a). *Research tool for time warp activity.* Retrieved December 15, 2006, from http://coe.k-state.edu/nlbemuseum/resource/lessonplans.html

Mott. L. (2006b). *The dirty laundry of segregation.* Unpublished manuscript.

National Multiple Sclerosis Society. (2004). *Glossary.* Retrieved March 26, 2006, from http://www.nationalmssociety.org/I%20-%20N.asp

NaturalReader. (2006). Retrieved October 15, 2006, from http://www .naturalreaders.com/index.htm

Nebraska Department of Education. (n.d.). *Glossary.* Retrieved December 19, 2006, from http://www.nde.state.ne.us/READ/FRAMEWORK/glossary/general_u-z.html

Negro Leagues Baseball Museum. (n.d.). Retrieved March 29, 2006, from www.nlbm.com

North Central Regional Educational Laboratory. (2004). *Glossary of education terms and acronyms.* Retrieved February 17, 2006, from http://www.ncrel.org/sdrs/areas/misc/glossary.htm

Nunley, K. (1996). Going for the goal: multilevel assignments cater to students of differing abilities. *The Science Teacher, 63*(6), 52-57. Retrieved November 30, 2006 from http://proquest.umi.com.er.lib.ksu.edu/pqdlink?vinst=PROD& fmt=6&startpage=-1&ver=1&clientid=48067&vname=PQD&RQT= 309&did=10096127&exp=11-29-2011&scaling=FULL&vtype=PQD&rqt =309&TS=1164916196&clientId=48067

Nunley, K. (2003). Layered curriculum brings teachers to tiers. *Education Digest 69*(1), 31-37. Retrieved November 30, 2006 from http://proquest.umi.com .er.lib.ksu.edu/pqdlink?Ver=1&Exp=11-29-2011&FMT=7&DID =424927581&RQT=309&clientId=48067

Orkwis, R. (1999). *What is curriculum access?* The ERIC Clearinghouse on Disabilities and Gifted Education. Retrieved March 26, 2006, from http://ericec.org/digests/e586.html

Peirce, R., & Adams, C. (2004). Tiered lessons: One way to differentiate mathematics instruction. *Gifted Child Today, 27*(2), 58-67.

Prestia, K. (2004). Incorporate sensory activities into the classroom. *Intervention in School and Clinic, 39*(3), 172-175.

ReadPlease. (2005). *Readplease.* Retrieved October 15, 2006, from http://www.readplease.com/english/readplease.php

Rehabtool. (2004). *What's assistive technology?* Retrieved December 19, 2006, from http://www.rehabtool.com/at.html#Speech%20and%20Augmentative%20Communication%20Aids

Robinson, S. (2005). Universal design for learning. Retrieved November 26, 2006, from http://www.specialconnections.ku.edu/cgi-bin/cgiwrap/specconn/main.php?cat=instruction&section=main&subsection=udl/main

Rose, D., & Meyer, A. (1998). *Learning to read in the digital age.* Retrieved October 1, 2006, from http://www.cast.org/teachingeverystudent/ideas/tes/

Rose, D., & Meyer, A. (2002). *Teaching every student in the digital age: Universal design for learning.* Retrieved October 1, 2006, from http://www.cast.org/teachingeverystudent/ideas/tes/

Savage, R., Cornish, T., Manly, T., & Hollis, C. (2006). Cognitive processes in children's reading and attention: The role of working memory, divided attention, and response inhibition. *British Journal of Psychology, 97*(3), 365-386.

Schumm, J. S., Vaughn, S., & Harris, J. (1997). Pyramid power for collaborative planning. *Teaching Exceptional Children, 29*(6), 62-66.

Siegil, M. (1995). More than words: The generative power of transmediation for learning. *Canadian Journal of Education, 20*(4), 455-475.

Slater Software. (2006). *Free stuff.* Retrieved November 26, 2006 from http://www.slatersoftware.com/document.html

Students for the Exploration and Development of Space. (2005). Retrieved November 19, 2006, from www.seds.org

System for Adult Basic Education Support. (n.d.). *Glossary of useful terms.* Retrieved April 14, 2006, from http://www.sabes.org/assessment/glossary.htm

Tokar, S. (2003). *Universal design: An optimal approach to the development of hands-on exhibits in science museums.* Retrieved January 12, 2006, from http://www.stevetokar.com/images/pdf_files/Tokar_UD_thesis.pdf

Tomlinson, C. (1995). *How to differentiate instruction in mixed ability classrooms.* Alexandria, VA: Association for Supervision and Curriculum Development.

Tomlinson, C. (1999). *The differentiated classroom: Responding to the needs of all learners.* Alexandria, VA: Association for Supervision and Curriculum Development.

Tomlinson, C. (2000). Reconcilable differences? Standards-based teaching and differentiation. *Educational Leadership, 58*(1), 6-11.

Tomlinson, C., & McTighe, J. (2006). *Integrating differentiated instruction and understanding by design: Connecting content and kids.* Alexandria, VA: Association for Supervision and Curriculum Development.

Trackstar. (2006) Retrieved November 19, 2006, from http://trackstar.4teachers.org/trackstar/;jsessionid=A9516CD0521917594BB7095D5BE69D40

United States Department of Education. (2003). *Overview: Fact sheet on the major provisions of the conference report to H.R. 1, The No Child Left Behind Act.* Retrieved February 16, 2006, from http://www.ed.gov/nclb/landing.jhtml

United States Department of Education. (2005). *History of IDEA*. Retrieved March 26, 2006, from http://www.ed.gov/policy/speced/leg/idea/history30.html

United States Department of Justice. (2005). *ADA references and technical materials*. Retrieved February 12, 2006, from http://www.usdoj.gov/crt/ada/publicat .htm#Anchor-ADA-44867

United States National Library of Medicine. (2006). *Medical encyclopedia*. Retrieved November 19, 2006, from http://www.nlm.nih.gov/medlineplus/ency/article/ 002286.htm

Van Garderen, D., & Whittaker, C. (2006). Planning differentiated, multicultural instruction for secondary inclusive classrooms. *Teaching Exceptional Children, 38*(3), 12-20.

VanSciver, J. (2005). Motherhood, apple pie, and differentiated instruction. *Phi Delta Kappan, 86*(7), 534.

World Fact Book. (n.d) Retrieved November 19, 2006, from www.odci.gov/cia /publications/factbook

WordReference. (2005). *English dictionary*. Retrieved April 1, 2006, from http:// www.wordreference.com/definition

GLOSSARY

Accessibility: The ability of a product to have the user actively engage and use that product (Orkwiss, 1999). Capable of being reached (WordReference, 2005).

Assistive Technology: The use of a device, item, piece of equipment, or product system, whether acquired commercially off the shelf, modified, or customized, that is used to increase, maintain, or improve functional capabilities of a child with a disability (Library of Congress, n.d.).

Auditory Processing: The ability of the brain to process incoming auditory signals. The brain identifies sounds by analyzing their distinguishing physical characteristics frequency, intensity, and temporal features. These are features that are perceived as pitch, loudness, and duration. Once the brain has completed its analysis of the physical characteristics of the incoming sound or message, it then constructs an "image" of the signal from these component parts for comparison with stored "images." If a match occurs, the brain can then understand what is being heard (Katz, Stecker, & Henderson, 1992).

Augmentative Communication Device: Alternate methods of communicating needs, feelings, ideas, and perceptions through the use of electronic and non-electronic devices that provide a means for expressive and receptive communication for persons with limited or no speech. Exam-

Handbook on Developing Curriculum Materials for Teachers:
Lessons From Museum Education Partnerships, pp. 371–374
Copyright © 2010 by Information Age Publishing
371

ples include communication boards, speech synthesizers, text-to-speech software and hardware, head wands, light pointers, mouth sticks, signal systems, telephony equipment, and so on (Rehabtool, 2004).

Cognition: High level functions carried out by the human brain, including comprehension and use of speech, visual perception and construction, calculation ability, attention (information processing), memory, and executive functions such as planning, problem-solving, and self-monitoring (The National Multiple Sclerosis Society, 2004).

Cognitive Prosthesis: A device that replaces or improves the function of a thinking process (Cole & Matthews, 1999).

Cognitive Rescaling: An adaptation that modifies the difficulty of cognitive processes needed to process content (Edyburn, 2004).

Curricular Scaffold: An instructional technique in which the teacher breaks a complex task into smaller tasks, models the desired learning strategy or task, provides support as students learn to do the task, and then gradually shifts responsibility to the students. In this manner, a teacher enables students to accomplish as much of a task as possible without adult assistance (North Central Regional Educational Laboratory (NCREL), 2004).

Differentiated Instruction: A method of teaching that requires teachers to begin where students are rather than at the front of a curriculum guide, and to accept and build upon the premise that learners differ in important ways (Tomlinson, 1999).

Digital: Referring to the electronic storage and presentation of information (Center for Applied Special Technology, 2006).

Diorama: A picture or series of pictures representing a continuous scene (WordReference, 2005).

Educator: One trained in teaching; a teacher; a specialist in the theory and practice of teaching; a person whose occupation is to educate (System for Adult Basic Education Support, n.d.).

Emotiocons: A group of keyboard characters that take on facial expressions and are used to express emotion in text-based electronic communication, that is, e-mail, discussions, or conferencing (Sacramento State, n.d.).

Engagement: That part of the learning process in which the learner is occupied with the content (Rose & Meyer, 2002).

Executive Functioning: A cognitive process that operates to schedule competing action plans, and is related to the control of attention through habituation and/or inhibition processes (Savage, Cornish, Manly, & Hollis, 2006).

Individuals With Disabilities Education Act (IDEA): HR1350, Federal legislation reauthorized in 1997, then again in 2004. The title was changed to the Individuals with Disabilities Education Improvement Act (IDEIA) with the 2004 reauthorization (United States Department of Education, 2005).

Icons: A pictorial image used in a graphical user interface to represent a program, a command, a link to a Web page, and so forth (Amberton, n.d.).

Negro Leagues Baseball Museum (NLBM): A privately funded, non-profit organization dedicated to preserving the rich history of African American Baseball (NLBM, n.d.).

No Child Left Behind: H.R. 1, The No Child Left Behind Act is a reform of the Elementary and Secondary Education Act (ESEA), enacted in 1965. It redefines the federal role in kindergarten through 12th grade education to help improve the academic achievement of all American students. It has four major components (a) accountability for results, (b) flexibility at the state and local level, (c) expanded options for parents, and (d) emphasis on research-base teaching methods (U.S. Department of Education, 2003).

Personal Digital Assistants (PDAs): A handheld device that combines computing, telephone/fax, and networking features. A typical PDA can function as a cellular phone, fax sender, and personal organizer. Many PDAs incorporate handwriting and/or voice recognition features. PDAs also are called palmtops, handheld computers, and pocket computers (CITES, 2006).

Portable Document Format (PDF): Portable Document Format. PDF is a universal file format that preserves the fonts, images, graphics, and layout of any source document, regardless of the application and platform used to create it. Adobe PDF files are compact and complete, and can be shared, viewed, and printed by anyone with free Adobe Reader software (DataCore, Inc., 2006).

Prosthesis: A device designed to replace a missing part of the body or to make a part of the body work better (United States National Library of Medicine, 2006).

Readiness: A way of looking at a learner's academic functioning skills, that includes current knowledge, understanding, and skill as it relates to what is being studied. Readiness varies from learner to learner, and within an individual learner; either according to content area, daily attitude, state of health, and so on (Tomlinson, 1999; Van Garderen & Whittaker, 2006).

Shape Story: A type of graphic organizer in which the learner takes notes in a non-linear fashion. The text creates a design that reflects an important aspect of the content.

Tiered Lessons: A method of differentiating instruction by planning lessons in which learners may be assigned different learning objectives, and be assigned different learning activities. However, the activities in which they engaged reflect a consistent learning path toward those objectives (Tomlinson, 1999).

Universal Design: The design of products and environments to be usable by all people, to the greatest extent possible, without the need for adaptation or specialized design (Mace, 1997).

Universal Design for Learning: A blueprint for creating flexible goals, methods, materials, and assessments that accommodate learner differences (Center for Applied Special Technology, 2006).

Venn Diagram: in concept mapping, overlapping circles that show those features either unique or common to two or more concepts (Nebraska Department of Education, n.d.).

WebQuest: This inquiry-oriented activity that involves interacting with resources on the Internet. They can be appropriate for almost any age learner or content. According to Dodge (2001), WebQuests contain the following six elements: introduction, task, process, resources, evaluation and conclusion.

APPENDIX A

COMPLETE NEGRO LEAGUES BASEBALL EMUSUEM LESSON PLAN

This lesson plan was developed by Lori Mott, Negro Leagues Scholar in March, 2006.

NEGRO LEAGUES SCRAPBOOK

Key Features of Powerful Teaching and Learning: (National Council for the Social Studies. A Vision of Powerful Teaching and Learning in the Social Studies: Building Social Understanding and Civic Efficacy. http://www.socialstudies.org/positions/powerful/)

Meaningful: Emphasizes social, political, and cultural issues of Black America and the Negro Leagues in the twentieth century.

Grade Level: 9-12

Subject: Social Studies

Standards:

NCSS Standards: I, II, III, IV, V, X

ISTE Standards: 2,3,4,5

Missouri Standards: 2, 5, 6, 7

Time allotment: 8, one-hour periods

Handbook on Developing Curriculum Materials for Teachers:
Lessons From Museum Education Partnerships, pp. 375–383
Copyright © 2010 by Information Age Publishing
All rights of reproduction in any form reserved.

Integrated: Students will use technology to explore Black America and the Negro Leagues in the twentieth century.

Challenging: Students will use a variety of skills to demonstrate their understanding of major ideas, eras, themes, and turning points in the history of the United States during the first 75 years of the twentieth century.

Active: Students will work in teams to create a scrapbook. Each member will play a role in the development of the final project.

Purpose/Rationale/Introduction:

Students will compile a scrapbook of photographs, quotations, and notes, representing the perspective of a Negro Leagues baseball player. The scrapbook will be from the point of view of a fictional character, and will include artifacts examining the Negro Leagues, travels, family, and life during segregation and the civil rights movement. The scrapbook should include photographs with captions, letters, news headlines, and any other materials students wish such as maps, souvenirs, and mementos.

Objectives:

1. Students will be able to identify key events in the United States and the Negro Leagues from 1900-1975.
2. Students will create a detailed timeline of the key events in the United States and the Negro Leagues from 1900 to 1975.
3. Students will create a historical-fiction scrapbook using key events in history.

Materials/Primary Resources:

- Electronic scrapbook resources: Internet access, PowerPoint, and handouts;
- Rubric;
- Physical scrapbook resources: construction paper, scissors, glue, and markers.

Procedures & Activities:

- *Day 1 & 2:* Students will receive the Quest Page with the assignment and rubric. The instructor should explain the assignment and discuss the requirements of the rubric. Students will work in teams of three to five to complete assignment 1.

- *Day 3:* Students will begin work on assignment 2. In assignment 2 students will begin to organize their research. They will also begin to sketch the layout of the scrapbook.
- *Day 4-6:* Students will work on the construction of the scrapbook following the criteria in the rubric and assignments two and three.
- *Day 7 & 8:* Students will present their finished scrapbook to the class.

Extension and Enrichment:

Create of scrapbook of your own detailing your life experiences and key historical events.

Online Resources:

- Negro Leagues Sites

  http://www.nlbm.com/

  http://mlb.mlb.com/NASApp/mlb/mlb/history/
     mlb_negro_Leagues.jsp

  http://www.nlbpa.com/index.html http://www
     .negroLeaguesbaseball.com/index.html

  http://www.blackbaseball.com/

- History Sites

  http://memory.loc.gov/ammem/

  http://www.thehistorymakers.com/

  http://lcweb2.loc.gov/ammem/aap/timelin3.html

Assessment:

Students should be assessed using the rubric. Students should receive the rubric prior to the start of the project.

Alternate Assessment:

Students will write an obituary for their great grandfather or grandmother detailing the events in his/her life.

THE SCRAPBOOK OF A NEGRO LEAGUES BASEBALL PLAYER

Introduction:

Last summer you were visiting your grandparents. While watching a baseball game on TV your grandfather mentions that your great grandfather played professional baseball in the Negro Leagues. This piqued your interest and you began to ask your grandparents questions about your great-grandfather and the Negro Leagues. Your grandfather asks if you would like to look at a box of his photographs, letters, and journals. As you are looking through the large box, your grandfather states that he always wanted to organize his memorabilia into a scrapbook for others to see. He asks if you would be willing to complete this project.

The Task:

You will create a scrapbook detailing the experiences of your great grandfather both as a baseball player and a Black male living during segregation. The scrapbook will be from the point of view of a fictional character, and will include artifacts examining the Negro Leagues, travels, family, and life during segregation and the civil rights movement. The scrapbook should include journal entries, photographs with captions, letters, news headlines, and any other materials students wish such as maps, souvenirs, and mementoes.

A scrapbook is a collection of artifacts and personal memorabilia, organized in an album. The album may be organized chronologically or by theme.

Your scrapbook will be historical fiction meaning the character will be fictional but the setting and events will be rooted in actual history.

Process:

You will work as a team of three to five to complete the following assignments. Within your team you should assign individual roles to complete the project.

- Project Manager (Team Leader): The role is to keep the team on task, monitor progress, and assists the technology leader and researchers.
- Technology Leader: Responsible for the building the electronic scrapbook.
- Researcher(s) - Responsible for collecting and organizing information and maintaining historical accuracy. Researchers are also responsible for the creation of artifacts to support each event.

Assignment 1: Your great grandfather lived from 1901 to 1975. Complete a timeline of key events that he would have experienced or would have impacted his life, both on and off of the baseball diamond. As a team, determine which of these events would have had the most impact and include them in the timeline

- The timeline should include at least 15 key historical events.
- Each event should have a detailed description. (Who, What, Why, Where, When, How)

Assignment 2: As a team, decide how you will present and organize the material for the scrapbook. The information can be organized either chronologically or by themes. Students have the option of creating an electronic journal with PowerPoint, Microsoft Publisher, etc. or creating a hard copy scrapbook. Use the graphic organizer and storyboard to map out the layout of your scrapbook. Your scrapbook should:

- Include at least three baseball-related experiences.
- Include at least seven events outside of baseball that would have made an impact on him during his lifetime.
- A journal entry and at least two other artifacts such as photographs with captions, letters, news headlines, and any other materials such as maps, souvenirs, mementoes, and so on, should support each of these events.

Assignment 3: Create an electronic scrapbook using the specifications listed above. Your scrapbook should also include:

- A title page with the names of each student.
- Bibliography page

Assignment 4: Present your scrapbook to your grandparents (class).

SCRAPBOOK RUBRIC

Scrapbook Rubric

	Beginning 1	Developing 2	Accomplished 3	Exemplary 4	Score
Preparedness	Unable to accomplish any assignments by the required due date	Unable to accomplish most assignments by the required due date	Able to complete most of the assignments by the required due date	Able to complete all assignments by the required due date	
Cooperation	Team members did not work together to complete assignments	Team members rarely worked together to complete assignments	Team members usually worked together to complete assignments	Team members worked together to complete assignments	
Historically Accurate *The scrapbook is historical fiction. Some events will be fictional but should reflect the time period.	Scrapbook is not historically accurate	Scrapbook contains some historical inaccuracies	Scrapbook is virtually historically accurate	Scrapbook accurately represents important ideas and events	
Use of Artifacts	Artifacts are not related to topic and do not meet assignment criteria	Artifacts adequately related to topic but do not meet assignment criteria	Artifacts are relevant and meet most of assignment criteria	A variety of artifacts are used to portray event and meet assignment criteria	
Scrapbook Design/ Creativity	No organization of page layout. Background and graphics are not appealing.	Page Layout somewhat organized. Some of the background and graphics are appealing and enhance the scrapbook.	Most of the page layout is organized. Most of the background and graphics are visually appealing and enhance the scrapbook.	The scrapbook is well organized and background and graphics are visually appealing and enhance the scrapbook.	
Spelling and Grammar	More than six spelling and grammar errors found on final scrapbook	Four or more spelling and grammar errors found on final scrapbook.	Two or more spelling and grammar errors found on final scrapbook	One or less spelling and grammar errors found on final scrapbook	
Citations	No Citation Page	Some citations. Cited incorrectly	Most of the scrapbook is cited. Some citations incorrect	All of the scrapbook is cited correctly	

Figure A.1.   Scrapbook rubic.

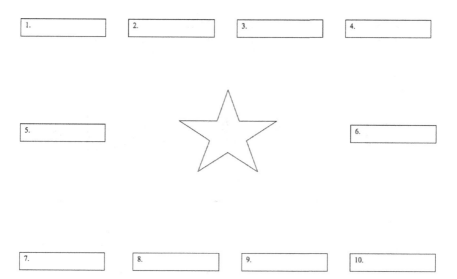

Figure A.2.   Quest Page to record main ideas.

Event	Journal Topic	Artifacts	Resources
1.		1. 2.	1. 2. 3.
2.		1. 2.	1. 2. 3.
3.		1. 2.	1. 2. 3.
4.		1. 2.	1. 2. 3.
5.		1. 2.	1. 2. 3.
6.		1. 2.	1. 2. 3.
7.		1. 2.	1. 2. 3.
8.		1. 2.	1. 2. 3.
9.		1. 2.	1. 2. 3.
10.		1. 2	1. 2. 3.

Figure A.3.   Quest Page to record details.

Timeline of your Great Grandfathers Life

Include at least 15 events in your timeline. Each event should be detailed be sure to include who, what, why, where, and when.

Events

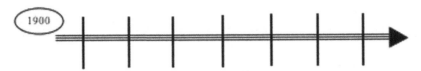

Event	Year
1.	
2.	
3.	
4.	
5.	
6.	
7.	
8.	
9.	
10.	
11.	
12.	
13.	
14.	

Figure A.4.

Figure A.5.

APPENDIX B

PERSUASIVE WRITING

Instructional Unit Resource Guide

Based on Principles of Universal Design and Differentiated Instruction and developed by Carolyn Dale and Barbara Melvin, Auburn Washburn School District #437

Barbara Melvin and Carolyn Dale, Auburn Washburn, USD 437

Handbook on Developing Curriculum Materials for Teachers:
Lessons From Museum Education Partnerships, pp. 385–391
Copyright © 2010 by Information Age Publishing

Authors' Note

This instructional resource guide is intended for use in the high school English classroom for persuasive writing techniques. This aligns with the Kansas State Writing Standards. The purpose of the guide is to assist teachers in finding additional resources to engage students with the use of technology, particularly students with disabilities. This guide contains both teacher resources and student-centered websites and activities.

In this unit the students will learn to present a position or an opinion in a written format, using one or details necessary to expand the main topic to support the writer's position of a quality to present to others. The student will have an introduction, body, and conclusion to reinforce the organized structure of the writing.

Standards

- Standard 1 Writing: The students write effectively for a variety of audiences, purposes, and contexts.
- Benchmark 4: The student writes persuasive text using the writing process.

Instructional Examples:

The teacher

- Instructs students to make posters intended to persuade viewers to subscribe to a point of view (i.e., access to web sites, homework, school uniforms, laws about noise).
- Encourages students to try to sell not only ordinary, realistic goods and services, but also bizarre and unusual ones.
- Have book talk groups read (or re-read) novels or chapter books set in the time of the American Revolution in which main characters start off with one point of view or opinion, then change, amend, or bolster their opinion as the story progresses.
- Presents other common examples of persuasive writing, such as film or book reviews, theater reviews, restaurant reviews, editorial articles, political position papers, government proposals, proposed legislation, and advertisements.

Resources for Locating State Standards:

- Kansas Curricular Standards

  http://www.ksde.org/outcomes/siacurrstds.html

Planning Pyramid:

Review the following article: Schumm, J. S., Vaughn, S., & Harris, J. (1997). Pyramid power for collaborative planning. *Teaching Exceptional Children, 26*(6), 62-66.fif

Planning Pyramid

What should students know?

Review the following article: Schumm, J.S., Vaughn, S., & Harris, J. (1997). Pyramid power for collaborative planning. Teaching Exceptional Children, 26(6), 62-66.

Some students will

-develop a clear and purposeful thesis statement and sufficient ideas to persuade reader
-build a focused argument in the persuasive mode that uses the persuasive techniques of logical thinking, appeals to reason, authority, and /or emotion.
-provide sufficient evidence, examples, and expert opinions to support author's position
-properly cite information from other sources
-effectively argue opposing arguments
-edit and produce final product of a quality to present to others following -research format specified by teachers

Most students will
-create a thesis sentence stating opinion
-use one or more of the following to support opionion: research, personal experience, prior knowledge, observations
-arrange information in logical sequence
-write an organized piece that includes intoduction, body and conclusion.
-edit and produce a final product of a quality to present to others

All students will

-develop an opinion statement
-provide and organize ideas of support in paragraph form
-conclude with a statement that reinforces the original opinion statement
-provide a finished document of a quality to present to others

Figure B.1. The planing pyramid.

Teacher Library:

Resources for locating instructional materials:

1. Writing: Instructional Philosophy and Teaching Suggestions
    http://www.sasked.gov.sk.ca/docs/mla/write.html

2. TrackStar
    http://trackstar.4teachers.org/
    Track#264620: Use this track and its resources for learning how to write a persuasive essay as well as find support activities. It includes a very good graphic organizer.

    Track #137738: This Track will teach persuasive writing techniques by exploring "up-to-date" movie, music, restaurant, video game, and automobile reviews. Students will be asked to identify elements of persuasive language, facts and opinions, and finally create their own persuasive review and publish it on the Web.

    Track #137738: This track includes persuasive writing tips, rubrics, and ideas for topics.

3. Study Guides and Strategies
    http://www.studygs.net/wrtstr4.htm
    This provides the teacher and student a very useful step by step guide to writing a persuasive essay

4. Student Samples
    http://www.eduplace.com/kids/hme/k_5/showcase/5-6/persuasive.html
    A student sample providing a sample of a basic persuasive essay
    http://www.janschipper.com/Example_Persuasive.htm
    Another student sample including research

5. Writing Prompts for Persuasive Essays
    http://home.earthlink.net/~jhholly/persuasive.html
    http://www.leeogle.org/byron/bhs/library/persuasion.htm
    http://www.leeogle.org/byron/bhs/library/persuasion.htm
    http://www.delmar.edu/engl/wrtctr/handouts/persuasive.htm
    http://www.leeogle.org/byron/bhs/library/persuasion.htm
    http://www.tengrrl.com/tens/018.shtml

6. 4 Teachers
    http://4teachers.org/

Learner Activities:

Resources for locating instructional materials:

1. TrackStar
   http://trackstar.4teachers.org/

Guides to the Writing Process

http:// http://www.geocities.com/fifth_grade_tpes/five.html   *(see five areas of writing)*

curry.edschool.virginia.edu/go/edis771/98webquests/student/scarlyoung/WQ2Powers1.html

http://www.tengrrl.com/tens/018.shtml   *(see persuasive topics)*

http://www.delmar.edu/engl/wrtctr/handouts/persuasive.htm   *(see guide for students)*

http://www.engl.niu.edu/wac/persuade.html   *(more student guides)*

http://www.janschipper.com/Example_Persuasive.htm   *(see student sample)*

http://www.eduplace.com/kids/hme/k_5/showcase/5-6/persuasive.html *(see sample)*

http://www.studygs.net/wrtstr4.htm   *(see student guide)*

http://www.studygs.net/wrtstr4.htm   *(see GOOD break down of how to write persuasive)*

http://search.lycos.com/index.php?src=sf&query=persuasive+essay&offset=20hhttp://www.ttms.org/PDFs/04%20Writing%20Process%20v001%20(Full).pdf

Assessment:

Resources for locating assessment materials:

1. Scoring Guide for Student Projects
   http://www.ncrtec.org/tl/sgsp/index.html

2. RubiStar
   http://rubistar.4teachers.org

3. Ruberic
    http://www.mcps.k12.md.us/departments/isa/elit/hs/RUBRIC.HTM

    Evaluation Rubric
    http://170.142.130.39/rubric/search.htm

4. Electronic Quizzes
    http://school.discovery.com/quizcenter/quizcenter.html
    http://www.funbrain.com
    http://quizstar.4teachers.org/
    http://www.studygs.net/wrtstr4.htmhttp://home.cogeco.ca/
        ~rayser3/paradev.txt
    http://home.earthlink.net/~jhholly/persuasive.html
    http://cctc.commnet.edu/HP/pages/darling/grammar.htm

If students **need test taking practice** as a study strategy for mastering the content of the unit, then ...

5. Try Quia
    http://www.quia.com

6. Quiz Hub
    http://www.kidshub.org/

Modifications:

Planning for academic diversity

1. For **students that cannot read at grade level**

    Try text to speech http://www.readplease.com

2. If students have **difficulty mastering the vocabulary** of the unit, some suggestions include ...

    Try a picture dictionary: http://www.enchantedlearning.com /Dictionary.html

    Try a talking dictionary: http://www.webster.com/

    Try the visual thesaurus: http://www.visualthesaurus.com

3. If you have students who **need the instructional materials in a language other than English** ...

    Try Babel Fish http://babelfish.altavista.com

4. If you have students who have **difficulty with organization,** then ...

   Consider using computer programs such as

   Inspiration http://inspiration.com

   Draft Builder http://www.donjohnston.com/catalog/writeco/ver/writecoverfrm.htm

5. If you have students who have **difficulty with handwriting** (either speed or accuracy), then ...

   Consider voice control computer programs such as...

   www.e-speaking.com/free_computer_voice_control_dictation_software.htm

   www.dragontalk.com/NATURAL.htm

   Consider allowing them to speak their answers in Kidspiration

   http://www.inspriration.com

   or Dragon Naturally Speaking

   www.dragontalk.com/NATURAL.htm

6. If you have students that have **difficulty with spelling,** then ...

   Consider allowing the student to use a computer word prediction program such as Co-Writer from Don Johnston Company:

   http://donjohnston.com/catalog/catalog.htm

7. If you have students who **need to hear what they have written,** then ...

   Consider using a computer reader program such as Read Please or Write Out Loud

   http://donjohnston.com/catalog/catalog.htm

   http://www.readplease.com

8. If you have **students who need additional challenge,** then...

   Search Google or TrackStar for enrichment activities

9. If your unit **requires students to conduct research,** you might want to...

   Use the NewsTracker http://my.yahoo.com

APPENDIX C

Civil Rights WebQuest

Home

Task

Process - General

Resources

Rubric

Evaluation

Conclusion

RESOURCES FOR:

Thurgood Marhsall

Martin L. King., Jr.

Malcolm X

Adding Sound & Video

EXAMPLE PPT AS WEB PAGE

EXAMPLE PPT AS PPT FILE

As we have read in the textbook, the Civil Rights movement took place over decades, with plenty of people playing important roles.

Using the information you gained in the Treasure Hunt and some other sites I will have you visit (or revisit), you will be placed in the shoes of those leaders. And you will have a decision to make and defend.

Click TASK on the menu buttons on the left to begin.

Picture of Thurgood Marshall	Picture of Martin Luther King Jr.	Picture of Malcom X

(c) 2001-2003 William Duck
Wicomico HS
201 Long Avenue
Salisbury, MD 21804
bduck@wcboe.org

Figure C.1.

Handbook on Developing Curriculum Materials for Teachers: Lessons From Museum Education Partnerships, pp. 393–395
Copyright © 2010 by Information Age Publishing

Task

Your job is to visit web sites to gather information on the philosophies of either Thurgood Marshall, Martin Luther King, or Malcolm X, depending on your assignment.

> ## Picture of elementary age students loading school buses

Using that information, you will craft a reaction to a fictional civil rights crisis in a Northeastern city that is opposing school integration by not enforcing busing routes.

You and your group partners will create a 10-slide PowerPoint presentation showing how your leader would react—what he might do, and what he might say. It MUST be consistent with his beliefs on Civil Rights and integration and how to achieve to gains.

You will utilize the philosophies and methods used by the Civil Rights leader you researched, and be able to cite principles of that leader's philosophy to show that your reaction is consistent with that leader's beliefs.

Let's begin by clicking on PROCESS on the left menu buttons....

Figure C.2.

Process - General

By 1970, the Rev. Dr. Martin Luther King, Jr. and Malcolm X were dead and Thurgood Marshall was an Associate Justice of the U.S. Surpreme Court.

In that year, South Boston, MA, found itself torn aprt by protests concerning a U.S. District Court order mandating the busing of students to schools outside their neighborhoods to integrate the city's schools.

Many white parents protested the busing, and many moved outside the city to avoid busing. the situation took many years to resolve in the courts and the streets and left many with feelings of racial hatred that would never completely disappear.

You have chosen one of these three Civil Rights Leaders. You will research the beliefs and actions of this leader, and you will craft a Powerpoint Presentation to give your group's response to the nonenforcement of the busing routes that is aligned with the beliefs and actions of the assigned leader.

Picture of Thurgood Marshall	Picture of Martin Luther King Jr.	Picture of Malcom X

Figure C.3.

Resources

POWERPOINT TUTORIAL

WEBSITES

U.S. Dep't. of Justice - Description of different Civil Rights protected by the federal government.

WithyLaw - Short timeline featuring main Civil Rights laws.

Cornell Law School - Detailed discussion of federal laws that define our Civil Rights.

The Boston Herald - A look back at the busing crisis after busing ended in 1999.

School Integration in Boston - A detailed look at the entire Boston busing crisis, including details of the first demonstrations against busing.

Associated Press - AP article about the end of busing in Boston 25 years after its start.

Photo Tour - Seattle Times site of photos from Civil Rights movement.

BOOKS	Book Cover:	Book Cover:	
Book Cover: Williams, J. (1998) Thurgood Marshall: American Revolutionary New York Times	Rowan, C.T. (1997) Dream Makers, Dream Breakers: The World of Justice Thurgood	King, M.L. Jr. (1998 ed.) The Autobiography of Martin Luther King Jr. New York: Intellectual Properties Management/Warner Books	Book Cover: X, M. and Haley, A. (1965) The Autobiography of Malcom X New York: Ballantine

This WebQuest was developed by William Duck, Wicomico High School, Salisbury, MD. He can be contacted at bduck@wcboe.org It was retrieved November 26, 2006 from http://webquest.org/

Figure C.4.

ACKNOWLEDGMENTS

This handbook was reviewed and validated using a research and design model that relied on three sets of experts in the fields of museums and education. Their feedback was crucial to both the format and the content of the handbook. Special thanks go to these professionals who gave their time and expertise to the study.

Expert Reviewers	*Profession/Organization*
Dr. Dave Edyburn	Associate Professor, University of Wisconsin
Ann Fortescue	Director of Education and Visitor Services, Senator John Heinz Pittsburgh Regional History Center, in association with the Smithsonian Institution
Tom Coleman	Accessibility Specialist (Retired), National Park Service, United States Department of the Interior
David Bakke	Naturalist and Education Liaison, Muscatine Nature Center, Muscatine Iowa
Sherry Reed	Professional Development and Curriculum, Greenbush Educational Service
Dr. Vicki Smith	Assistant Director of Special Education, Holton Special Education Cooperative, Holton, Kansas
Linda Rosenblum	Training/Education Specialist, *Brown vs. Board of Education* National Historic Site, Topeka, Kansas
Dan Carey-Whalen	Education Coordinator, Kansas Historical Society
Mary Madden	Education and Outreach Division, Kansas State Historical Society